The Political Economy of European Social Democracy

For many years European social democrats have aspired to create a 'Social Europe' to compensate for the ascendance of an international neoliberal consensus. Despite the promises of European integration, however, the European Union has thus far been largely a market-building project. EU-level market-correcting policies have either been curtailed by national opposition (such as the EU Social Chapter) or steered in a market-friendly direction (such as the Lisbon Strategy).

This book argues that rather than presenting an opportunity for European social democrats, the European Union instead provides the *appearance* of an opportunity, which ensures that 'new' social democratic party initiatives are complicit with the neoliberal international political economy. Included as part of this examination are case studies from the UK, France, Sweden, Spain, Italy and the transnational Party of European Socialists.

Providing a theoretically innovative explanation for the 'new' social democratic turn to Europe, this book will be of interest to postgraduate students and academics focusing on social democratic parties.

David J. Bailey completed his PhD at the London School of Economics, and is currently lecturer in political science at the University of Birmingham. His research focuses on social democratic parties and European integration. He has published articles in the *Journal of Common Market Studies*, and *Comparative European Politics*.

Critical realism: Interventions
Other titles in this series:

(Mis)recognition, Social Inequality and Social Justice
Nancy Fraser and Pierre Bourdieu
Edited by Terry Lovell

After International Relations
Critical realism and the (re)construction of world politics
Heikki Patomäki

Being and Worth
Andrew Collier

Beyond East and West
Roy Bhaskar

Capitalism and Citizenship
The impossible partnership
Kathryn Dean

Critical Realism and Marxism
Andrew Brown, Steve Fleetwood and John Michael Roberts

Dictionary of Critical Realism
Edited by Mervyn Hartwig

A Social Theory of the Nation-State
The political forms of modernity beyond methodological nationalism
Daniel Chernilo

Rethinking Marxism
From Kant and Hegel to Marx and Engels
Jolyon Agar

Transcendence
Critical realism and God
Margaret S. Archer, Andrew Collier and Douglas V. Porpora

The Political Economy of European Social Democracy

A critical realist approach

David J. Bailey

LONDON AND NEW YORK

First published 2009
by Routledge
2 Park Square, Milton Park, Abingdon, Oxon, OX14 4RN

Simultaneously published in the USA and Canada
by Routledge
270 Madison Avenue, New York, NY 10016

First issued in paperback 2010

*Routledge is an imprint of the Taylor & Francis Group,
an informa business*

© 2009 David J. Bailey

Typeset in Times New Roman by Swales & Willis Ltd, Exeter, Devon

All rights reserved. No part of this book may be reprinted or reproduced or utilized in any form or by any electronic, mechanical, or other means, now known or hereafter invented, including photocopying and recording, or in any information storage or retrieval system, without permission in writing from the publishers.

British Library Cataloguing in Publication Data
A catalogue record for this book is available from the British Library

Library of Congress Cataloging in Publication Data
A catalog record for this book has been requested

ISBN13: 978–0–415–46213–6 (hbk)
ISBN13: 978–0–415–60425–3 (pbk)
ISBN13: 978–0–203–86766–2 (ebk)

For my parents

Contents

	Acknowledgements	ix
	List of abbreviations	xi
1	The paradox of the 'new' social democratic turn to 'Social Europe'	1
2	Analysing party change: a critical realist method	20
3	Decommodification, recommodification, and crisis: the transformation to 'new' social democracy	41
4	'New' social democratic party relations and the turn to 'Social Europe'	95
5	(The absence of) social democracy at the EU-level	128
	Conclusion	157
	Notes	173
	List of interviewees	175
	Bibliography	177
	Index	192

Acknowledgements

This book is the product of a long research project that began with my PhD thesis. As a result, I owe a deep debt of gratitude to a number of people who helped me throughout this process. My PhD supervisors, Simon Hix and Eiko Thielemann, both provided me with invaluable advice, assistance and support for the duration of my PhD studies, often spotting holes in my argument and requiring me to either defend, remove or fill those holes. In the early stages of the thesis Eiko Thielemann provided me with both extremely useful advice on how to actually go about doing a PhD, and the right amount of steering to make sure I could work out for myself what that meant in practice without getting completely lost in the process. During the later stages of writing the thesis Simon Hix consistently and constructively identified weaknesses in my argument, the correction of which, I hope, are reflected in the argument as it now appears in this book. I am also grateful for a series of conversations with a fellow PhD student, Sara Motta, who introduced me to a number of new ideas that I would otherwise not have considered and which ended up having a significant impact upon my own intellectual development. I also wish to acknowledge the extremely detailed and constructive comments of my PhD examiners, Colin Hay and Philippe Marlière, both of whom, based on a very close reading of the text, provided me with positive feedback and very useful advice on how to improve the viability of the argument made herein, for which I am extremely grateful. I am also grateful to the Party of European Socialists for granting me access to their archives, providing me with the opportunity to work in and observe their office in Brussels, and to the individuals who took part in my interviews during my field research in late 2002. I was also fortunate enough to gain a small research grant from the British Academy (SG-48128), which allowed me to travel to each of the non-UK countries that form case studies in the present book, to interview leading political actors in each case. I am extremely grateful to the interviewees in each country, the British Academy, and the assistance I received from Magalie Bourblanc, Claudio Corradetti, Borja Lasheras, and Tove Linden. For reading and critically commenting in depth on a number of earlier drafts of this work, I am grateful to Abby Innes, Sebastian Balfour, Bob Hancke, the students who attended GV502 European Politics and Policy, and the anonymous Routledge reviewer. I also acknowledge ESRC award R42200034145. I am also grateful for the chance to discuss some of the claims of the book with Luis Cabrera, who was particularly insightful in pointing me towards the way someone more optimistic about the prospects of European integration might engage with the argument. I am absolutely indebted to Saori Shibata, without whose constant and unwavering support this book is one of many things I would never otherwise have achieved. Finally, I dedicate the book to my parents, who did so much to provide me with the initial conditions necessary to engender an enjoyment of study, for which I will always be grateful.

List of abbreviations

AES	Alternative Economic Strategy
AEU	Amalgamated Engineering Union
AMS	National Labour Market Board
BLP	British Labour Party
CAP	Common Agricultural Policy
CERES	*Centre d'Etudes de Recherches et d'Education Socialistes*
CGIL	*Confederazione Generale Italiana del Lavoro* (General Confederation of Italian Workers)
CLP	Constituency Labour Party
CLPD	Campaign for Labour Party Democracy
CMU	*Couverture Maladie Universelle*
CR	Critical Realism
CSPEC	Confederation of the Socialist Parties of European Community
DS	*Democratici di Sinistra* (Democrats of the Left)
ECB	European Central Bank
EDC	European Defence Community
EEA	European Economic Area
EEC	European Economic Community
EES	European Employment Strategy
EFTA	European Free Trade Association
EIB	European Investment Bank
EIF	European Investment Fund
EMU	European Monetary Union
EMS	European Monetary System
EPA	European Parliamentary Assembly
ESF	European Social Fund
FI	*Forza Italia*
IGC	Intergovernmental Conference
IMF	International Monetary Fund
LO	*Landsorganisationen i Sverige* (Swedish trade union confederation)
MEP	Member of European Parliament
NUM	National Union of Miners
NUR	National Union of Railwaymen

OECD	Organisation for Economic Co-operation and Development
OMC	Open Method of Coordination
OMC/SISP	Open Method of Coordination in Social Inclusion and Social Protection
OPEC	Organization of the Petroleum Exporting Countries
PCF	*Parti Communiste Français* (French Communist Party)
PCI	*Partito Comunista Italiano* (Italian Communist Party)
PD	*Partito Democratico* (Democratic Party)
PDS	*Partito Democratico della Sinistra* (Party of the Democrats of the Left)
PES	Party of European Socialists
PLP	Parliamentary Labour Party
PS	*Parti Socialiste* (Socialist Party)
PSDI	*Partito Socialista Democratico Italiano* (Italian Democratic Socialist Party)
PSOE	*Partito Socialista Obrero Español* (Spanish Socialist Workers Party)
QMV	Qualified Majority Voting
RC	*Rifondazione Comunista* (Refoundation Communists)
SAF	*Svenska Arbetsgivareföreningen* (Swedish Employers Federation)
SAP	*Sveriges socialdemokratiska arbetarparti* (Swedish Social Democratic Party)
SDP	Social Democratic Party
SEA	Single European Act
SFIO	Section Française de l'Internationale Ouvriere
SGP	Stability and Growth Pact
SI	Socialist International
SPD	*Sozial Demokratische Partei Deutschlands* (Social Democratic Party of Germany)
TGWU	Transport and General Workers' Union
TUC	Trades Union Congress
UGT	*Union General de Trabajadores* (Workers' General Union)
UMP	*Union Pour un Mouvement Populaire* (Union for Presidential Majority)

1 The paradox of the 'new' social democratic turn to 'Social Europe'

> In the long run, the European Social Model can only be secured by European integration, for should it falter then global forces will inevitably force down standards.
> (Albers, *et al.*, 2006: 5)

> Europe's common values correspond strongly with those that have defined the labour movement since its inception – internationalism, solidarity, equality and the belief that economic life should be compatible with the needs of society. Labour needs partners in order to realise its political goals and there is nowhere in the world it is more likely to find them than in Europe. It should view any proposal that strengthens Europe's capacity to apply its values in the form of common policies and practical achievements with enthusiasm.
> (Clark *et al.*, 2006: 95).

Social democratic parties across Europe have, over the past thirty years, adapted to a new economic and/or political climate following the end of the post-war consensus and the Bretton Woods system within which it was embedded. 'Traditional' social democratic goals, such as Keynesian demand management, welfare expansion, fiscal redistribution, full employment, and corporatist decision-making have increasingly come to be seen as impracticable. This has prompted several commentators to speak of the demise of social democracy (at least in its 'traditional' form) as a viable political project (Gray, 1996; Giddens, 1998; Kitschelt, 1994; Kuisma, 2007). In an attempt to adjust to this apparent demise of their 'traditional' social democratic programme, social democratic parties have adopted, to varying degrees, alternative policies and programmes. These changes crystallized over time into a 'new' social democratic programme characterized by a focus on supply-side economic policies that incorporate many of the neoliberal criticisms aimed at 'traditional' social democracy. 'New' social democratic programmes thus include active labour market policies, greater conditionality in welfare provisions, a fiscal policy geared towards incentivizing entrepreneurialism and work, and the prioritization of tackling inflation over unemployment (see, for instance, Scharpf, 1991; Kitschelt, 1994; Gamble and Wright, 1999; Callaghan, 2000a; Glyn, 2001; Moschonas, 2002; Schmidtke, 2002; Bonoli and Powell, 2004). At the same time, and as a central part of the same transition process, the goal of a supranational

2 The paradoxical turn to 'Social Europe'

'Social Europe'[1] has increasingly been adopted as a central pillar in 'new' social democratic party programmes. Social democratic actors have increasingly come to believe and/or state that, through supranational cooperation, social democratic parties can overcome many of the obstacles, preventing the address of their 'traditional' concerns, that they have experienced at the national level. Thus, Hooghe, Marks and Wilson show how, 'majorities in one [social democratic] party after another have come to perceive European integration as a means for projecting social democratic goals in a liberalizing world economy' (2002: 975).

This transition from 'traditional' to 'new' social democracy has prompted a number of important questions to be raised. Are the (arguably) more egalitarian (and certainly more interventionist) policies of 'traditional' social democracy still feasible within the contemporary international political economy (Beramendi and Rueda, 2007; Huo *et al.*, 2008; Pierson, 2001)? To what extent can meaningful social and economic reforms still be achieved by social democratic parties (Paterson and Sloam, 2006; Powell, 2004)? Does the demise of 'traditional' social democracy reflect the end of a distinctive partisan party politics (Allan and Scruggs, 2004; Huber and Stephens, 2001)? Questions have also focused on the turn by many social democratic parties and party actors towards the opportunities perceived at the European Union level. In particular, given the oft-noted market-conforming nature of European integration, a number of commentators have questioned the extent to which the European Union actually does offer, in Hooghe, Marks and Wilson's (2002) terms, 'the means for projecting social democratic goals in a liberalizing world economy' (see, for instance, Gray, 2004; Cafruny and Ryner, 2007; Bailey, 2005). Indeed, in raising this final question, commentators have pointed to the predominantly 'neoliberal', or non-interventionist, nature of much of EU-level economic and social policy, characterized by both a reluctance and an inability to adopt policies that would produce such traditional social democratic goals as the reintroduction of redistributive policies through the institutions of the European Union (see Scharpf, 1999 for the classic statement along these lines; see also Cafruny and Ryner, 2003; Bailey, 2008). For instance, Falkner (2000) describes EU social policy as an 'empty shell'. Leibfried discusses how, in contrast to the development of national-level social policy, which emerged as something '*against* markets', at the EU-level 'social policy interventions have developed as *part of* the process of market-building itself' (2005: 274–5). Many commentators have therefore noted the way in which EU-level social policy does little to redistribute resources in an egalitarian direction, and indeed acts predominantly to facilitate the technical operation of the single European market (Scharpf, 2002: 645; Hantrais, 2007: ch. 1; Büchs, 2007: 6–7). Whilst many social democrats have come to support European integration as a means through which to promote political aims that are increasingly (viewed as) unattainable at the national level, European integration itself has thus far produced little sign that such aims are actually feasible at the European level. Indeed, many scholars argue that European integration makes 'traditional' social democratic goals *less* likely to be implemented across the European Union (Scharpf, 2006; Streeck, 2001). The 'new' social democratic turn to 'Social Europe' therefore presents a paradox: *Why, given the predominantly market-making and liberalizing effect of European integration, have social democratic parties, and party actors, increasingly supported European integration as a potential means to reverse the apparent impracticability of 'traditional' social democratic policy aims?*

This book seeks to contribute to these debates by providing an answer to this paradox. In doing so, therefore, it also seeks to answer the wider questions regarding the possibility, likelihood and/or desirability of a return to the more substantive and redistributive ambitions of 'traditional' social democracy, at either the national or supranational level. Before we can attempt to provide an answer to the paradox of the 'new' social democratic turn to 'Social Europe', however, we must first examine in more detail both the historical processes that form the background to these developments and existing attempts to provide an explanation for them.

A brief and stylized history of European social democracy

Despite certain reservations (see, especially, Fitzpatrick, 2003), a number of scholars have sought to present a stylized history of European social democracy which roughly divides into four stages: 'revolutionary', 'reformist', 'traditional', and 'new' social democracy (Przeworski, 2001; Whickam-Jones, 2003). Thus, according to this stylized history, the revolutionary stage in the history of social democracy emerged with the ascendance of class politics and the promotion of communism associated with Marx and Marxism at the end of the nineteenth century. The First International Workingmen's Association (from hereon the First International) (1864–76) had been divided between 'communists' (Marxists), 'collectivists' (anarchists), and 'socialists' (moderates). In contrast, the Second International (founded in 1889) was explicitly Marxist (officially so since 1896) and adopted 'social democracy' as the label for its ideological position. Thus, both the German Social Democratic Party (founded in 1875) and Lenin's revolutionary Russian Social Democratic Labour Party adopted the title, 'social democracy'. As a result, 'from the 1880s onwards the term "social-democratic" referred to parties influenced by Marxism' (Moschonas, 2002: 18). The social democratic movement therefore began its life constructed around a commitment to Marxism, to the revolutionary emancipation of the working class, and to overthrowing capitalism and replacing it with a communist society.

Around the turn of the twentieth century, social democratic parties increasingly began to turn towards parliamentary activity, which prompted a now classic debate between those advocating a 'reformist' strategy, which included parliamentary activity as a means to both improve the lives of the working class and to solidify a collective working-class identity, and those proposing a 'revolutionary' alternative that refused any form of conciliation with either capitalism or the capitalist state. Those parties that eventually adopted the reformist approach (mainly within western Europe) retained the label 'social democratic', in contrast to those advocating a revolutionary strategy, which came to be known as 'communist' parties. Whilst the 'reformist' social democrats accepted the need for a partial accommodation with parliamentary politics and capitalism (at least in the medium term), communists expounded the need to overthrow (without any involvement in) both the liberal democratic (or 'capitalist') state and capitalist relations of production. This ideological division continued throughout the first quarter of the twentieth century, with Rosa Luxembourg (1900) and Lenin (1902) making the most vociferous arguments for 'revolutionary' communism, and the west European social democratic parties largely advocating (or at least practising) 'reformist' social democracy. It should be stressed, however, that 'reformist' social democracy (at least in the form advocated by leading proponents, such as Karl Kautsky) did not represent a rejection of the Marxist end-goal to transcend capitalism. It did, however, represent a rejection of revolutionary insurgency as the *only* means through which the interests of the working class could be furthered (Sassoon, 1996: 5–26). Following the October Revolution and the end of the First World War, the Second International itself imploded under the strain of these internal ideological divisions, with Lenin leading the revolutionary wing to form the Third (Communist) International in 1919, and the 'reformist' social democratic wing remaining to form the Socialist International in 1923 (Moschonas, 2002: 20–1).

Having adopted a parliamentary strategy, but not having abandoned the Marxist condemnation of 'bourgeois' democracy, 'reformist' social democratic parties found themselves in a dilemma. They stood for, and were often relatively successful in, parliamentary elections (in an attempt to promote working-class interests), but they refused to advocate or support policies that would administer capitalism as this would represent implicit support of it. As Berman (2006) documents, this strategy effectively paralysed 'reformist' social democratic parties, as they were unable to enter positions of real influence within democratic states, and thereby implement reforms that might benefit their constituents, but were also unable to advocate a real challenge to capitalist relations, which they argued would only be possible during a revolutionary period (which had not yet materialized). As a result of the frustration that arose from this effective paralysis, a further divide occurred between those that advocated a fundamental revision (or abandonment) of Marxism, and those who remained loyal to a more 'orthodox' interpretation of Marx. Revisionist social democrats, such as Eduard Bernstein in the SPD (German Social Democratic Party) and Jean Jaurés of the French socialists, argued for a further step towards conciliation and engagement with the instruments of power within capitalist nations (in particular, by accepting ministerial posts within national governments). In advocating the management, stabilization, and pacification of (rather than simply the promotion of pro-worker reforms within) the capitalist economy, revisionists believed they could improve the lives of their constituents (both within, and beyond, the industrial working class), and therefore also increase their party's electoral appeal. This revisionist view was largely based on the belief that the demise of capitalism, long anticipated by orthodox Marxists, was not, after all, inevitably forthcoming, and that capitalism could (and should) be improved through effective public policy. Opponents to this view, on the other hand, such as August Bebel in the SPD and Jules Guesde in France, claimed that to use the instruments of capitalist power would compromise their attempt to advocate working-class interests. In doing so, a 'revisionist' strategy would implicate social democratic parties too deeply in the process of managing capitalism, thereby diverting them from the pursuit of its transcendence. The revisionists were, however, unsuccessful in their attempts to revise social democratic ideology. The Second International's 1904 Amsterdam Congress voted to renounce any attempt by 'revisionist' social democrats to assume positions of office within national 'bourgeois' political systems, and revisionists were routinely unsuccessful in their subsequent attempts to reverse this decision (Berman, 2006: 54–7).

Despite consistently refusing to adopt a revisionist strategy, however, 'reformist' social democratic parties nevertheless continued to face the same intrinsic dilemma. On the one hand, successful engagement with the democratic nation-state required that social democratic parties secure a majority (or close to majority) of the support of the electorate in order for it to successfully achieve pro-worker reforms. On the other hand, by restricting the scope of its agenda to the promotion of working-class interests, and by excluding themselves from office-holding posts, social democratic parties limited the size of their natural constituency *and* the extent to which they could effectively influence policy-making (and thereby bolster their popular appeal) (Przeworski, 1985). In part as a response to this problem, but also due to both the inability of reformist social democratic parties to prevent the rise of fascism during the inter-war period and the experience of government intervention in capitalist economies during the Second World War, social democratic parties came increasingly after 1945 to adopt a managerial approach to capitalism, similar to that which had been advocated by revisionists such as Bernstein prior to the war. This post-war manifestation of social democracy is referred to here as 'traditional' social democracy. During this 'traditional' stage social democratic parties came increasingly to abandon their outright rejection of capitalism. Thus, before the Second World War, the adoption of social democratic programmes that sought to govern national capitalist economies was limited to the Swedish Social Democratic Party (SAP) (Berman, 2006: ch. 7). However, after 1945, social democratic parties across western Europe increasingly adopted programmes that included both a commitment to Keynesian macroeconomics and an extension of the welfare state, as the means to promote the interests of *both* the traditional working-class constituency of social democratic parties *and* the remainder of the national electorate (and, in particular, sections of the middle-class and public-sector employees, whom social democratic parties courted) (Berman, 2006). Whilst the content of 'traditional' social democratic party policy varied across countries, in each instance we can nevertheless witness an attempt to access national instruments of policy-making in order to manage national capitalism in a form that would promote the interests of both the working-class *and* the national interest. For instance, the success of 'traditional' social democracy in Sweden was built in part upon an attempt to represent the interests of the Swedish working *and* middle classes, notably in the form of a generous pension policy that benefited citizens within both groups, thereby securing a cross-class electoral alliance in support of the SAP (Esping-Andersen, 1985). Across western Europe, therefore, social democratic parties increasingly abandoned the attempt to exclusively promote working-class interests.

The Keynesian macroeconomic policy adopted by most 'traditional' social democratic parties, therefore, sought to reconcile the national interest with the promotion of more long-standing social democratic interests (Przeworski, 2001), particularly by advocating government spending in order to rectify downturns in the business cycle. Moreover, by directing this counter-cyclical spending towards the working class and the expansion of public sector services, 'Keynesianism made possible an *electorally ideal juncture* between the sectoral interests of the working class (fairer distribution of wealth, full employment, strengthening of the role of trade-unionism) and the national interest (sustaining growth)' (Moschonas, 2002: 21). It is during this stage that 'traditional' social democracy was classically defined in the following terms:

> First, an acceptance of a capitalist economy is coupled with extensive state intervention to counteract uneven development. Second, Keynesian steering mechanisms are used to achieve economic growth, high wages, price stability, and full employment. Third, state policies redistribute the economic surplus in progressive ways, through welfare programs, social insurance, and tax laws. And, finally, the working class is organized in a majority-bent social democratic party closely linked to a powerful, centralized, disciplined trade-union movement.
>
> (Kesselman, 1982: 402; quoted in Pierson, 2001)

'Traditional' social democracy therefore accepted the ongoing existence of both the capitalist economy and the liberal democratic state. However, it retained a conviction in the possibility of tempering the most erratic effects of capitalism and, thereby, advancing the interests of its traditional constituency (the working class). This was to be achieved through a programme geared towards redistribution, at the same time as benefiting the national electorate as a whole through the promotion of stable economic growth, and thereby becoming a viable electoral force.

The period from 1945 to the mid-1970s is often seen as a golden age for social democratic parties, and is particularly associated with the promotion of a 'traditional' social democratic programme. Indeed, three points of success are particularly noteworthy. First, the rise of the Keynesian welfare state in the post-war period coincided with strong economic performance across the developed world, consistently averaging above 4 per cent per annum (Aldcroft, 2001: 130, 213–14), and thereby negating concerns regarding the affordability of 'traditional' social democratic policies. Second, and partly as a result of this, 'traditional' social democratic policies, and especially a commitment to welfare state expansion, were adopted by rivals to social democratic parties, particularly Christian democratic parties. Whilst the partisan preference of the incumbent party in government did effect the *type* of welfare state developed within each country, the de-selection from office of social democratic parties, particularly if replaced by a Christian democratic party, frequently resulted in the continued expansion of the welfare state (Huber and Stephens, 2001: 352–3). Finally, 'traditional' social democratic parties were relatively successful electorally. As Gallagher *et al.* (2006: 232) show, in the 16 European countries which they observe, the mean electoral support for social democratic parties reached a peak in the 1950s. Moreover, Bartolini (2000: 54–5) shows how left parties achieved a higher share of total European votes in the period after the war than it did before.

Since the mid-1970s, however, the success of 'traditional' social democratic parties appears to have gone into reverse. Many of the policy and political achievements that had been promoted by 'traditional' social democratic parties were themselves associated with the experience of sustained economic growth during the *Trente glorieuses*. Following the Bretton Woods crisis of 1971–73, the stagflation of the 1970s, and the OPEC price shocks, however, Keynesianism and national economic intervention increasingly came to be seen as impracticable policy aims (Scharpf, 1991). This eventually resulted in the rise to power of the neoliberal New Right, most notably with the election to office of Thatcher in the UK and Reagan in the United States, marking the end of the post-war Keynesian consensus. Given that Keynesianism had been central to the success of 'traditional' social democracy, its decline was highly problematic for social democratic parties, thereby presenting them with a considerable dilemma (Thomson, 2000; Scharpf, 1991). Whilst the policies of the Keynesian consensus had enabled social democratic parties to reconcile their ideological commitment to working-class interests with more pragmatic electoral, governmental and office-seeking concerns, once Keynesian policies ceased to work (or be viewed as workable) and the welfare state was therefore problematized as an institution that might actually *destabilize* economic growth, social democratic parties were faced with equally unattractive options. On the one hand, they could reject their established programme (and alienate a large section of their core constituency). On the other hand, they could continue with an unsuccessful (but largely impracticable) programme, which was therefore electorally unviable.

In a gradual, and partly successful, resolution of this dilemma, European social democratic parties have increasingly adopted a 'new' social democratic programme. In brief, this 'new' social democratic agenda is characterized by an acceptance of much of the neoliberal critique of 'traditional' social democracy (Przeworski, 2001: 320–2), including the need for balanced budgets, a focus upon low inflation in macroeconomic policy, a reduction in the level of disincentivizing income transfers,[2] the limiting of economic intervention to the supply-side in order for macroeconomic policy to facilitate (rather than temper) the role of the market,[3] and an acceptance of 'the association between collective provision and bureaucratic inertia'[4] (Sassoon, 1996: 735; Thompson, 1996; Thomson, 2000: 156–7). Within these limits, political intervention in the economy may take the form of public service provisions that benefit the *national* interest (such as health and education), but not those that are specifically in the interest of the working class. Thus,

> the parties aim to follow national policies that reflect the interests of the whole of the population. This it is hoped will replace the notion of some social

democrats being too closely associated with sectional interests such as the trade unions.

(Thomson, 2000: 157)

Further, economic policy is geared towards ensuring the supply of a skilled and flexible labour force. Social democratic party policy has also undergone a shift in focus towards equality of opportunity, rather than equality of outcome, to be achieved through meritocratic mechanisms such as education and training (Powell, 2004; Sassoon, 1996).

Whilst national variation in the extent and form of the transition to 'new' social democracy clearly exists, there is nevertheless a discernible trend towards 'new' social democracy which can be observed across social democratic parties (Volkens, 2004). In the UK, for instance, Labour Prime Minister James Callaghan famously renounced his faith in Keynesian-oriented deficit spending to the 1976 Labour Party conference, prompting a long-term transformation of the party's programme that ultimately resulted in the 'new' social democratic programme of 'New' Labour. Similarly, in Germany, the SPD was kept out of office from 1982 to 1998, proving unable to adopt a party programme that could convince either the electorate or potential coalition partners that it possessed an economic policy that would produce a stable German economy with a low public deficit and acceptable growth levels (Braunthal, 1998). This was partly reversed with the selection of business-friendly candidate, Gerhard Schröder, in 1998, and party reform was more firmly completed (although with some detrimental electoral effects) with the launch of the Agenda 2010 initiative of 2003 (Dyson, 2005). In France and Sweden, the transformation from 'traditional' to 'new' social democracy was prompted by a series of policy failures. In the case of France, this came in the form of the now-infamous U-turn in Mitterrand's presidency, following the inability to combine the experiment of 'Keynesianism in one country' between 1981 and 1983 with a stable *franc* (Lordon, 2001). In the case of Sweden, there was a more gradual series of policy reversals, including the gradual end to the system of centralized wage negotiations throughout the 1980s, a major deregulation of capital markets in 1985, and the decision in 1990 to replace the historic prioritization of full employment with a commitment to low inflation (Ryner, 2002). Meanwhile, in Spain, the Socialist Workers' Party (PSOE) adopted a programme of economic liberalization (prompting general strikes in 1988, 1992 and 1994), in an attempt to pre-empt the experience of Keynesian programmatic failure witnessed in other European countries (Recio and Roca, 1998; Smith, 1998).

Over the course of the twentieth century, therefore, social democratic parties have travelled through a number of significant ideological and programmatic changes, from 'revolutionary' social democracy, through 'reformism' and 'traditional' social democracy, to the current 'new' social democracy. Whilst each of these stages obviously witnessed national variation, and at times overlapped with each other (both within and across countries), we can, nevertheless, identify a broad chronological process that provides an indicative overview of the development of social democratic parties throughout the twentieth century and up until the present.

The following section examines social democratic parties' positions on European integration during the latter part of this development as social democratic parties moved from 'traditional' to 'new' social democracy. Before we turn to this overview, however, we should first attempt a more formal definition of what we mean when we refer to social democratic parties. As we have seen in the foregoing discussion, social democratic parties have proceeded through a number of quite different ideological and organizational forms. Indeed, as Marlière notes, in using the term 'social democracy' or 'social democratic', 'we immediately encounter a significant problem in that the term "social democracy", the substantive "social democrat", or the adjective "social democratic" can be used to refer to a number of different realities' (Marlière, 1999: 1). To further complicate matters, a distinction is often made between the type of social democracy that exists (or has existed) in northern and southern Europe. Thus, in northern Europe, social democratic parties have historically been highly organized, with a well-developed bureaucratic party machine, strong connections to the organized labour movement and a moderate stance towards capitalism. In contrast, in southern Europe, social democratic parties have tended to be more loosely organized, have weaker links to organized labour and have adopted a position that espouses a more explicit rejection of capitalism. Indeed, this distinction between northern and southern European social democracy at one time reached the point where, for southern European social democratic parties, who preferred to see themselves as democratic socialists, 'the very notion of "social democracy" or the substantive "social democrat" almost constituted a term of abuse', coming to be viewed as 'synonymous with excessive compromise with capitalism and a tag of ideological vacuum' (Marlière, 2001: 6–7; see also Thomson, 2000; Marlière, 1999: 5–6). However, in an attempt to overcome some of these terminological problems, the present study looks to a common factor which unites those parties referred to here as 'social democratic parties'. This is their membership of the First, Second and Socialist Internationals. For the purposes of this study, therefore, and in keeping with the practice adopted by most commentators who have written in the past two decades, social democratic parties will be considered to be those parties that are currently members of the Socialist International (see Marlière, 2001; Ladrech and Marlière, 1999; Powell, 2004; Thomson, 2000; Kitschelt, 1994; Pierson, 2001; Przeworski, 1985; Vandenbroucke, 1999; Keman, 1993; Pontusson, 1995; Koelble, 1992; Callaghan, 2000a, 2003; Martell et al., 2001; Ladrech, 2000; Moschonas, 2002; Clift, 2002; Green-Pedersen and van Kersbergen, 2002; Roder, 2003). Whilst this definition is obviously open to the claim that we could label a party in the present study 'social democratic', despite its non-adherence to social democratic aims, modes of organization, or practices, nevertheless, it does provide a clear (and commonly used) method of identifying those parties that identify themselves as part of a single ideological party family. For this reason, therefore, we shall use the term 'social democratic' to refer to member parties of the First or Second Internationals (in the past), or of the Socialist International (in the present). For this reason, moreover, we shall refer to the different stages in the development undergone by social democratic parties in inverted commas, thereby recognizing that these are conceptual labels rather than formal terms adopted by social democratic parties themselves.

The 'new' social democratic turn to 'Social Europe'

As already noted in the introduction to this chapter, a central aspect of the most recent transformation from 'traditional' to 'new' social democratic parties was the adoption of a much more firmly pro-European position. Whereas 'traditional' social democratic parties tended to adopt a degree of scepticism towards the EU, ranging from indifference to open hostility, new social democratic parties have been much less equivocally supportive of European integration (Hooghe *et al.*, 2002; Hix, 2005: 186; Featherstone, 1988; Holmes and Lightfoot, 2007: 146–7). This shift in support was largely associated with a discourse adopted by 'new' social democratic parties that viewed European-level action as an opportunity to promote more interventionist and/or redistributive policies than that considered feasible at the national level. The European Union therefore came to be heralded as the institutional tier through which social and economic policy could continue to produce a redistribution of power and wealth throughout society, in keeping with more 'traditional' social democratic concerns.

The case of the British Labour Party (BLP) perhaps most clearly illustrates this process. Thus, in 1983 the Labour Party infamously committed itself to withdrawal from the European Commission as part of a wider socialist agenda promoted by the then-dominant left-wing of the party (Seyd, 1987). However, from 1983 onwards, following the party's worst electoral performance since 1918, individuals on both the left and right of the Labour Party began to consider the opportunities presented by coordinated social democratic activity at the European level. With the Labour Party leadership equally keen to move away from the more extreme position of advocating withdrawal from the EC, by the time of the 1988 Labour Party conference it was possible for the party to adopt a resolution stating, 'the Labour Party, in conjunction with the other socialist parties of the EC, must seek to use and adapt Community institutions to promote democratic socialism' (Labour Party, 1988b: 180). By the early 1990s, therefore, the Labour Party had become the pro-European party in British politics, contrasting itself effectively to a Conservative Party heavily divided over the issue. This pro-EU position was retained throughout the construction of the 'new' social democratic New Labour project (see, for instance, Mandelson and Liddle, 1996: 27–8). This move towards a more optimistic view of European integration was echoed within social democratic parties across the European Union. Thus, in the case of France, for instance, the 1983 U-turn was followed by an explicit increase in the French Socialist Government's enthusiasm for European integration (Clift, 2003b: 181), in part reflected in the presence of French Socialist Jacques Delors as European Commission president. Thus, Delors argued that Europe required, 'an organized space endowed with common rules to ensure economic and social cohesion' (quoted in Ross, 1995: 43). Moreover, this was an agenda that grew in importance within the *Parti Socialiste* (PS) throughout the 1990s, coming to represent a distinguishing feature of the PS's centre-left programme in the 1997 general election and during Jospin's incumbency as prime minister (Ross, 1998b: 22; Howarth, 2002).

In the case of Sweden, having maintained a position outside of the European Community throughout most of the post-war period, the SAP Government announced in 1990 that it would be applying to join the EC, witnessing the party leadership consistently argue, in debates on both the 1994 and 2003 referendums on accession to the EU and on EMU membership, respectively, that Swedish integration within the European Union would safeguard the social provisions of the Swedish model as part of a wider austerity package attempting to stabilize the Swedish economy. Finally, in Italy, the promise held by a unified 'European Left' represented a key source of optimism for the Italian Communists during their transformation from Eurocommunism to the post-communist Party of the Democrats of the Left (PDS) (Fouskas, 1998: 120; Abse, 2001; Dunphy, 2004).

Social democratic parties operating at the national-level, therefore, have become increasingly positive about the opportunities for policy-making that exist at the European level. This optimism was also mirrored by social democratic party actors operating at the supranational level itself, witnessing an increasing attempt to coordinate social democratic policy positions particularly from the early 1990s onwards (Hix, 2002; Hix and Lord, 1997; Lightfoot, 2005; Ladrech, 2000). The programmes adopted at the European level, moreover, have sought to utilize the opportunities provided by supranational policy-making to overcome some of the limitations, already noted above, experienced at the national level. For instance, the PES (Party of European Socialists) adopted a resolution in 2006, in which it argued that,

> [T]here are those who argue that Europe can no longer afford its welfare states due to the unrelenting pressure of globalization. That the welfare state will have to be 'downsized' in the future and the role of government limited to averting the worst forms of poverty. They also argue that societies should compete with each other to set the lowest rates of taxation. That the primary purpose of the European Union should be to promote free trade and competitiveness.
>
> But Europe's socialists and social democrats know there is another way – not only in theory but in practice. We set out our commitment: that the European Union shall not be reduced to a competition among states, or a marketplace for social dumping. Europe's socialists and social democrats firmly reject such a short-sighted view of the economy, society and democracy. *We stake our claim for a New Social Europe.*
>
> (PES, 2006, emphasis added).

Thus, the goal of Social Europe, as an antidote, or counterweight, to the pressures of globalization, has become central to the European agenda of 'new' social democratic parties. The supranational level has increasingly come to be viewed by 'new' social democratic actors as a key institutional opportunity through which more 'traditional' concerns such as inequality and welfare provision remain viable goals despite the obstacles to unilateral activity at the national level.

12 *The paradoxical turn to 'Social Europe'*

As outlined in the introduction to this chapter, however, this 'new' social democratic turn to 'Social Europe' is somewhat paradoxical. In particular, there are a number of institutional and political obstacles to 'Social Europe' which cast considerable doubt on the possibility of realizing such an agenda (Bailey, 2008). Moreover, whilst 'new' social democratic parties increasingly view the EU-level in terms of the opportunities for economic and social policy-making it provides, the history of European integration to date is largely characterized by the limits its imposes upon market-correcting policy-making in the areas of economic and social policy (Scharpf, 2002; 2006; see also Verdier and Breen, 2001; Cafruny and Ryner, 2007). For example, having managed to secure the adoption of the Social Protocol in the Maastricht Treaty, and the Social and Employment Chapters in the Amsterdam Treaty, advocates of market-correcting intervention have had to contend with substantial obstacles, including the minimal nature of the competences ceded to the EU-level in these areas, the 'market-conforming' nature of the policy instruments that exist under these Chapters,[5] and the high level of consensus required in order to reach policy agreements. As a result, EU-level social policy consists largely of minimal forms of labour market regulation. Attempts to go beyond this (such as the end to the opt-outs of the Working Time Directive and the adoption of a Temporary Workers' Directive) have thus far struggled to secure sufficient support from the member states or otherwise been significantly scaled-down in the course of the legislative process. Even the renewed attempt at the relatively unimposing 'open' coordination of national economic and social policies contained in the Lisbon Strategy adopted in 2000 has proven difficult to implement, with the Kok Report stating in 2004 that the process has been characterized by 'slow progress' and 'disappointing delivery ... due to an overloaded agenda, poor coordination and conflicting priorities' (High Level Group chaired by Wim Kok, 2004). What perhaps makes these developments more surprising still is that commentators have been arguing that these constraints would limit the scope for substantive policy-making throughout the history of European integration (see, for instance, Pinder, 1969; Holland, 1980). The paradoxical nature of the 'new' social democratic turn to 'Social Europe', which effectively consists of an attempt to achieve more 'traditional' social democratic policy goals through an institution that apparently limits the scope for realizing such goals, thus prompts further investigation. This forms the purpose of the present book.

Existing explanations

The 'new' social democratic turn to 'Social Europe'

Explanations for the 'new' social democratic turn to 'Social Europe' can be placed broadly into two groups – those focusing on 'structural-push', and those that identify an 'institutional-pull'. Whilst these represent different accounts of the processes through which 'new' social democratic parties have become more pro-European, they should not necessarily be viewed as incompatible, and indeed some scholars have emphasized both processes in their explanations for change within social democratic views on European integration. Nevertheless, for analytical purposes they are presented below as distinct approaches.

The 'structural-push' account perhaps fits most closely with the optimism found in much official social democratic party discourse and literature on the EU. According to this view, 'new' social democratic parties have become increasingly positive about EU-level policy-making opportunities due to the socio-economic, political and/or ideological obstacles to 'traditional' social democratic goals which came into existence at the national level during the last quarter of the twentieth century. Thus, whilst redistributive and/or macroeconomic regulative measures are no longer feasible at the national level, they can nevertheless be pursued within the supranational institutions of the European Union. According to this account, therefore, the limits to national-level policy-making have created a 'structural-push' for social democratic parties, leading those parties to reconsider their commitment to national-level policy-making and to seek instead a coordinated supranational strategy in response. As a result, 'because social democracy depends on state power, it must either reassert national autonomy with all the problems entailed by this strategy or work toward a federalist system to re-regulate the economy at the level of the EU' (Cafruny, 1997: 122; see also Paterson and Sloam, 2006: 238–9). As such, European integration enables states to improve their ability to engage with international processes, including the international economy, which we would expect social democratic party actors, unable to implement the policies they seek at the national-level, to therefore support.

The 'institutional-pull' account, in contrast, explains the 'new' social democratic turn to 'Social Europe' in terms of changes to the political institutions governing Europe. In particular, as the EU has become an increasingly important and permanent political institution since the mid-1980s, so social democratic parties (along with all parties that wish to be effective political actors) have been required to develop a substantive political agenda at the EU-level. In this sense, the European Union has become a permanent institutional fixture within European politics, rendering the question of whether parties should advocate policies at the European level, or not, increasingly redundant. Moreover, as part of the increasing institutional permanence of the EU-tier that has developed from the mid-1980s onwards, the possibility of a 'Social Europe' agenda being adopted at that level was viewed as having been improved by a number of initiatives, including the rise in structural funds and the adoption of the Social Charter. Thus, as the question of the supranational level as an institutional opportunity for political activity was increasingly becoming irrelevant, signs emerged that a 'Social Europe' agenda was becoming increasingly realizable at the European level. As a result, 'new' social democratic actors increasingly sought to promote such an agenda at the EC/EU-level. In the words of Hooghe and Marks, 'as regulated capitalism at the European level became a feasible goal and as social democratic parties came to realize that they could not exit the single market, they sought to deepen the European Union' (Hooghe and Marks, 2001: 174; for similar views, see also Ladrech, 1993; 2000; Holmes and Lightfoot, 2007).

Both the 'structural push' and 'institutional pull' accounts, however, leave a number of questions unanswered. First, whilst in both types of explanation a number of contextual changes are identified as having prompted a particular response by 'new' social democratic parties – the rise of socio-economic, political and/or ideological obstacles to redistributive/regulative measures at the national level (in the case of the 'structural-push' account), and the increasing permanence and openness to social policy developments of the EU-level institutional apparatus (in the case of the 'institutional-pull' account) – it nevertheless remains unclear why social democratic parties chose to respond to these contextual changes in the way that they did. Indeed, given the detrimental impact that European integration has had upon the prospects for 'traditional' social democratic action (as already noted above), such accounts need to at least acknowledge the obstacles to 'Social Europe' that exist, in order to provide an account regarding why, and/or whether, these obstacles have been underestimated by social democratic party actors. They need also to explain why these contextual changes have prompted the response that they did, rather than one characterized by an attempt by social democratic parties to reverse the particular contextual change in question. Why, for instance, did social democratic party actors not seek to reverse structural obstacles to national-level redistribution through an emboldened opposition to European integration? Why did the increased permanence of EU institutions not result in an increased Euroscepticism? Why were the limited opportunities for EU-level social policy viewed as a reason to support European integration, rather than the highly constrained nature of those opportunities being viewed as a reason to reject it? We need, therefore, an explanation for the 'new' social democratic turn to 'Social Europe' that is able to account for the agential response to the contextual changes that are identified as having occurred by existing accounts. In particular, as this study is concerned specifically with the *'new'* social democratic turn to 'Social Europe', in seeking to understand agential responses to particular contextual changes we should also consider the nature of *'new'* social democracy and why *'new'* social democratic party actors might be predisposed towards the responses to the given contextual changes that we have thus far observed. Our attempt to explain the 'new' social democratic turn to 'Social Europe' therefore requires additional insight into the nature of 'new' social democratic parties. In seeking to provide this additional insight, the following section provides an overview of existing explanations for the transformation to and therefore creation of, 'new' social democratic parties.

The transformation from 'traditional' to 'new' social democracy

As with accounts for the turn to 'Social Europe', attempts to model the transition to 'new' social democracy can also be located within one of two broad approaches. The first, structuralist, approach views the transition from 'traditional' to 'new' social democracy as the result of changes in the contemporary international political economy. From this perspective, some of the commonly noted changes including the shift to post-Fordist production techniques, the internationalization of finance and trade, the shrinking of the organized manual working class, and the diversity, flexibility and complexity of contemporary organizational practices have each reduced both the viability and the desirability of 'traditional' social democratic goals. This process, it is argued, has created a shift in the political opportunity structure faced by social democratic parties, rendering 'traditional' social democratic policies unfeasible and therefore necessitating the transformation to 'new' social democracy (Kitschelt, 1994; Pontusson, 1995; Giddens, 1998; Cerny, 1996; Klitgaard, 2007). Thus, for Giddens, the increased social complexity which characterizes the contemporary international socio-economic environment renders 'traditional' social democracy impracticable, necessitating its replacement with 'positive' welfare which acts to empower the individual: 'the guideline is investment in *human capital* wherever possible, rather than the direct provision of economic maintenance' (1998: 117). Similarly, Kitschelt (1994) argues that the transition to a post-Fordist, service-based economy across western Europe implies that society is no longer populated with a large enough number of people wishing to challenge the operation of the market. This therefore requires social democratic parties to accept the ongoing existence of the market and to focus instead upon the promotion of a left-libertarian programme (in opposition to a right-authoritarian one). According to this 'structuralist' approach, therefore, the inability of social democratic parties to successfully implement 'traditional' social democratic programmes has necessitated the transition to 'new' social democracy in order both to remain electorally viable and to implement those social democratic goals that remain practicable.

Whilst this structuralist account may be accurate in identifying certain changes within the international political economy, it has also been criticized by a number of scholars for the deterministic way in which it fails to give sufficient attention to the ideas, values and preferences that mediate these structural changes. These views therefore represent a second, 'ideational', account of the transformation to 'new' social democratic parties. Crucially, these scholars are keen to point out that political opportunity structures are themselves defined in part by the ideas held by members of a political community. As such, the claim (implicit within the materialist accounts above) that material social structures determine the viability and content of individual political preferences is rejected on the grounds that those preferences are themselves (relatively) autonomous from the material structures within which they are located. As a result of this (relative) autonomy, political opportunity structures are invariably contestable, and therefore also malleable. The corollary of this explanation, therefore, is that we must consider the impact of the *perception* of international economic constraints upon social democratic parties in the post-Bretton Woods era in order to understand how such parties have responded to these perceived constraints. Several scholars adopting such an ideational approach, therefore, have argued that the constraints that result from the contemporary structure of the international political economy have been exaggerated by actors who are *ideologically* committed to the erosion of social democratic policies (Hay, 2000; 2004; 2006). Moreover, these ideas have become dominant within social democratic parties themselves due to an empirically inaccurate conviction that 'traditional' social democracy has ceased to be a viable political project. In particular, the persistence of regional and national variation in macroeconomic policy illustrates the absence of insurmountable pressure upon social democratic parties to converge upon a 'neoliberal' revision of 'traditional' social democracy (Hay, 1997, 2006; Hirst, 1999). For instance, in discussing the specific case of the British Labour Party, Watson and Hay claim that, 'it was Labour's perceived electoral expediency that drove it to adopt a necessitarian discourse of globalization rather than the converse' (2003: 302). Further, for a number of EU-focused scholars of social democracy, the dominance of a 'neoliberal' ideology at the EU-level has influenced social democratic actors as they seek to engage with EU-level policy-making opportunities (see, for instance, Ladrech, 2000, McGowan, 2001). According to this 'ideational' account, therefore, the transition to 'new' social democracy results from the internalization of a prevalent, neoliberal, 'logic of no alternative' by social democratic actors themselves (both party actors and social democratic voters). In these terms, 'new' social democracy represents an (unnecessary) acquiescence to neoliberal norms by social democratic party actors.

As with the existing explanations for the 'new' social democratic turn to 'Social Europe', however, whilst both the structuralist and ideational accounts of social democratic party transformation rightly identify contextual changes that have prompted the transition from 'traditional' to 'new' social democratic programmes, they nevertheless fail to fully account for the agential responses that have occurred in response. Thus, in the case of the structuralist account, we are left without an explanation for the apparent acceptance of the structural changes observed. Why not adopt a 'traditional' social democratic strategy of macroeconomic demand management as a means to adapt to the internationalization of the political economy? Why not seek to *re*-nationalize regulation and control over flows of both goods and financial speculation? And why not seek to re-democratize organizational interactions that currently evade the democratic capacity of contemporary political institutions? In brief, why did 'traditional' social democratic parties choose to *adapt to* contextual changes that were hostile to their original programmatic aims and identity, rather than seeking *to adapt* the context itself. Similarly, whilst the ideational approach rightly identifies change in ideas as an important element in the transition process, we are nevertheless left without an explanation for the process of ideational change itself. Most importantly, the ideational approach fails to fully explain the reasons that social democratic parties capitulated to the pressures of the neoliberal consensus in the first place. Why did 'traditional' social democratic parties not simply seek to reverse or challenge the neoliberal consensus with which they were faced? What we need, therefore, is to be able to explain the transformation to 'new' social democracy in a form that is both able to identify the structural and ideational contextual changes that have prompted the transformation, *and* to account for the particular agential responses that constitute it.

To summarize, existing accounts of the 'new' social democratic turn to 'Social Europe' identify the 'structural-push' created by changes to the contemporary international political economy, and the impeding affect they apparently have upon the unilateral pursuit of 'traditional' social democratic goals at the national level, and the 'institutional-pull' of increased European integration. Nevertheless, they fail to account for the particular response of social democratic parties to these contextual changes, most notably the decision to acquiesce to (rather than to seek the reversal of) both of these 'push' and 'pull' effects; a question that is especially pertinent as the opportunities that social democratic actors are apparently pursuing at the supranational level are far from straightforwardly realizable. We need, therefore, greater understanding of the particular agential response – i.e., the turn to 'Social Europe' – to the contextual changes that both the 'structural push' and 'institutional pull' accounts provide. This, in turn, requires greater understanding of 'new' social democratic parties and party actors. In order to achieve this improved understanding, we can examine existing accounts of the emergence of 'new' social democratic parties. However, existing accounts of the transformation to 'new' social democratic parties exhibit a similar problem to those of the turn to 'Social Europe'. Thus, existing accounts for the transition to 'new' social democracy identify changes to the structural and/or ideational context within which 'traditional' social democratic parties were located, and which prompted a transition to 'new' social democracy, but we are nevertheless left without an explanation for the particular response adopted.

The present study therefore claims that, in order to answer the paradox of the 'new' social democratic turn to 'Social Europe', we need an account that is able to account for the response by 'new' social democratic parties and party actors to both the structural and institutional changes that prompted the turn to 'Social Europe'. This, in turn, requires an account of the emergence of 'new' social democratic parties which is able to account for the decision by 'traditional' social democratic parties and party actors to respond to structural and ideational contextual changes by undertaking a transformation to 'new' social democracy. The remainder of this book attempts to provide these explanations, beginning in the following chapter with what it argues is the necessary adoption of a critical realist approach to social scientific explanation, in order to successfully integrate both contextual changes and agential responses in explanations for social outcomes.

Plan of the book

The book proceeds through a series of arguments. The following chapter outlines, and makes the case for, a critical realist approach to the conduct of social science. In contrast to the positivist conception of causality, whereby causation is considered the constant conjunction of (causal and caused) events, the critical realist approach is introduced. Accordingly, causation is considered the ability of particular structures of social relations to generate particular outcomes. Social scientific research, therefore, seeks to conceptualize structures of social relations, and to use those conceptualizations to facilitate the creation of analytical narratives that illustrate the way in which particular events occurred, or were 'caused'. The chapter goes on to argue that this method of social science is able to integrate both an analysis of contextual (or 'structural') developments and the agential responses which those developments prompt (Hay, 2002a, presents the critical realist approach in a similar light). As such, the critical realist approach provides an important methodological underpinning to the attempt to address some of the problems in existing explanations for the paradox of the 'new' social democratic turn to 'Social Europe'. In particular, it is argued, we need to derive a real definition of the specific social relations under investigation in order to engender a more adequate explanation of them. In seeking to undertake such an aim, the chapter produces a real definition of 'traditional' social democratic party relations derived from both the existing literature on social democratic parties and from a number of theoretical insights within the wider literature. In particular, it draws upon both Marxist and anarchist conceptions of the wider social relations that 'traditional' social democratic parties acted to reproduce.

Chapter 3 uses this real definition of 'traditional' social democratic party relations to provide an analytical narrative of the process whereby 'traditional' social democratic parties adopted 'new' social democratic policies, in the cases of the British Labour Party, the Swedish Social Democratic Party (SAP), the French *Parti Socialiste* (PS), the Italian Communist Party (PCI) and its successor parties, and the Spanish Socialist Workers Party (PSOE). It illustrates how, in each case, the tensions embedded within the social relations that constituted 'traditional' social democratic parties ultimately proved unsustainable. As a result, and in an attempt to resolve the crises that resulted from these overwhelming tensions, 'traditional' social democratic party elites sought to downscale both the promise of, and demand for, the decommodifying policies that had historically formed the basis for the electoral appeal of 'traditional' social democratic parties. In adopting 'new' social democratic policy programmes, therefore, the chapter argues, each of the parties under investigation witnessed a transformation of party relations. The chapter concludes by drawing on these analytical narratives to derive a real definition of 'new' social democratic party relations.

Chapter 4 proceeds to use this real definition of 'new' social democratic party relations to inform another series of analytical narratives that this time seek to uncover the process through which 'new' social democratic parties embraced the goal of 'Social Europe'. Observing the attempt by 'new' social democratic party elites to maintain the electoral support of a constituency historically constructed on the basis of an appeal to decommodifying public policies, whilst simultaneously moving away from the promotion of such policies, the chapter presents an alternative explanation for social democratic party transformation. Rather than the paradox lying in the pursuit of a 'Social Europe' agenda in an institutional context that does much to restrict its realization, instead the adoption of this strategy by 'new' social democratic party leaders arises from the contradictory nature of 'new' social democratic party relations themselves. As such, the 'new' social democratic turn to 'Social Europe' represents an understandable attempt by social democratic party elites to reconcile some of the contradictory pressures generated by the structure of 'new' social democratic party relations.

Chapter 5 provides further support for these claims, examining both the development of the 'Social Europe' agenda at the supranational level, and the obstacles to its realization. It argues that, whilst social democratic party actors have sought to coordinate policy advocacy within the European Union, attempts to do so have nevertheless run into a number of significant obstacles preventing the realization of a substantive redistributive, market-correcting, or decommodifying policy framework. The existence of such institutional obstacles, therefore, enables social democratic party elites to both promote a decommodification agenda and legitimate its non-realization.

The book concludes with a discussion of some of the initial questions posed in this first chapter. Having argued that both the transformation from 'traditional' to 'new' social democratic party relations, and the pursuit of a 'Social Europe' agenda, are the result of the tensions inherent within the 'traditional' social democratic and 'new' social democratic party structures, the book is explicitly sceptical regarding the possibility of social democratic parties realizing a 'Social Europe' agenda, either within or without the institutions of the European Union. This need not, however, necessarily be a cause for concern.

2 Analysing party change
A critical realist method

The key claims of critical realism have been discussed at length elsewhere (Bhaskar, 1975; 1998; Sayer, 1992; Collier, 1994; Cruickshank, 2003; Outhwaite, 1987; Hay, 2002a). What this chapter aims to do, therefore, is, first, provide an overview of the merits of the critical realist (CR) approach, and, second, use this approach to derive the foundations for an alternative account of the transformation from 'traditional' to 'new' social democratic parties. Thus, the present study uses a critical realist approach to underpin an analysis of the transformation from 'traditional' to 'new' social democratic parties that occurred across western Europe over the last quarter of the twentieth century. In doing so it seeks to facilitate a subsequent re-examination of the 'new' social democratic turn to 'Social Europe'. In particular, the critical realist method is adopted on the grounds that it is able to underpin explanations that integrate both contextual stimuli and agential reactions to those stimuli (Hay, 2002a). This is particularly useful for the present study, it is argued, due to the inability, as argued in Chapter 1, of existing accounts to achieve such an integration, and the detrimental impact this inability has had upon their analytical adequacy. The approach adopted here draws particularly on Margaret Archer's attempt to provide a 'practical methodological embodiment of the realist social ontology' (1995: 16). In doing so, it seeks to provide the methodological apparatus required for the production of an 'analytical narrative' able to highlight the emergence of underlying structural properties (or mechanisms), the role of these properties in conditioning the context within which agents operate, the interactions between those agents, and the outcomes that therefore result (Archer, 1995: 343).

The critical realist approach and its merits

The merits of the CR approach are best illustrated, at the risk of caricature, through a comparison with alternative positivist and interpretivist approaches (for a similar discussion, see Patomäki and Wight, 2000). This section proceeds, therefore, with a discussion of the main differences between critical realism, positivism and interpretivism, seeking in particular to highlight the advantages of adopting a critical realist approach.

It is, perhaps, in its ability to provide an alternative conception of causality that critical realism is most able to assist our present investigation. Thus, positivist conceptions of causality typically view causal processes as consisting of events prompting (or causing) subsequent events to occur. The occurrence of event X (globalization, for instance) causes event Y (such as increased income inequality) to occur. In contrast, critical realism views the process of causality in terms of the *generation* of particular outcomes by social relations by virtue of their particular internal structures. Thus, as Bhaskar shows, the positivist view of causality is steeped in a Humean conception of independent entities, whereby the repeated observation of co-existence between certain entities suggests that one entity is able to 'cause' the occurrence of the other. In contrast, the critical realist approach asserts that particular outcomes are the product of social relations (Bhaskar, 1975: 24–5). The critical realist approach, therefore, views events such as the coincidence of globalization and an increase in inequality as explicable in terms of the generative mechanisms that make up the social relations (for instance, capitalism) which produced the particular observed coincidence in question. Thus, undertaking a positivist approach, causally-linked events are viewed as independent but nevertheless co-occurring, whilst according to a critical realist approach, a caused event is viewed as the product of the social relations that generated it. In contrast to the positivist conception of causality, according to which it is only possible to identify (and observe) the coincidence between causally-related events and outcomes (but not, implicitly, the process of causation itself), therefore, the CR approach claims that we are able to identify and observe the causal mechanisms that exist, and the process through which they occur, particularly as we get to know them through engagement with them (Bhaskar, 1975: 31, 143–8). Whilst causal mechanisms may not, therefore, be *immediately* observable (indeed, if they were, a rigorous scientific process would not be necessary in order to identify them), social science is driven by the attempt to identify and conceptualize the structures of the social relations that make up the human world, and which enable, cause, or 'generate', the occurrence of particular social outcomes, and the process through which these developments occur. The critical realist scientific method consists of the attempt to identify and describe the generative mechanisms contained within particular structures of social relations in reality, and the particular outcomes those mechanisms are able to, and do, produce (Bhaskar, 1975: 51–2). In this sense, 'social theorizing [from a critical realist perspective] is an attempt to construct "principles of visuality" that will allow us to "grasp" or "see" empirical evidence of the existence of social objects, and the manner of their functioning' (López, 2003: 78). Whilst a positivist explanation might account for increasing global inequality in terms of the occurrence of globalization (evinced through the repeatedly observed coincidence of variables measuring the occurrence of each phenomenon), therefore, a critical realist explanation would seek to *show* the process whereby an aspect of the internal structure of global social relations generated increased inequality.

One important observation of the critical realist method, moreover, is that, given that social relations are constituted by conscious human agents, the reproduction of those social relations in question is always dependent on the (ultimately contingent) decision of those constitutive agents to act to ensure that reproduction (Bhaskar, 1998: 17–54). As such, we might expect those individuals that benefit most from the reproduction of the social relations of which they are a part to do most to secure that reproduction. In contrast, those benefiting least (or actually being harmed), might be expected to resist the process of reproduction, or actively seek a transformation of the social relationship(s) in question. Moreover, due to this potential for change social relations themselves can never be assumed to be fixed. The social scientific process of knowledge-creation itself is therefore ongoing, as existing knowledge always contains the potential to become obsolete (or, perhaps more likely, in need of refinement) as a result of (potential) changes to the social relations to which that knowledge refers.

Further, the CR philosophy of social science rests upon an acceptance of the claim that reality is stratified, with each stratum generated by the sub-stratum from which it emerges. Each stratum is viewed as *emergent from* – rather than *determined by* – the sub-stratum which generates it. This refers to the way that social relations have properties that are not reducible to the individuals that form them – social relations are greater than the sum of their individual parts. Social relations have emergent properties that exist as a result of the interactions between individuals, and cannot therefore be explained solely through reference to those individuals (requiring an account of the structure of relations themselves) (Elder-Vass, 2008; Bhaskar, 1975: 113). This notion of emergence is particularly important to the CR approach because it allows for the possibility that social relations might *enable* certain actions and outcomes to emerge (and, therefore, 'cause' them), whilst also acknowledging that those relations do not directly *determine* (in a linear way) those actions/outcomes. This is important because it enables outcomes to be viewed as having been made possible by the social relations that exist, but nevertheless to have occurred as a result of the conscious (and therefore contingent) agency of those individual(s) who utilized the opportunities that are emergent properties of the social relations within which they are located. Events are therefore the result of the interaction between contingent human agency and the emergent opportunities that arise from the social relations within which those agents are located. Moreover, the failure to view reality in terms of emergent strata (which, to use Bhaskar's terms, would result in the adoption of a 'flat ontology') would imply that a posited causal event will always (and invariably) lead to the claimed caused outcome, as there would otherwise be no ontological basis according to which we could expect a causal property to exist but not be activated (or, in Bhaskar's terms, 'actualised') (on this, see also Outhwaite, 1987). In this sense, critical realism is able to produce non-deterministic (and, therefore, necessarily *post-hoc*) explanations for events, in terms of an interaction between conscious human agency and the underlying social relations that are able to generate them. Generative social structures provide the range of feasible options available to human agents, but do not determine which of those options actors choose to pursue (Bhaskar, 1998: 33–5). From a CR perspective, moreover, each stratum is viewed as the emergent product of a deeper underlying sub-stratum, which contains its own causal structures, thereby allowing (and, indeed, necessitating) a 'process of successive discovery and description of new and ever deeper ... strata' in order to complete existing knowledge and explanation (Bhaskar, 1975: 169).

Adopting a critical realist method in social science, therefore, means viewing explanation as the attempt to uncover the underlying structure of social relations that enables and motivates the generation of particular outcomes. Yet, this critical realist notion of underlying (but not necessarily (immediately) observable) generative structures is highly problematic from a positivist perspective of social scientific explanation. This is because, according to the positivist approach, explanation largely consists of identifying variation between pre-existing conditions, events or contexts, and explaining different social outcomes in terms of that variation. For instance, King, Keohane and Verba (1994: 81–2) define causality as 'the difference between the systematic component of observations made when the explanatory variable takes one value and the systematic component of comparable observations when the explanatory variable takes on another value.' Put more simply, their (positivist) notion of causality refers to the different outcomes that different causal events produce. However, once we permit that, from a critical realist perspective, the reflexivity of human agency ensures that action is always ultimately contingent, it becomes entirely plausible that similar pre-existing conditions, events or contexts result in *different* social outcomes, and indeed that different conditions result in similar events. It is not immediately clear, therefore, how one would 'test' for the existence of these structures once we accept that what they produce is contingent upon the reflexive human agency through which they are instantiated. Thus, for Bhaskar,

> it is a necessary condition for the concept of action that the world is open, in the sense that the agent's activity makes a difference to the state of affairs that would (normally) otherwise have prevailed. As the world is open, and agency is real, and as society is only materially present in intentional human action, it follows that social phenomena only ever manifest themselves in open systems. And from this it follows that any possible social (or psychological) laws must be analysed as tendencies.
>
> (Bhaskar, 1998: 14)

According to the positivist approach to social science, such an admission would render social scientific explanation redundant. Indeed, for King, Keohane and Verba, 'only repeated tests in different contexts ... enable us to decide whether to define a pattern as systematic or just due to the transient consequences of random processes' (1994: 62). Without the certainty that causal properties will produce empirical regularities, therefore, positivist science lacks an empirical base upon which to ground valid statements about causality. From a critical realist perspective, in contrast, the awkward ontological fact of human reflexivity (and the unpredictable open systems which that reflexivity implies) cannot be elided for the sake of social scientific convenience, and must, therefore, be incorporated into the way in which we study (an albeit inconvenient) social reality. In order to do so, the critical realist approach advocates that social scientists present explanations for events in terms of the (theoretically) known properties of the social relations, mechanisms and structures in existence at any one point in time (provided theoretical knowledge is sufficient to do so). This is the process, referred to as 'retrodiction' in critical realist terminology, whereby 'events are explained by postulating (and identifying) mechanisms which are capable of producing them' (Sayer, 1992: 107; Bhaskar, 1975: 125–6). This therefore requires that we draw upon a pre-existing conceptual and explanatory 'tool box' in our attempt to conceptualize and explain phenomena under investigation. In this way, we avoid the impossibility of causal explanation presumed by the absence of a closed system, whilst also enabling a process of confirmation, repudiation, and (importantly) improvement of existing knowledge, through the process of applying that knowledge to reality. If existing knowledge is *insufficient* to provide an explanation for the outcomes observed, we must refine that knowledge in order that it might become (more) sufficient (Bhaskar, 1975: 194). This process of constructing new conceptualizations of causal mechanisms is referred to as 'retroduction' – whereby potential causal processes that exist as a result of the structure of social relations are 'retroduced' through a consideration of what the structure of the social relations being investigated must have been in order that the outcomes observed could have been generated (Bhaskar, 1993: 109).

Critical realism also provides important insights into how we might understand and explain social change. Indeed, in positing the importance of social relationships in explaining social outcomes, we can also expect to be able to understand and explain changes to those relationships in terms of the contradictions and tensions that they contain. Thus, for Collier, a 'structural contradiction' produces change 'by virtue of the inner antagonism that it generates in the system in which it is a contradiction' (2002: 159). Whilst the social relations and generative mechanisms that constitute social reality might enable particular social outcomes to occur, therefore, there is nothing to prevent a situation whereby the reproduction of multiple, co-existing, social relations acts to mutually impede the reproduction of each other. Under this situation, different social relations exist in an antagonistic relationship, necessitating either change or, at least, some type of modifying compromise (Archer, 1995: 218).

Whilst the foregoing has focused predominantly upon the distinctions between the positivist and critical realist approaches to social science, interpretivist approaches also contrast with the CR approach, although on quite different grounds. Indeed, from an interpretivist perspective, the process of observing, understanding and interpreting particular social structures, mechanisms, and, indeed, the particular events they generate, is ultimately a question of perception. Thus, whilst the critical realist perspective presumes a degree of judgemental rationality, and therefore an ability to advance towards increasingly firm knowledge as a result of social scientific enquiry (Sayer, 1992; see also Bates and Jenkins, 2007), interpretivists deny that such a process can occur and, further, that such an attempt would anyway be undesirable and therefore counter-productive. For instance, Bevir and Rhodes announce that,

> we reject explicitly the idea of given truths whether based on pure reason or pure experience: all perceptions, and so 'facts', arise within the context of a

prior set of beliefs or theoretical commitments. As a result, we typically look suspiciously on any claim to describe neutrally an external reality.
(Bevir and Rhodes, 2004: 132)

In contrast, a critical realist approach presumes the knowledge-independent nature of reality, which, as mentioned earlier, due to the fact that we are able to interact with and affect it, can be known, and that knowledge of it can be refined and revised on the basis of that interaction. Whilst accepting that our access to reality is always concept-dependent, critical realism rejects the interpretivist view that there can be no judgement between different concepts, whilst nevertheless recognizing the ultimate fallibility of those concepts. The more useful and coterminous with actual experience that certain concepts are, the more adequate they are in their conceptualization of the real social relations, structures, and generative mechanisms that exist within reality (Sayer, 1992: 65–71).

In sum, from a critical realist perspective, the structures of social relations and the real generative mechanisms that are emergent from those relations come to be known through the development, application and revision of conceptualizations of those structures and mechanisms. Bhaskar terms these conceptualizations, 'real definitions', which, he claims, seek to capture the 'real essence of things and their intrinsic structures' (1975: 174). Thus, in the social sciences, real definitions seek to describe the structure of relations and the generative mechanisms, or causal properties, which these structures contain. Explanation for observed empirical developments, therefore, involves a series of 'backward' steps, whereby theoretically-known, potentially-causal, generative mechanisms are identified, and their ability to generate the particular event under investigation is evaluated. We are, therefore, engaged in a process of refining, revising and/or constructing a conceptual apparatus that seeks to provide real definitions of the nature of social reality and the social relations that constitute that reality.

The CR method therefore provides a number of important insights that have the potential to enable us to overcome some of the problems with the existing accounts of the 'new' social democratic turn to 'Social Europe' that we identified in the earlier chapter. Perhaps most importantly, it provides the methodological basis upon which to integrate, within causal explanations, actors' interactions and the social relations within which they are located. The CR approach outlined above views agents and social relations as mutually constitutive, but nevertheless undetermining of each other, with social relations creating the prompts for, and limits to, agential responses, which in turn act to reproduce and/or transform those relations. Whilst we might expect those benefiting most from particular social relations to seek their reproduction, we might equally expect those benefiting least, or being harmed, by particular relations to seek their reform, transformation, or transcendence. Finally, we should consider the possibility that social relations contain multiple and potentially contradictory mechanisms, a situation which is likely to necessitate change. This ability to integrate agency and the social relations that comprise the context for this agency is obviously of particular importance to the present study as it was the inability of existing explanations to perform such an integration which we argued in Chapter 1 was their most important failing. This book therefore seeks to employ this CR approach in order to provide a more adequate account of the 'new' social democratic turn to 'Social Europe'. As a first step in this process, the following section attempts to employ the critical realist approach in seeking to derive a real definition of the structure of 'traditional' social democratic party relations, which will in turn facilitate a more adequate explanation for the transformation to 'new' social democracy.

A real definition of 'traditional' social democratic parties

As outlined above, the critical realist approach to explanation requires a conceptualization, or real definition, of the structure of social relations that pertain to the particular observation, event or outcome for which an explanation is being sought. According to Archer (1995), once we have such a conceptualization, it is possible to present an explanatory, or 'analytical', narrative that illustrates the interaction between agency and the structure of social relations that produced the explanandum in question (Archer, 1995). In Chapter 1 we identified the absence of an adequate account for the transformation to 'new' social democracy as an obstacle to sufficient understanding of the emergence of 'new' social democratic parties and party actors, which in turn prevents an adequate analysis of the particular agential response to those (structural, institutional and ideational) contextual changes that produced the 'new' social democratic turn to 'Social Europe'. As such, the remainder of this chapter seeks to utilize the foregoing discussion of critical realist method to provide the basis for a more adequate account of the emergence of 'new' social democratic parties. In seeking to perform such a task, we first require a 'real definition' of the structure of 'traditional' social democratic party relations, in order that we might use this to inform an analytical narrative of the transition to 'new' social democracy.

In seeking to derive such a real definition we turn first to a consideration of existing definitions of 'traditional' social democratic parties within the literature. It is argued that, whilst these definitions provide an important account of the activity undertaken by social democratic parties during their 'traditional' phase, they nevertheless fail to provide a 'real definition' due to their focus upon what social democratic parties did during this period, rather than upon the social relations that constituted those parties and the means by which those relations were reproduced. This section therefore attempts to build upon the existing literature in order to derive a 'real definition' of 'traditional' social democracy that draws attention to the structure of social relationships that were constitutive of social democratic parties during their 'traditional' phase.

In keeping with the scheme outlined in Chapter 1, the term 'traditional' social democracy refers broadly to the type of social democracy most closely associated with the post-war period up until the late 1970s. It is, therefore, the form of social democracy most often referred to when speaking of the post-war (or Keynesian) consensus, the *Trente Glorieuses*, or the Bretton Woods era. However, whilst many commentators agree that social democratic parties entered a recognizable ideological, organizational and programmatic phase during this period, the terms used to depict it nevertheless vary. This results in a series of alternative labels being used to describe what is in effect the same phase in social democratic parties' history. For instance, different commentators have referred to 'revisionism' (Sassoon, 1996), 'traditionalist social democrats' (Leggett, 2007), and 'classical social democracy' (Pierson, 2001). What follows, therefore, is an attempt to go beyond the stylized history presented in the previous chapter in order to look in more detail at what elements different studies have identified as characteristic of (what we refer to in this study as) 'traditional' social democracy.

Towards a real definition of 'traditional' social democratic parties

In what is one of the most comprehensive histories of west European socialism and social democracy, Sassoon (1996) identifies three phases in social democratic parties' post-war history – welfare socialism, revisionism, and neo-revisionism. In terms of the stylized history introduced in chapter one, we can view the first two of these phases as different stages of 'traditional' social democracy. Thus, in the first, welfare socialism, phase, Sassoon shows how social democratic parties were committed to the introduction of welfare-oriented social reform through a centralized state. As a result, 'a centralized state was considered everywhere to be a useful instrument for the introduction of welfare socialism' (1996: 131). This therefore required a commitment to the pursuit of electoral victory within such centralized states. Indeed, as social democratic parties in this early post-war phase defined themselves explicitly in terms of not being communists, they thereby rejected any kind of revolutionary path to socialism in favour of a commitment to electoral means (1996: 135). According to Sassoon, moreover, the electoral strategy adopted appealed to the entire national electorate, rather than simply the working class. In seeking to appeal across class lines, therefore, welfare socialist 'traditional' social democratic parties increasingly adopted nationalism as the means through which to integrate popular appeals (1996: 132–3). However they also retained a symbolic commitment to working-class politics, as 'the more reformist their practice became, the more necessary it was to remain anchored to some of the symbols of the past' (1996: 134).

In Sassoon's second, revisionist, phase 'traditional' social democratic parties increasingly came to de-emphasize the abolition of the private ownership of the means of production as the long-term goal of socialist and social democratic parties (1996: 241). As a result, 'revisionism quite deliberately obliterated the painstakingly established border between socialist and non-socialist thought', largely in an attempt to increase its electoral appeal (1996: 242). This was the social democratic tradition most closely associated with the work of Crosland (1956), and with the SPD's Bad Godesberg programme, and also with a more comprehensive commitment to Keynesianism and its attempt to regulate, and maintain, capitalism in a form which would ensure positive social reform. Thus, Sassoon's revisionist 'traditional' social democracy witnessed a commitment to equitable life chances, a well-managed capitalist economy, and an electoral strategy that went more explicitly beyond the core industrial working-class constituency. Each of these aims were to be achieved through a commitment to a welfare state that sought to both successfully manage the national economy and to produce more equitable social outcomes, whilst rejecting Marxist claims regarding the incompatibility of these aims with the private ownership of property.

A number of other studies have sought to identify key characteristics of 'traditional' social democratic parties, focusing at times on different aspects of the parties' organization, ideology and/or electoral strategy. Thus, in referring to the 'Postwar Social-Democratic Model', Moschonas (2002) focuses more upon the organizational form taken by 'traditional' social democratic parties, identifying seven shared characteristics: mass organization; an institutional relationship with organized labour; an electoral appeal centred around (but extending beyond) the working class; a domination of the left of the ideological spectrum in the party system; a mainstream party strategy that (successfully) sought to enter government (rather than overturn it); an ideological commitment to political liberalism, the welfare state, social justice and ideological moderation; and a loose commitment to neo-corporatist decision-making. In contrast, in his discussion of the 'the golden age of social democracy', Callaghan (2000a) focuses more on the redistributive policies that 'traditional' social democratic parties were committed to. Thus, Callaghan shows how social democracy came to be understood as 'the creation and further extension of welfare-state capitalism, in the name of equality and social justice' (2000a: 1). 'Traditional' social democratic parties accepted that capitalism was the most effective mode of economic organization (often alongside a commitment to the Keynesian management of it), and therefore sought to advocate 'social justice in the context of an expanding, full-employment economy' (2000a: 11). This included a commitment to fiscal redistribution, welfare services and economic planning (2000a: 11–18).

In contrast to the focus on electoral, organizational and programmatic strategy found within the studies outlined above, Berman (2006) focuses in her study of 'postwar social democracy' upon the self-definition of 'traditional' social democratic parties, and in particular the process whereby they sought to define themselves in terms of what they were not. For Berman, 'postwar social democracy', or in our terms, 'traditional' social democracy, is understood as a dual commitment to, on the one hand, 'the primacy of politics' (as opposed to the economic determinism of orthodox Marxism, and the related conviction that intervention in bourgeois politics is futile), and 'communitarianism' (as opposed to the individualism, and aversion to the expansion of the welfare state, of liberalism). In an attempt to realize these dual ideals, Berman argues, 'traditional' social democratic parties committed themselves to a practical reorientation to 'policies such as Keynesianism and the welfare state' (2006: 200–1). In contrast, in his discussion of 'classical' social democracy, Pierson (2001) argues that any definition fails to capture the empirical variation that existed across west European parties. As a result, he adopts a more abstract definition, according to which social democracy can be viewed more in terms of being 'an approach to the political process – above all, a commitment to piecemeal and 'progressive' change through legal-constitutional and generally parliamentary methods' (2001: 56). For Pierson, this co-exists alongside a faith in the capacity of the public sector and state bureaucracy (2001: 57–8). Further, in understanding social democratic parties in terms of their commitment to 'progressive' reforms, Pierson points to a commitment to tackling both class and non-class forms of inequality. Finally, he claims that 'classical', or 'traditional', social democratic parties accepted the ongoing existence of the market – despite being committed to ensuring that those individuals able to form a meaningful electoral constituency were not too severely disadvantaged by it – and to engendering economic growth (2001: 61–2). For Pierson, therefore, 'classical', or 'traditional', social democracy was characterized by an approach to the political process that included a commitment to equality-oriented state-led reform of (but not opposition to) the market economy.

The final definition of 'traditional' social democracy considered here is that of Przeworski, who refers to a period of 'remedial social democracy'. In his account, Przeworski provides a convincing and popular argument regarding the non-feasibility of the social democratic strategy for overturning capitalism (Przeworski, 1985; 2001; Przeworski and Sprague, 1986), focusing particularly on the electoral dilemma faced by socialist parties in the first half of the twentieth century. For Przeworski, as already noted, this was an electoral dilemma in the sense that, in attempting to achieve popular electoral appeal, social democratic parties at the same time undermined the cohesion of the social group upon whom they relied for the electoral success of their political programme. Thus, for Przeworski,

> [I]f political parties do not mobilize people qua workers but as 'the masses', 'the people', 'consumers', 'taxpayers', or simply 'citizens', then workers are less likely to identify themselves as class members and, eventually, less likely to vote as workers. By broadening their appeal to the 'masses', social democrats weaken the general salience of class as a determinant of political behaviour of individuals.
>
> (1985: 27).

As a result of this dilution of class identity, therefore, social democratic parties were increasingly unable to appeal to the electorate on a class-focused political programme. In discussing the way in which social democratic parties sought to overcome this dilemma, by adopting an electorally-viable programme that would nevertheless be compatible with working-class interests and identities, Przeworski charts how socialist and social democratic parties first adopted nationalization (1985: 32–5), and then (following a lack of success due to insufficient electoral support) moved, from the mid-1930s onwards, to the adoption of Keynesianism as a means through which to grant 'a universalistic status to the interests of workers' (1985: 37). The 'Keynesian revolution' therefore enabled 'traditional' social democratic parties to reject nationalization and to move to a policy of managed capitalism that would redistribute resources towards its own constituents. This 'remedial', or 'traditional', social democracy is therefore characterized by (1) Keynesian demand management of the economy (and a rejection of nationalization as a necessary step to overturn capitalism), and (2) redistribution of resources and incomes to the working class (Przeworski, 2001: 319–20). Despite the apparent improvement in social democratic parties' fortunes that resulted from their adoption of a Keynesian strategy, however, Przeworksi (1985) shows how it also led to the abandonment of any attempt to reform or change capitalist relations of production. As a result, social democrats remained reliant upon the continued profitability of capitalism (1985: 38–43), which rendered them dependent upon the demands of

Table 2.1 Major interpretations of 'traditional' social democracy

Author	Term used	Main characteristics
Sassoon	Welfare Socialism	Welfare-oriented social reform through a centralized state.
		Committed to electoral victory within centralized state.
		Appeal to entire national electorate; embrace nationalism, but with continued commitment to 'working-class' politics. Rejection of revolutionary/communist politics.
	Revisionism	De-emphasize long-term aim of abolishing private ownership of the means of production.
		More comprehensive commitment to Keynesianism and regulation of capitalism.
		Commitment to equal opportunities, economic effectiveness, and an appeal beyond the industrial working class.
		Strong attachment to the welfare state.
Moschonas	Postwar Social-Democratic Model	Mass organization.
		Link to the organized working class.
		Electoral link centred around (but extending beyond) the working class.
		Main party on the left of the ideological spectrum.
		Mainstream reformist parties of government.
		Ideological commitment to political liberalism, the welfare state, social justice and ideological moderation.
		Loose commitment to neo-corporatist decision-making.
Callaghan	Golden Age of Social Democracy	Aim to create and extend 'welfare state capitalism', including fiscal redistribution, welfare services, and economic planning.
Berman	Postwar Social Democracy	Dual commitment to: • Primacy of politics • Communitarianism.
Pierson	'Classical' Social Democracy	Commitment to gradual change and parliamentary methods.
		Commitment to reducing inequality.
		Commitment to both the state and the (relatively fair and well-functioning) market.
Przeworski	Remedial Social Democracy	Commitment to the Keynesian demand management of the economy.
		Attempt to redistribute resources and incomes to the working class.

capitalists and the capitalist economy, particularly under conditions of lower levels of profitability and economic growth (Przeworski and Wallerstein, 1988).

Whilst these existing depictions of 'traditional' social democratic parties clearly and accurately identify defining elements of 'traditional' social democratic policies, ideas, modes of organization, and political strategies, they nevertheless fail to provide 'real definitions' that conceptualize the structure of social relations that constituted 'traditional' social democratic parties. Put differently, existing definitions of 'traditional' social democratic parties identify what social democratic parties *did* during their 'traditional' phase, but not the structure of social relations that constituted what they *were*.

Despite this distinction, it is possible to use these existing definitions as the basis for the derivation of a real definition that seeks to conceptualize the social relations that constituted 'traditional' social democratic parties. Table 2.1 provides an overview of the key characteristics identified by the existing studies of 'traditional' social democratic parties, as surveyed above. In reviewing these definitions, and in terms of the social relations that comprise social democratic parties, of most obvious importance is the electoral constituency upon which 'traditional' social democratic parties were constructed. Thus, Sassoon (1996), Moschonas (2001), and Przeworski (2001) all note that 'traditional' social democratic parties consisted of a core industrial working-class constituency, but one that also appealed to voters beyond that class. As noted by Przeworski (1985) and Berman (2006), this attempt to extend the electoral appeal of 'traditional' social democracy was largely pursued through the commitment to ensure the successful management of the national economy. Moreover, as a number of the studies reviewed earlier identified, social democratic parties also sought to implement progressive redistributive public policies that would benefit their constituency through the reduction of (various forms of) social inequality, alongside the more general commitment to oversee the successful performance of the national economy (Sassoon, 1996; Callaghan, 2000a; Pierson, 2001). As such, an initial attempt at deriving a real definition of the structure of social relations that constitute 'traditional' social democratic parties, based on a review of existing accounts within the literature, can be stated as follows:

> ***A real definition of traditional social democracy (1):*** *'Traditional' social democratic parties are constituted by party actors acting to represent the interests of an electoral constituency that includes, but extends beyond, the industrial working class, through the pursuit and realization of public policies that produce both the redistribution of resources to their electoral constituency and the enhancement of the economic well-being of the national capitalist economy.*

This real definition therefore provides a conceptualization of the social relations that constituted 'traditional' social democratic party relations. In particular, it focuses upon the relationship between the electoral constituency that provided the basis for social democratic party actors, and the way in which the actions of those actors sought to ensure the consistent support of its electoral base. In this way, the real definition seeks to conceptualize the relationships that constituted 'traditional' social democratic parties. However, it is the contention of the present study that, in keeping with a critical realist method, we should seek to uncover the deeper underlying strata of social relations that underpin the more immediate social relations conceptualized in this first real definition. In particular, our first real definition alludes to two further structures of social relations, a conceptualization of which can facilitate the derivation of a more adequate real definition. First, in seeking to oversee the successful management of the national capitalist economy, 'traditional' social democratic parties needed to reproduce the capital–labour relationship that constitutes capitalist economies. Second, the promotion and realization of redistributive public policies, in an attempt to maintain a 'traditional' social democratic electoral constituency, also implied the reproduction of the relations that constitute the representative-democratic state, within which those goals could be pursued. Our initial real definition of 'traditional' social democracy therefore includes, by implication, reference to two further structures of social relations – those of the national capitalist economy and those of the representative-democratic state within which the party was based – both of which needed to be reproduced in order to achieve the successful reproduction of the more immediate relations that constitute 'traditional' social democratic parties. It is to these two related structures of social relations that this chapter now turns in an attempt to further improve our real definition of the social relations that comprised 'traditional' social democratic parties.

'Traditional' social democracy and the management of the national capitalist economy

This section draws upon Marxist conceptions of capitalist relations in order to argue that the 'traditional' social democratic attempt to reproduce the national capitalist economy engendered tensions that problematized the reproduction of 'traditional' social democratic party relations themselves. A Marxist approach is particularly well suited to such a study due to the common concern, in both the CR method and Marxist approaches to capitalism, to secure a sound conceptualization of the structure of social relationships under investigation (on the compatibility between critical realism and Marxism, see Nielsen, 2002; and Creaven, 2002). Indeed, as Aglietta notes, 'such is in fact the nature of the concepts introduced by Marx. They are representations of the relationships that structure society' (1979: 16). What follows, therefore, is an attempt to draw upon Marx's discussion of the reproduction of capitalist relations in order to further develop our real definition of 'traditional' social democratic parties.

The central relationship within a capitalist economy, from a Marxist perspective, is that between capital and labour, which exists in a mutually dependent (but nevertheless antagonistic) relationship. As such, Marx observes:

> Without a *class dependent on wages* [i.e., the working class], the moment individuals confront each other as free persons, there can be no production of surplus-value; without the production of surplus-value there can be no capitalist

production, and hence no capital and no capitalist! Capital and wage-labour ... only express two aspects of the self-same relationship.

(1867: 1005–06)

Further, Marxist accounts view the antagonistic nature of the capital–labour relationship, alongside its centrality to capitalist production, as acting to destabilize the reproduction of the capitalist economy. Thus, from a Marxist perspective, there is a fundamental contradiction at the core of capitalist economic relations. On the one hand, capital and labour are mutually constitutive; whilst, on the other hand, they are mutually antagonistic. Capital depends upon labour in order to exist, but constantly strives to expel labour from the capital–labour relation through labour-saving efficiency gains. This central contradiction underpins much of the Marxist critique of capitalism (the account presented below draws largely from Harvey's (2006) reading of Marx's *Capital*; for similar accounts, which focus on the contradiction between the production and realization of profit, see Kotz, 2008; Fung, 2008). Indeed, for Marx, individual capitalists exist in a competitive relationship and must, therefore, seek, through their engagement with the wider capitalist economy, to accumulate further capital in order to be able to compete with rival capitalists. The smooth reproduction of a capitalist economy, therefore, requires that capitalists in general are able to accumulate additional capital, which itself therefore requires a general expansion of capital and (by implication) the labour it employs in order to reproduce itself. As such, 'capitalist production is not merely the reproduction of the relationship [between capital and labour]: it is its reproduction on a steadily increasing scale' (Marx, 1867: 1062). This process of expansion, however, engenders a number of tensions and contradictions. In particular, Marx argued that the combination of antagonistic relations of production (the exploitative relationship between capital and labour), and competitive relations of distribution (as found within the free market), create a tendency for the rate of profit to fall. Moreover, as profit is central to the process of capitalist production, its decline problematizes the more general reproduction of the capitalist economy, and thereby produces recurrent (economic) crises (Marx, 1894: 357–9).

Whilst the validity, or otherwise, of Marx's theory of the tendency for the rate of profit to fall has been subject to lengthy and, as yet, unresolved theoretical debate (for a useful overview of these debates, see Wright, 1999), Harvey (2006) presents a more abstract statement of some of its core claims in a way that is arguably less susceptible to such sustained critique. Indeed, for Harvey, it is not so much a decline in the rate of profit that is problematic for the reproduction of capitalism, but rather a more general tendency for crises to occur as a result of the overaccumulation of capital (2006: 192). Thus, Harvey argues that the competition between individual capitalists for greater shares of profit ensures that technological adjustments are pursued which reduce the cost of producing commodities below the average market price and thereby enable their sale at prices which yield supernormal profit.[1] Provided that this occurs within a competitive market, however, supernormal profit will only exist temporarily, until other capitalists are able to utilize the same technological adjustments, resulting in industry-wide adaptation to the new, more innovative and efficient, process of production. The problem, however, is that as a result of this process of innovation and competitive restructuring, the capital–labour relation itself is destabilized. In particular, the generalized improvement in productivity that results from the competitive restructuring creates a surplus of capital, as the same quantity of commodities can now be produced using fewer resources. In order to avoid making this surplus redundant, therefore, it must be re-invested profitably elsewhere. However, two additional developments problematize this search for re-investment. First, the process of competitive restructuring creates a tendency for sections of the workforce to become redundant, as labour-saving measures imply that some workers will no longer be required for production. This therefore acts to dampen demand. Second, competitive restructuring reduces the cost, and therefore market value, of commodities produced under the new method of production. For those commodities that have *already* been produced using the old method, however, the same reduction in market value occurs. This therefore prevents capital invested in commodities produced under the superseded method of production from earning the revenue originally anticipated, bringing associated risks of losses, reduced capacity for subsequent investment, and/or bankruptcy, each of which will have a further dampening effect upon general levels of demand within the marketplace (Harvey, 2006: 183–203).

In sum, capitalist innovation and the pursuit of profit have a tendency to create a situation in which capital is faced with the need to search for new opportunities for profitable investment, within a general context of dampened demand within the market. There is a serious risk, therefore, that capital will be unable to identify such opportunities for profitable investment, which itself disincentivizes investment in production, prompting further declines in demand, and profitability, and so on. Harvey terms this situation a 'crisis of overaccumulation', referring to a situation characterized by the inability of capital to identify opportunities for profitable investment, often alongside a pool of labour that is unable to identify employment opportunities, all of which arises through the 'normal' pursuit of profit within a capitalist economy. As such, the capital–labour relation is self-destabilizing – the normal pursuit of profit by capitalists problematizes the ability of capital to identify subsequent (and necessary) opportunities for profitable investment, which in turn disincentivizes capital from (re)entering, and thereby reproducing, the capital–labour relation itself. As Harvey puts it,

> individual capitalists, acting in their own self-interest under the social relations of capitalist production and exchange, generate a technological mix that threatens further accumulation, destroys the potentiality for balanced growth and puts the reproduction of the capitalist class as a whole in jeopardy. Individual capitalists, in short, necessarily act in such a way as to de-stabilize capitalism.
>
> (2006: 188)

As a result of these processes, we can expect to witness the ongoing occurrence, and recurrence, of crises that, even when they are (temporarily) resolved through the

Analysing party change 35

discovery of new opportunities for profitable expansion, nevertheless merely create the conditions for a repetition of the same reproduction of the capital–labour relation, and, therefore, subsequent crises. In Marx's words, 'capitalist production constantly strives to overcome these immanent barriers, but it overcomes them only by means that set up the barriers afresh and on a more powerful scale' (Marx, 1894: 358). Given the ongoing recurrence of crises of overaccumulation, therefore, actors committed to successfully reproducing or managing the capitalist economy must seek resolutions to these crises. As a result, 'traditional' social democratic parties in office (or seeking election to office) were required to facilitate (or propose means by which to facilitate) the identification of new opportunities for profitable investment. Our real definition of 'traditional' social democratic parties, therefore, requires a conceptualization of the process through which crises of overaccumulation can be resolved (at least in the short term). As Harvey transforms Marx's tendency of the rate of profit to fall into a more plausible account of capitalist crises of overaccumulation through the re-consideration, at a higher level of abstraction, of the processes identified by Marx (Harvey, 2006: 183–203). So, in much the same way, we can reconsider at a more abstract level the factors that Marx identifies as having a counteracting effect upon the tendency of the rate of profit to fall.

Those factors which Marx claimed have a counteracting effect upon the tendency for the rate of profit to fall include: an increase in the degree to which labour was exploited by any given amount of capital, a reduction in the amount of wages paid to labour, a reduction in the value of capital, and the expansion of capitalism to less-developed national economies (Marx, 1894: 338–48). Considered at a more abstract level, however, each of these potential resolutions act simply to intensify the work that capitalists are able to demand in exchange for the investment of capital. Moreover, if, following Castree we understand commodification to be 'a process where qualitatively distinct things are rendered equivalent and saleable through the medium of money' (2003: 278), then we might consider this process, whereby the amount of work performed by labour increases without a proportional increase in reward to be a *re*commodification of labour. In more abstract terms, therefore, we can consider each of Marx's counteracting effects upon the tendency of the rate of profit to fall as a 'recommodification' of labour. This therefore contrasts with Esping-Andersen's (1990) notion of the decommodification of labour, typically central to 'traditional' social democratic party programmes, whereby individuals become *less* dependent upon the exchange of their working time (on the role of decommodification in social democratic party identity, see also Huo, *et al.*, 2008). Under conditions of recommodification, therefore, workers become *more* dependent upon the exchange of their working time, and are coerced into working more intensively and/or for longer periods of time, without a related increase in reward. Through such a process of recommodification, therefore, the overaccumulation of capital is (temporarily) resolved through the discovery of new opportunities for profitable investment.

Returning to 'traditional' social democratic parties, the problem they were always likely to face was that, in the light of recurrent crises of overaccumulation, and given that they were committed to the successful reproduction of the national capitalist economy, they would need to promote the recommodification of the working-class population which formed the core of their electoral constituency. This therefore represents a significant tension at the centre of 'traditional' social democratic party relations. On the one hand, 'traditional' social democratic parties needed to promote the recommodification of labour in order that recurrent crisis tendencies inherent to the national capitalist economy could be resolved. On the other hand, they needed to promote the redistribution of resources towards their working-class constituency (in order to maintain their electoral viability). This was itself an attempt to achieve the 'decommodification' of labour, which was a core 'traditional' social democratic aim (Esping-Anderson, 1990). This tension can therefore be used to revise our initial real definition of 'traditional' social democracy, as follows:

> ***A real definition of traditional social democracy (2):*** *'Traditional' social democratic parties are constituted by party actors acting to represent the interests of an electoral constituency which includes, but extends beyond, the industrial working class, through the pursuit and realization of redistributive public policies that produce a decommodification of labour, whilst simultaneously seeking to secure the successful reproduction of the capital–labour relations that constitute the national capitalist economy over which they govern, through the promotion of the recommodification of labour in response to recurrent crises of overaccumulation.*

'Traditional' social democratic parties, conceptualized in this way, were therefore characterized by an internal instability arising from the contradictory, but constitutive, mechanisms generated by their wider structure of party relations. The following section seeks to further develop this real definition through the introduction of a conceptualization of the social relations that comprise the representative-democratic state.

'Traditional' social democratic parties and the representative-democratic state

As already noted, the attempt by 'traditional' social democratic parties to promote and realize redistributive public policies, on behalf of a 'traditional' social democratic constituency, presumes the existence of a representative-democratic state within which to pursue such policy outcomes. As such, the reproduction of the structure of 'traditional' social democratic party relations requires the reproduction of relations that constitute the representative-democratic state. This section argues that, in seeking to conceptualize these relations that constitute the representative-democratic state, we can draw upon some of the insights of anarchist political theory. Indeed, two critical conceptions of representative-democratic state relations in anarchist political theory are of particular relevance. First, the state constitutes a coercive and unequal relationship. Second, that the relation of representation should be conceptualized as an attempt by a representative elite to regulate and contain the demands of those being represented, in order that those demands might be 'representable'. Each of these claims, and their implications for our conceptualization of 'traditional' social democratic party relations, are elaborated below.

Whilst it is hardly controversial to claim that the modern state is coercive in nature, what distinguishes the anarchist perspective on the state, however, is its focus on the state's role in both acting to reproduce, and in turn requiring for its own reproduction, unequal power relations throughout society. Thus, one of the key critiques of the state presented by classical anarchists is the claim that, in centralizing decision-making capacity, the state acts to disempower citizens and thereby undermine their capacity for self-determination. Moreover, in order that this centralization of decision-making capacity can both come into existence and be sustained, it is necessary that wider patterns of inequality are maintained throughout society. Thus, Kropotkin (1897) argues that the modern state was able to come into existence at a time when both power and wealth inequalities were increasing as modern capitalism developed. This, he claims, concentrated power and wealth in the hands of the European political and economic elite during the late medieval period. As inequality grew in European society, two factors encouraged a further consolidation of this concentration of power, eventually resulting in the emergence of the modern state. First, the concentration of power created elites powerful enough to achieve a monopolization of coercive force. Second, the rise in inequality created a context within which non-elites were increasingly vulnerable to domination and therefore came to desire and support an overbearing monopoly of force in the hands of a recognizable authority – i.e., the state – in order to stabilize power relations. As such, according to Kropotkin, the state came into existence as an effect of, but nevertheless acting to consolidate, the political and economic inequality that characterized early capitalist society. Perhaps more importantly, for Kropotkin, the continued existence of the state itself depends upon the continuation of political and economic inequality within the society that the state governs over. As such, 'a whole mechanism of legislation and of policing has to be developed in order to subject some classes to the domination of others' (Kropotkin, 1897: 10).

As a result of these criticisms, the classical anarchist critique of ('traditional') social democratic parties views their participation in, and reproduction of the state, which itself depends upon a system of social inequality that centralizes decision-making capacity within the hands of the state, as (explicitly or implicitly) acting to ensure the continuation of social inequality, and the subordination and disempowerment of citizens governed by that state. In the words of Kropotkin:

> Just as the Florentines at the end of the fifteenth century knew no better than to call on the dictatorship of the State to save themselves from the Patricians, so the socialists can only call upon the same Gods, the dictatorship of the State, to save themselves from the horrors of the economic regime created by that very same State!
>
> (1897: 55)

Drawing upon a classical anarchist political theory, therefore, we can reconceptualize 'traditional' social democratic party relations in terms of their intrinsic dependence upon wider patterns of social inequality. In this sense, therefore, 'traditional' social democratic party engagement with the state can be conceptualized as the attempt to ensure the subordination of subaltern classes to the centralized decision-making capacity of the state.

Whilst the foregoing has discussed the coercive role of the state in general, however, we are particularly concerned here with 'traditional' social democratic parties' engagement with the *representative-democratic* state. Indeed, the process of representation is perhaps the central legitimating factor for contemporary state relations, and as such is crucial to our understanding. We can, however, also derive from both classical and poststructuralist anarchist political theory a reconceptualization of relations of representation that might aid our present analysis. Indeed, according to May (1994), what connects both classical and poststructural anarchist theorists is a common critique of representation. According to this critique, the process of representation is one whereby the demands of those being represented must be suppressed in order that they can be 'represented' by those who are acting as representatives. For classical anarchists, as already alluded to above, the attempt (or claim) by one group of people to make decisions, and thereby rule, *on behalf of* another group merely acts to establish a power relationship whereby decision-makers are empowered at the expense of those on whose behalf decisions are being made. Thus, for Bakunin,

> [I]rrespective of their democratic sentiments or intentions, the rulers by virtue of their elevated position look down upon society as a sovereign regarding his subjects. But there can be no equality between the sovereign and the subject. ... Political power means domination. ... and subjects will naturally hate their rulers, who will then naturally be forced to subdue the people by even more oppressive measures, further curtailing their freedom.
>
> (1870: 221)

Similarly, for Kropotkin, the attempt by subordinate groups to emancipate themselves through reliance upon the decisions made by a centralized site of decision-making is ultimately unsustainable. As a result, 'any external authority cannot be anything other than an impediment, an obstacle to this organizational undertaking which has to be carried out, and, from the outset, a source of discord and hatred' (Kropotkin, n.d. [2005]: 322).

Contemporary theorists have also sought to develop this classical anarchist critique of representation, often drawing insights from recent developments in poststructuralist philosophy, and especially the work of Gilles Deleuze (see, for instance, May, 1994; Newman, 2001; Tormey, 2006). From this perspective, the critique of representative democracy is less focused upon the centralization of decision-making capacity, and rests instead upon a problematization of the notion of representation itself. Thus, in one of his earlier works, *Difference and Repetition*, Deleuze presents the problem whereby difference always precedes identity. In order for identity to exist, there must first be two *different* entities between which that identity occurs. Identity, therefore, presupposes difference, ensuring that what we call identity is actually the *appearance* of identity between differences: 'It is always differences which resemble one another, which are analogous, opposed or identical: difference is behind everything, but behind difference there is nothing' (Deleuze, 1994: 69). This observation significantly problematizes the notion of representation, therefore, as representation seeks to deny that which is different. It seeks to claim an identity between the represented and the representative, and therefore seeks to deny a difference that always already exists. As such, representation is an attempt to repress, control or regulate the difference that exists amongst those being represented. Representation 'is a site of transcendental illusion', which seeks 'the subordination of difference to resemblance' (Deleuze, 1994: 67, 334–5). Deleuze therefore views the process of democratic representation as an act of control and repression. Thus, he speaks of, 'the politician, who is above all concerned to deny that which "differs", so as to conserve or prolong an established historical order, or to establish a historical order which already calls forth in the world the forms of its representation' (Deleuze, 1994: 64). As Colebrook notes, therefore, 'to affirm difference eternally is to take difference beyond representation. Any *represented* difference has fallen into identity' (2005: 247). Moreover, contemporary political theorists have used this discussion of difference, identity and representation to reconsider the classical anarchist critique of representative democracy (see, for instance, Tormey, 2006; May, 1994). From this perspective, we can reconceptualize the reproduction of relations of representative democracy as a process whereby the different demands of represented citizens must be regulated and contained in order that they can become 'representable', and thereby 'represented' by a democratically elected political elite.

Returning to our discussion of 'traditional' social democratic party relations, therefore, we can draw upon anarchist critiques of the state to derive a number of important observations. Thus, in seeking to engage with the institutions of the representative-democratic state, 'traditional' social democratic parties acted to consolidate unequal social relationships, including those between the centralized authority of the state and those of its subordinate citizens. Indeed, in requiring actors to seek office within the state, 'traditional' social democratic party relations were in part constituted by an elected political elite that sought, in the terms introduced above, to ensure the continued subordination of those citizens it sought to govern over. Moreover, in seeking to represent a particular constituency, which included, but extended beyond, the industrial working class, 'traditional' social democratic party elites were required also to regulate and contain the demands of that constituency, in order that they might be 'representable' and therefore be successfully 'represented'. We can therefore draw upon these observations to further revise our real definition of 'traditional' social democracy:

A real definition of traditional social democracy (3): *'Traditional' social democratic parties are constituted by a party elite seeking to regulate and contain the demands for decommodification made by an electoral constituency which includes, but extends beyond, the industrial working class, in order that those demands might be* both *(a) 'representable' within the institutions of the representative-democratic state,* and *(b) compatible with attempts to achieve*

> *the successful reproduction of the capital–labour relationship that constitutes the national capitalist economy, through the promotion of the recommodification of labour in response to recurrent crises of overaccumulation.*

The successful reproduction of 'traditional' social democratic party relations therefore required a balance between, on the one hand, the provision of policy outputs that acted to decommodify labour, and on the other hand, the recommodification of labour necessary for the reproduction of capital–labour relations which constituted the contemporary national capitalist economy. Whilst this could therefore be considered, on one level, a straightforward balance between decommodification and recommodification, the process of representation also required that the demands of 'traditional' social democratic constituents be sufficiently contained. As such, the balance between recommodification and decommodification was one in which we would ultimately expect party elites to favour recommodification, as the realization of constituents' demands for decommodification, and the empowerment they would obtain as a result, contained the potential to disrupt relations of representation themselves.

'Traditional' social democratic party relations also contained a number of potential sites of tension. In particular, there could be no guarantee that 'traditional' social democratic constituents *would* actually sufficiently limit their demands for decommodification. Moreover, their failure to do so had the potential to destabilize both the relations of representation and the capital–labour relations upon which the successful reproduction of 'traditional' social democratic party relations rested. There was, therefore, an ever-present source of tension at the centre of 'traditional' social democratic party relations.

It is the claim of this book that, through the adoption of this revised real definition of 'traditional' social democracy we are able to provide the basis for a more adequate analytical narrative of the transformation from 'traditional' to 'new' social democracy. This is presented in Chapter 3, which represents a first step towards a more plausible explanation for the paradox of the 'new' social democratic turn to 'Social Europe'.

3 Decommodification, recommodification, and crisis

The transformation to 'new' social democracy

The aim in this chapter is to use the real definition of 'traditional' social democratic party relations, developed in Chapter 2, as the conceptual basis for an analytical narrative charting the transformation from 'traditional' to 'new' social democracy in the cases of the UK, Sweden, France, Italy and Spain. In each case, the aim is to identify the way in which the structure of social relations that constituted 'traditional' social democratic parties, and in particular the tensions they gave rise to, generated the transformation to 'new' social democracy.

Before we proceed, however, it is necessary to comment on the empirical cases selected for the present study. Whilst, as noted in Chapter 2, in adopting a critical realist approach, the validation of social scientific explanation is not confirmed through the identification of invariant empirical regularities (as sought by positivist approaches to social science), nevertheless, the present study does seek to uncover the structure of social relations that has produced two developments – the transformation to 'new' social democracy, and the 'new' social democratic turn to 'Social Europe' – which have occurred across multiple countries. In Chapter 2 we sought to reconceptualize the structure of 'traditional' social democratic party relations. In seeking to examine the way in which (if at all) this alternative conceptualization can provide insights into these developments, therefore, the present study seeks to provide a series of analytical narratives, applied to a number of country cases. To borrow from the language of positivist social science, the cases selected in this study are chosen using a 'most different systems design'. This means that the range of cases chosen has sought to combine as wide a variety of contextual factors as possible, whilst controlling case selection so that within each case we nevertheless experience the two key developments that we are interested in investigating (Landman, 2008: 32, 70–1). In adopting such a research design, therefore, the aim is to provide a series of different cases within which we can investigate the way, if at all, that the structure of 'traditional' social democratic parties, as conceptualized in the preceding chapter, acted to generate the particular outcomes we are seeking to explain. As the cases chosen are 'most different', they provide the opportunity to examine the process whereby 'traditional' social democratic party relations generated a transformation to 'new' social democracy in a range of different contextual settings, thereby enabling greater exploration of the causal properties of those party relations.

As already noted, the cases that are considered in this and the following chapter are the social democratic parties in the UK, Sweden, France, Italy and Spain. These are chosen as they represent as broad a range as possible of the different contextual factors of relevance to social democratic parties. Combined, therefore, the cases include most different characteristics in terms of size, geographical location within Europe, length of time of membership of the EC/EU, types of capitalist economy, and traditions of organized labour. Thus, in terms of population size, the range of cases include small (Sweden), medium (Spain) and large (UK, France and Italy) countries. In terms of geographical location, the cases include what are commonly referred to as northern (Sweden and UK), and southern (Spain, France, and Italy) European social democratic parties (see Thomson, 2000, for a discussion of these different types). In terms of length of time of membership within the EC/EU, the cases range from those within the original member states (France and Italy), the 1973 accession (UK), the 1980s accessions (Spain), and the 1995 accession (Sweden). The cases selected represent each of Esping-Andersen's three types of welfare capitalism – social democratic (Sweden), liberal (UK), and conservative (France, and Italy). It also includes cases that fall into a more contested category, which Arts and Gelissen (2002: 142–6) refer to as the 'Mediterranean model' (Italy and Spain). Finally, the cases include those countries with high, medium and low levels of union density. Thus, between 1994 and 2003, the average rate of union density was low in France and Spain (8.4 per cent and 16.3 per cent, respectively), medium in the UK and Italy (30.7 per cent and 36 per cent, respectively), and high in Sweden (80.7 per cent) (own calculations, from Visser, 2006).

The remainder of this chapter therefore presents an examination of the transition from 'traditional' to 'new' social democratic parties in the five 'most different' cases chosen for this study, using the conceptualization of 'traditional' social democratic party relations derived in the previous chapter as the basis for this examination. In doing so, it seeks to uncover the causal processes leading to this transformation, based on the particular relations identified as important in the real definition of 'traditional' social democratic parties employed herein. As such, rather than provide a detailed documentation of all aspects of each party's history up to the present, the case studies provide instead a narrative that focuses in particular upon the period of transformation. In each case, therefore, the narrative ends at or around the end of the 1990s or early 2000s, by which point each of the social democratic parties in question had undertaken significant transitions to what we refer to here as 'new' social democratic party relations.

British social democracy

As noted in Chapter 2, the 'traditional' social democratic structure of party relations produced potential sites of tension which threatened to destabilize social democratic parties. Indeed, in the case of the British Labour Party, these tensions were present from the beginning of the post-war period. Thus, despite the Attlee Government of 1945–51 being heralded by many as the most successful of the 'traditional' social democratic governments in Britain (Shaw, 1996: 19; Howell,

1976: 135), it nevertheless implemented a series of restrictive, or 'recommodifying', fiscal, welfare and, particularly, incomes policies, that proved unpopular amongst, and significantly problematized its attempts to 'represent', its electoral constituency. What follows, therefore, is a historical overview of the more important tensions arising from the structure of Labour Party relations during this period. The aim is not, therefore, to provide a detailed history of the post-war Labour Party (a vast selection of which already exists, see, for instance, Reid and Pelling, 2005; Shaw, 1996; Panitch and Leys, 2001; Hay, 1999; Coates, 1975). It is, rather, to employ the real definition of 'traditional' social democratic party relations derived in the earlier chapter, in an attempt to uncover the way in which these party relations acted to generate a transformation to 'new' social democracy.

The problematic reproduction of 'traditional' social democratic party relations in the case of the British Labour Party

The 1945–51 Labour Government introduced a number of significant reforms which acted, to varying extents, to decommodify the lives of its working class-oriented electoral constituency. These included the creation of the National Health Service, the nationalization of the coal, railway, cable and wireless, much of road haulage, civil aviation, gas, electricity and iron and steel industries, the implementation of an extensive high-quality and government-subsidized council housing programme, and the introduction of two major social security initiatives (National Insurance and National Assistance). At the same time, however, these decommodifying measures were limited by the attempt to successfully reproduce British capital–labour relations. In particular, an attempt to maintain sterling convertibility in 1947, at the same time as running a serious trade deficit, led to a number of decisions which sought to control personal consumption and imports in order that profitable investment and exports could be stimulated. These included the freezing of food subsidies, the raising of purchase taxes, cuts to the housing programme, and reduction in rations for meat, sugar and other food. Similarly, the extent to which nationalization acted to decommodify the lives of those workers located within the nationalized industries was significantly limited as traditional management structures and practices remained largely intact, and new management boards were largely drawn from the private sector. In its management of industrial relations after the convertibility crisis of 1947, moreover, the Attlee Government consistently (and successfully) called upon the unions to temper their wage claims. For instance, in response to the 1948 government White Paper, a *Statement on Personal Incomes, Costs and Prices*, trade union leaders, led by the TGWU (Transport and General Workers' Union) leader, Arthur Deakin, accepted a proposed voluntary wage freeze, thereby limiting workers' demands (Shaw, 1996: 24–41; Morgan, 1984; Howell, 1976: 154–62).

Indeed, in an attempt to secure the consent of their core working-class constituency to their 'traditional' social democratic programme, the Labour Party leadership consistently sought to dampen its constituents' demands, largely by arguing that such a programme was the best possible alternative available to them, and particularly emphasizing the importance of the national, rather than class, interest. For instance, in 1945, the Labour Party secretary Morgan Phillips stated that there should be no 'lingering impression of the outworn idea that the Labour Party is a class party' (quoted in Panitch, 1976: 10). Similarly, in presenting its 1948 *Statement on Personal Incomes*, the government argued for a wage freeze in terms that emphasized the national interest (Panitch, 1976: 22–6). However, these early attempts to reproduce the 'traditional' social democratic party relations of the British Labour Party also exposed the tensions within those relations. Thus, whilst the union leadership showed 'unflinching support' for the government's wage policy due to the loyalty they felt towards the Labour Party in office, by 1950 the impact of a devaluation of sterling in 1949, combined with an increase in prices resulting from the Korean War, resulted in the growing intransigence of British trade unionists. As a result, key unions, such as the Amalgamated Engineering Union (AEU) and National Union of Railwaymen (NUR) refused to support the TUC's (Trades Union Congress) proposal for a tightening of the wage freeze, and wage negotiations witnessed both rising claims and demands that negotiations be settled at a faster pace (Panitch, 1976: 30–7). Nevertheless, the appetite for industrial conflict at this stage remained relatively weak, and as a result union leaders were largely able to discourage unofficial industrial action and, indeed, often sought to assist the government in its productivity drive (Shaw, 1996: 36–7).

Following its defeat in the 1951 general election, the Labour Party was in opposition until its re-election in 1964. During this period out of office, it experienced less direct pressure to manage the British economy and as a result was under less pressure to contain the demands of its constituents. On the one hand, therefore, this opened the possibility for more ambitious policy commitments to secure the decommodification of labour. For instance, the 1952 party conference agreed on a resolution calling for a more extensive commitment to nationalization. Nevertheless, in order to maintain its appearance as a viable party of government, the Labour Party had also to ensure that it retained a balance between the demands of its constituents and the requirements of the British capitalist economy. After the defeat of the 1955 general election, therefore, a new leadership, committed to more moderate forms of decommodification, reasserted control over the party. Thus, initiatives such as nationalization and the construction of the welfare state, which had come to be associated with the Attlee Government, were replaced between 1955 and 1964 with a 'revisionist' programme that placed much greater emphasis on Keynesian demand management (Coates, 1975: 76–8). The election of Hugh Gaitskell as party leader in 1955 (a contest in which he defeated the left-leaning Aneurin Bevan), and the publication in 1956 of the extremely important *The Future of Socialism* by Tony Crosland, therefore, both marked important steps in the consolidation of a 'traditional' social democratic programme characterized by Keynesian demand management and an accommodation with capitalist economic relations, which themselves represented a move away from nationalization and the further extension of the welfare state.

In making this transition, the Labour Party leadership adopted a programme that was more adequately suited to the tempering of working-class demands. In particular, it produced an articulate argument against demands by those on the left of the Labour Party – grouped around Bevan – for the continued expansion of both the generosity and extent of welfare provisions, and the further expansion of public ownership. It also witnessed a more vehement defence of the virtue of profit as a central element in the capital–labour relation. Thus, Crosland argued, 'so long as we maintain a substantial private sector ... socialists must logically applaud the accumulation of private profit' (quoted in Shaw, 1996: 53). Similarly, the Labour Party argued in a 1957 policy document, *Industry and Society*, that, 'under increasingly professional managements, large firms are as a whole serving the nation well ... [and] no organization, public or private, can operate effectively if it is subjected to persistent and detailed interventions from above' (quoted in Coates, 1975: 90).

It was during this period, however, that tensions within the structure of 'traditional' social democratic party relations became increasingly apparent. Thus, an increasingly demanding grassroots constituency within the Labour Party sought to challenge the institutional dominance of the right-wing leadership of Gaitskell, Crosland, Herbert Morrison, Hugh Dalton, Douglas Jay and much of the trade union leadership, witnessing a rise in grassroots support for the left-wing Bevanite group of MPs (Shaw, 1996: 58–66; Shaw, 1988). This attempt to challenge the moderate Labour Party leadership was, however, ultimately unsuccessful, and in 1964 the Labour Party, led by Harold Wilson, was elected to office. Characteristic of a 'traditional' social democratic electoral strategy that sought to appeal beyond a core industrial working-class constituency, the 1964 election campaign focused heavily on the demands of middle-class voters. Nevertheless, in actual voting terms, the Wilson Government retained its core working-class constituency, thereby retaining a 'traditional' social democratic structure of party relations (Panitch, 1976: 66; Butler and Stokes, 1969). Upon its election to office, however, the new government was immediately faced with an economic crisis producing significant downward pressure on the value of sterling, which again acted to destabilize the 'traditional' social democratic structure of party relations. Thus, in response to the pressure upon sterling, the government initially sought to combine voluntary wage restraint with increased taxes on capital (including the introduction of Capital Gains and Corporation Taxes in the 1965 budget), in an attempt to reduce domestic demand and thereby strengthen sterling through an improvement in the balance of payments. Wage restraint, which aimed at nominal rises of 3.5 per cent, was accepted by the TUC, in part as a display of loyalty to the Labour Party in office (Panitch, 1976: 67–78; Coates, 1975: 103–4). Nevertheless, these measures proved insufficient and in July 1965 the government announced a package of deflationary measures that sought to dampen government spending and therefore further restrict demand (Shaw, 1996: 70–2). The following month, the government moved towards a statutory incomes policy, requiring state approval for wage increases, and again successfully appealed to the TUC for its consent, on the basis of loyalty to both the Labour Party in office and to the national economic interest (Panitch, 1976: 90; Coates, 1975: 107; Brandon, 1966). As had occurred with the Attlee Government, within a year of being in office, the Wilson Government had actively sought to recommodify British labour, this time through a combination of deflationary public expenditure measures and statutory wage restraint, in response to a crisis of British capitalism. Moreover, it had succeeded in attaining the acquiescence of the trade union leadership in its attempt to do so. By the end of September 1965, therefore, the TUC had established an Incomes Policy Committee that would itself vet wage claims in line with government policy (Panitch, 1976: 92–5).

Despite the union leadership's support for the Labour Government's incomes policy, however, its grassroots constituency was less forthcoming. Thus, following re-election to office in 1966, the government soon entered into a bitterly fought industrial dispute with the National Union of Seamen. Such instances of industrial unrest, combined with continued currency speculation, prompted growing pressure for the devaluation of sterling. Rather than implement a currency devaluation, however, the government introduced in July 1966 a colossal deflationary package, including £500 million worth of cuts, increases in indirect taxation, and a £150 million reduction in public spending investment and overseas expenditure (Shaw, 1996: 72–4). This was combined with the re-introduction of statutory wage restraint, which included a six month wage freeze, to be followed by a further six months of 'severe restraint' (a development that was nevertheless endorsed by the TUC General Council). The government also abandoned its commitment to full employment, noting that unemployment up to 2 per cent would no longer be considered 'unacceptable' (Panitch, 1976: 113–8).

The Wilson Government clearly sought, therefore, to intensify the level of commodification of British labour in order that capital could be profitably invested in the British economy. Indeed, as both Coates (1975) and Glyn and Sutcliffe (1972) have argued, the Wilson Government was faced with low investment, an over-valued pound, low productivity and a well-entrenched working class, all of which combined to produce a fall in the rate of British profitability (or, in the terms introduced in the earlier chapter, a crisis of overaccumulation). As a result, in order

> to produce the economic growth which the Labour Party had promised, its profit margins *had* to be restored, its investment levels raised, its productivity increased, its resources concentrated in its export sector, and its working-class pressure on costs eased.
>
> (Coates, 1975: 113)

This in turn implied an attempt 'to spend the bulk of its period in office attempting to undermine the industrial power, job security and living standards' of the workforce within the UK (Coates, 1975: 113). Moreover, in an attempt to maintain 'traditional' social democratic party relations, the government continued to seek the containment of its constituents' demands for decommodification, arguing that its policy measures were in their long-term interest. Thus, shortly after the 1966 general election, the prime minister announced that the Prices and Incomes Policy is not a whim of a Government Department, not a bright idea that has occurred to [Secretary of State for Economic Affairs] George Brown and me. It is a necessary condition of maintaining full employment.

(quoted in Panitch, 1976: 106)

Similarly, in confronting the National Union of Seamen, Wilson condemned what he claimed was 'a strike against the state, against the community' (quoted in Panitch, 1976: 108). Finally, in welcoming the TUC's support for the government's wage freeze, Brown himself announced that the 'TUC, not for the first time is ahead in saying "we will surrender for the good of the country"' (quoted in Panitch, 1976: 119).

In 1967, however, the Wilson Government decided to devalue sterling to a new rate of $2.40 to the pound. This prompted severe disillusion amongst the Labour Party's 'traditional' social democratic constituency. The decision effectively meant that all the sacrifices that the government had asked of the labour movement and its traditional social democratic constituency – in the form of wage freezes, reduced public expenditure and increased indirect taxes – had nonetheless failed to avoid a devaluation of the pound. Indeed, speculation against the pound continued to the extent that widespread fear remained that yet another devaluation might be necessary. This therefore prompted yet more fiscal austerity measures (including the postponement of a planned raising of the school leaving age and the reimposition of prescription charges) and a continuation of statutory wage restraint. Whilst the balance of payments and budget deficit moved into surplus by 1970, therefore, this was largely at the cost of both private consumption and public expenditure (Shaw, 1996: 79–81). Moreover, the government's increasingly austere fiscal and income policies began to prompt increasing opposition from its grassroots constituency, thereby significantly destabilizing 'traditional' social democratic party relations (Shaw, 1996: 78). In particular, the trade unions became increasingly hostile to Labour Party policy, witnessing for instance the membership of the traditionally loyal NUM voting to oppose the 1966 Prices and Incomes Bill (against the recommendation of the union executive) and the 1967 TUC Congress adopting a motion opposing the 1967 Prices and Incomes Bill. Further, industrial unrest increased during the late 1960s, with growing trade unionist despondency towards the government prompting the election of a more radical union leadership (including Hugh Scanlon in the AEU, Arthur Scargill in the NUM, and Jack Jones in the TGWU). The ability of the Labour Government to regulate the demands of its core constituency was therefore coming under increasing strain. As a result, 'between 1964 and 1967, the average number of days lost through strikes ranged from 2–3 million. The following year this doubled to 4.7 million and reached 6.8 million in 1969'. Moreover, many of these were unofficial and 'unconstitutional' (Shaw, 1996: 82). In response to this rise of industrial unrest, the government published in 1969 a White Paper, *In Place of Strife*, which sought (unsuccessfully, as it was eventually defeated by opposition throughout the labour movement) to regulate industrial action and thereby recommodify labour through disciplinary means

(Shaw, 1996: 82–8). The defeat of *In Place of Strife* represented a major breakdown in 'traditional' social democratic party relations, as in the words of Leo Panitch, 'workers openly rejected the Labour Party's contention that they could best improve their lot in capitalist society by foregoing the expression of industrial class conflict.' (Panitch, 1976: 213).

Largely as a result of the tumultuous end to the 1960s under the Labour Government, the Labour Party was once again voted out of office in 1970 and, as with its earlier period out of office, the pressure upon the Labour Party leadership to pursue the recommodification of British labour was considerably reduced. As a result, the 1972 party conference reversed its support for statutory wage restraint and committed itself to a large extension of public ownership with minimum compensation and the introduction of industrial democracy (Panitch, 1976: 228). Nonetheless, and again in a way that repeated the experience of the Labour Party in opposition in the 1950s, the party leadership eventually reasserted control of the party and adopted more moderate policy commitments to decommodify the lives of the Labour Party's 'traditional' social democratic constituency. Thus, the 1973 Conference passed a resolution which granted considerable autonomy to the party leadership regarding the choice of policies to be implemented once it returned to office and the opportunity to reject conference demands for nationalization. Nevertheless, the 1974 general election manifesto did commit the Labour Party to nationalization of failing industries, the drawing up of planning agreements, a National Enterprise Board to invest in profitable sectors, and measures to introduce supervisory boards that resembled the practice of German codetermination. In terms of incomes policy, the manifesto committed the party to *voluntary* wage restraint, which it sought to present as a 'social contract', thereby marking a significant move away from the policy of statutory wage restraint of the 1964–70 period, (Panitch, 1976: 229–33). This 'Social Contract' therefore represented an attempt to secure stable cooperation between the Labour Party in office and the wider labour movement (Holmes, 1985: 6).

In February 1974 the Labour Party was elected on a 'traditional' social democratic platform that sought a 'climate of social justice, and the re-establishment of political, public control over market, private forces', and aimed to represent and benefit the organized working class, the public sector and the poor, in the interests of the British economy and the unity of British society as a whole (Coates, 1980: 7–12). Indeed, upon election to office, the government set about quickly seeking to implement key decommodifying elements of the 'Social Contract'. Thus, within two days of taking office the Wilson Government settled the ongoing miners' strike (that had effectively defeated the preceding Heath Government) with a deal above the miners' original claim. Similarly, statutory incomes policy was abandoned, food subsidies were introduced, pensions increased and the Heath Government's Industrial Relations Act was repealed (Holmes, 1985: 5–8). However, by 1975 the British capitalist economy was in crisis: price inflation was over 30 per cent, wage inflation was 27.4 per cent, the balance of payments deficit was around £3.3 billion, GDP had fallen by 2.5 per cent over the previous year, and unemployment had risen to over 1 million (Coates, 1980: 13–24). In the light of these developments, the government appeared to have seriously misjudged the level of labour commodification necessary to secure the reproduction of the capital–labour relations it sought to govern over. Having secured re-election to office in the October 1974 election, therefore, the government was now faced with the effects of its initial reflationary measures. Moreover, as a result of both the experience of the 1964–70 Wilson Government, and the commitments contained in the Social Contract, 'both compulsory wage restraint and deflationary measures were strictly ruled out' for the early period of the 1974–79 government (Holmes, 1985: 11). By 1975, however, the government chose to implement major spending cuts (of nearly £1 billion) in its April 1975 budget, including reductions in subsidies for nationalized industries, food and housing. Further, with wages rising at 10 per cent more than prices, the government adopted a flat-rate £6 wage rise limit with a zero increase for those on £8500 or above, to take effect from 1 August 1975. The TUC General Council and the 1975 TUC Congress accepted the policy, thereby avoiding the need for statutory control, although the move effectively ended the Social Contract. These initial restrictive measures were complemented in November 1975 by a further cabinet decision to implement public expenditure cuts of £3 billion, published as a White Paper in February of the following year, and the second stage of the incomes policy agreement in May 1976, which agreed a further restriction in wage rises to 4.5 per cent.

As the British economy entered recession, however, 'a growing fiscal crisis forced the government into heavy borrowing to meet increased demands for welfare as unemployment rose, undermining foreign confidence and forcing the value of sterling to historically low levels' (Rhodes, 2000: 35). The currency markets increasingly speculated against sterling, viewing the British economy as in serious need of a reduction in public expenditure. In response, the Callaghan Government was famously forced to introduce a further £1 billion of cuts in July, and to apply to the IMF for an emergency loan in September. Attached to this loan which was yet another package of £3 billion cuts in public expenditure over two years (Holmes, 1985), producing overbearing strain upon 'traditional' social democratic party relations. Moreover, in an attempt to acquire the consent of 'traditional' social democratic party constituents, Labour Prime Minister, James Callaghan, argued in a frequently quoted speech that,

> [W]e used to think that you could spend your way out of recession and increase employment by cutting taxes and boosting Government spending. I will tell you in all candour that that option no longer exists, and that insofar as it ever did exist, it only worked on each occasion since the war by injecting a bigger dose of inflation into the economy, followed by a higher level of unemployment as the next step.
>
> (Labour Party, 1976)

For many commentators, Callaghan's 1976 conference speech marked a turning point in the attempt to reproduce 'traditional' social democratic party relations in Britain as the tensions between the party leadership and its constituency proved overwhelming. Thus, in 1977 the government faced mounting resistance to its attempt to further restrain wages. Whilst trade union leaders continued to support the government's incomes policy, the union membership became increasingly recalcitrant. For instance, the 1977 TGWU conference rejected General Secretary Jack Jones' recommendation for a waiting period of 12-months after an initial pay rise before submitting a subsequent one, evincing a growing division between the union leadership and its membership as workers grew increasingly impatient with the practice of government pay restraint (Holmes, 1985: 109–10).

In July 1978, during a brief economic upturn, the government announced that stage 4 of its incomes policy would seek a 5 per cent pay limit. In doing so, it sought to maintain the support of its working-class constituency by arguing that it needed to contain wage demands so that low pay claims could lead to a reduction in unemployment, inflation, and therefore the need for public expenditure cuts. For instance, William Rodgers, Transport Minister, argued,

> In the national interest and not least in the interest of maintaining and improving public services it must be understood that if public sector wages take a bigger share of the national cake then – if we are not simply to finance inflation by printing money, as our predecessors did – the consequences are clear.
> (quoted in Holmes, 1985: 126)

However, the 5 per cent pay limit was rejected by the TUC General Council and the policy was immediately broken in September 1978 when an industrial dispute at Ford settled for 15 per cent. This in turn prompted a series of industrial disputes in which, having sensed that the incomes policy was on the brink of collapse, workers sought to catch up on the pay claims they had been forced to limit during the first three stages of the government's incomes policy. Petrol tank hauliers, lorry drivers, and, most damagingly, public sector workers entered a period of prolonged industrial disruption that included strikes and secondary picketing. The 1978–9 'winter of discontent' therefore witnessed strike numbers rise from 1 to 4.5 million (Rhodes, 2000: 35), and left the Callaghan Government with the distinct appearance of incompetence and an inability to either effectively govern or 'represent' the interests of its core constituency.

The crisis of 'traditional' social democratic party relations

Having charted the increasingly problematic reproduction of 'traditional' social democratic party relations in the case of the British Labour Party from 1945 to 1979, this section argues that, following the defeat of the 1979 election, these relations went into crisis. Thus, it proved impossible for the Labour Party leadership to reproduce 'traditional' social democratic party relations. If we accept Habermas' (1976) definition of crisis as the point at which a social system is no longer able to reproduce itself in accordance with its own internal relations, values and powers, therefore, we can consider 1979 to mark the beginning of a crisis period in Labour Party history. Indeed, between 1979 and 1995 (the point at which the Labour Party is largely considered to have adopted a 'new' social democratic programme), the 'traditional' social democratic party relations of the Labour Party were unable to successfully reproduce themselves. We witness during this period, therefore, an oscillation between alternative ideological stances and policy programmes, none of which were successfully able to reconcile the contending pressures emergent from the structure of 'traditional' social democratic party relations.

Indeed, as has been well documented elsewhere, the intense ideological struggle within the Labour Party that followed the 1979 general election defeat witnessed a schism between the left and right of the party (Seyd, 1987). On the one hand, the left, led by Tony Benn, mobilized around three interconnected goals: internal party democracy through the ascendant Campaign for Labour Party Democracy (CLPD); national economic democracy in the form of a political-economic programme that came to be known as the Alternative Economic Strategy (AES); and withdrawal from the EC. It had increasingly come to view the lack of accountability of the party leadership to the grassroots as one of the problems preventing 'traditional' social democracy from successfully representing the interests of its working-class constituency, thereby explaining the focus on internal party democracy. The AES was promoted as a programme of economic protectionism, state-financed reflation, fiscal redistribution, and the nationalization of industry, which it claimed would secure a more thoroughgoing intervention in, and democratization of, the British capitalist economy. Moreover, the left viewed the EC as antithetical to its interventionist programme and therefore pursued the withdrawal of the UK from the EC (Callaghan, 2000b). On the other hand, the right of the Labour Party resisted each of these initiatives on the grounds that they were economically impractical and therefore rendered the Labour Party electorally unviable. In particular, EC membership became one of the defining issues for the left of the Party as it was seen as an organization that limited the scope for national economic policy-making (and therefore the scope for implementing social democracy itself). This conflict would come to form the basis for intra-party divisions up until the general election of 1983. Thus, the Labour left was successful in the early 1980s in a number of attempts to reform internal Labour Party democracy. This included the adoption of Conference resolutions committing the Labour Party to the mandatory reselection of MPs by their constituency parties prior to each general election, and to the adoption of a new electoral college for selecting the Party leadership that included the PLP, CLPs and the trade unions. It also achieved the election of Michael Foot as party leader and, in 1983, the adoption of one of the most left-leaning manifestos in the party's history, committing the Labour Party to reflationary measures, redistribution, import and price controls, industrial democracy and withdrawal from the EC. In contrast, and in response to the rise of the Labour left, a significant proportion of the right of the parliamentary party left the Labour Party in 1981 to form the Social Democratic Party (SDP) (Seyd, 1987). The result of these developments, however, was a major defeat in the 1983 general election, witnessing the Labour Party gain only 27.6 per cent of the vote (its lowest since 1918), and losing 60 seats in the process. The 1983 manifesto was famously dubbed 'the longest suicide note in history'.[1]

As with previous periods out of office, however, following the radical turn of the 1979–83 period, the Labour Party leadership sought once again to reclaim control of the party and adopt more moderately decommodifying policy commitments. Nevertheless, the strength of the Labour left within the party, combined with the skilful utilization of the memory of the 1974–79 period of Labour Government by the Thatcher administration, created a context in which such a process of moderation proved unable to satisfactorily recombine the elements of 'traditional' social democratic party relations. Thus, following the 1983 general election defeat, Foot was replaced as leader by Neil Kinnock, who sought both to increase the control of the leadership's office and to significantly moderate the party programme (Panitch and Leys, 2001; Motta and Bailey, 2007). This process was given further impetus following the subsequent general election defeat of 1987 and, as a result, between 1988 and 1991 the party programme underwent a number of considerable changes as part of a policy review process comprised of seven policy review groups (a process that was tightly controlled by the leadership's office) (Taylor, 1997). This policy review witnessed the Labour Party officially accept much of the neoliberal critique of 'traditional' social democracy, including the claim that an oversized government was inefficient and therefore damaged the economy, either directly (through its inefficiency) or indirectly through its negative effect on the investment decisions of capital. Alongside these developments, the Labour Party began to argue for the importance of facilitating the market through the provision of important supply-side conditions, in order to stimulate investment and growth. As such, the policy review represented the first steps in the adoption of a 'new' social democratic programme. Thus, in the 1990 policy review document, *Looking to the Future*, the party stated,

> We welcome and endorse the efficiency and realism which markets can provide. The difference between ourselves and the Conservatives is not that they accept the market and we do not, but that we recognise the limits of the market and they do not. The market can be a good servant, but is often a bad master.
>
> Left to itself, the market cannot provide the education and training, the high-speed transport and telecommunications, the environmental protection, the investment in science and technology or the regional development which a modern economy needs.
>
> (Labour Party, 1990: 6)

However, the moderation of the Labour Party programme through the course of the policy review nevertheless proved unable to attain the sufficient support of a 'traditional' social democratic electoral constituency. Thus, whilst its commitment to radical decommodification in the 1983 election had left the party with an appearance of being unfit for office, its attempt to present a moderate balance of decommodification and recommodification following the policy review proved equally unable to appeal to a sufficiently broad electoral constituency to win election to office. In particular, the party's commitment to higher taxation and spending was of particular concern to many of the middle-class voters the Labour Party courted, and was successfully emphasized by the Conservative Party as a key sign of the implausibility of Labour's moderation (Butler, 1992). As a result, the experience of electoral defeat in the 1992 election convinced many on the right of the Labour Party that a more successful reproduction of Labour Party relations would in fact require a more thoroughgoing transformation of the structure of social democratic party relations. It was this prolonged experience of crisis within the 'traditional' social democratic Labour Party, therefore, that ultimately prompted the transition to 'new' social democracy under Blair. Thus, following a brief pause in the modernization of the Labour Party under the leadership of John Smith, the Labour Party was transformed into a 'new' social democratic party from 1995 onwards, under the leadership of Tony Blair.

The transformation to 'new' social democracy

The election of Tony Blair as leader of the Labour Party on 21 June 1994 represented a new direction for the Labour Party. Elected with 57 per cent of the vote[2] Blair and his entourage of 'modernisers'[3] argued that the failure of the Labour Party to win the 1992 General Election could be explained in terms of the failure of Labour to convince the electorate that it accepted the unfeasibility and unsuitability of its pre-policy review programme. In order to resolve this problem of mistrust amongst the electorate, Blair argued, it was necessary to prove that the Labour Party was committed to facilitating the operation of the market and was not comprised of covert radical socialists (Mandelson and Liddle, 1996: 92). This therefore marked the birth of New Labour, a political programme aiming to transform the image of the Labour Party in the minds of the electorate. Blair sought to contrast 'New' Labour, which advocated market efficiency, meritocracy, indirectly facilitating (rather than directly intervening in) the operation of the market, and a less centralized and overbearing state implementing efficient public services, with the popular conception of 'Old' Labour, which he viewed as being associated with heavy-handed state intervention and disproportionately influential trade unions (see Blair, 1998 for a coherent outline of this view). In doing so, he sought to broaden the electoral constituency of the Labour Party, in an attempt 'to reach out beyond Old Labour's traditional base in the ever-shrinking working class and among deprived minorities and to gain new recruits in the expanding middle classes and aspiring middle-income groups' (Heath *et al.*, 2001: 105). The main tool that Blair chose to symbolize this transformation was the reform to Clause IV of the Labour Party's constitution, thereby changing the party's constitutional *raison d'être* from the 'common ownership of the means of production'[4] to the aim to 'create for each of us the means to reach our true potential and for all of us a community in which power, wealth and opportunity are in the hands of the many not the few', an aim which would be realized through

> a dynamic economy, serving the public interest, in which the enterprise of the market and the rigour of competition are joined with the forces of partnership and co-operation to produce the wealth the nation needs and the opportunity for all to work and prosper.
>
> (Labour Party, 1995)

By the time of the 1997 general election, therefore, the Labour Party under Blair had fully adopted a 'new' social democratic programme. This included an avowed rejection of the statist approach of 'traditional' social democracy, of fiscal redistribution (and especially increases in income tax), of the expansion of the welfare state, and of a macroeconomic policy aimed at planning and direct management of the economy. Instead, 'New' Labour proposed a policy framework that was business-friendly, including a low tax regime with social and economic policies that focused on active labour market policies (education, training, support for technological research and development, and subsidies for work experience placements) and means-tested benefits (often conditional upon attempts to join the labour market) for the poorest (and most worthy, which was usually defined in terms of their preparedness to engage in paid employment) sections of society. This new policy programme was justified both in terms of its moral superiority over 'traditional' social democracy (see Blair, 1998) *and* in terms of the impracticability of 'traditional' social democracy given the scale of 'globalization' and the limits it places upon state activity (Watson and Hay, 2003). Thus, in outlining its 'new' social democratic programme to the electorate in its 1997 manifesto, *New Labour: Because Britain Deserves Better*, the Labour Party claimed:

> The old left would have sought state control of industry. The Conservative right is content to leave all to the market. We reject both approaches. Government and industry must work together to achieve key objectives aimed at enhancing the dynamism of the market, not undermining it.
> (Labour Party, 1997)

In order to further distance itself from the tainted image of 'Old' Labour, the manifesto stated,

> We have rewritten our constitution, the new Clause IV, to put a commitment to enterprise alongside the commitment to justice. We have changed the way we make policy, and put our relations with the trade unions on a modern footing where they accept they can get fairness but no favours from a Labour government.
> (Labour Party, 1997)

Further, to illustrate its replacement of class-based politics with national pragmatic politics, the manifesto stated,

> We are a national party, supported by people from all walks of life, from the successful businessman or woman to the pensioner on a council estate.
> [...]
> We are a broad-based movement for progress and justice. New Labour is the political arm of none other than the British people as a whole. Our values are the same: the equal worth of all, with no one cast aside; fairness and justice within strong communities.

But we have liberated these values from outdated dogma or doctrine, and we have applied these values to the modern world.

(Labour Party, 1997)

The Labour Party in its 'traditional' social democratic phase had sought to balance a commitment to the decommodification of the lives of its constituents with the necessary (particularly in office) recommodification of labour during periods of economic crisis. In its 'new' social democratic stage, however, the Labour Party sought rather to insist that it was its ability to achieve the successful management of the national capitalist economy – including the strategic promotion of recommodification – that was the basis of its electoral appeal. In this sense, therefore, the transition from 'traditional' to 'new' social democracy, in the case of the British Labour Party, can be considered a process whereby both the working-class element of the electoral constituency has been de-emphasized and the commitment to decommodifying policies has been replaced by an appeal to the technical administration of recommodifying measures that seek a more successful reproduction of capital–labour relations within the UK. Importantly, however, 'New' Labour's electoral appeal was less focused upon an *alternative* electoral constituency, than it was upon an *extended* one. In de-emphasizing the working-class element to its electoral core, therefore, the Labour Party leadership continued to seek the support of the working class, but to couple that with a large increase in support amongst the non-unionised middle class (Heath *et al.*, 2001: 134–9). In undertaking these revisions, and in attempting so thoroughly to project an image of reform and internal party transformation, the Labour Party, in its 'New' Labour guise, has since been considered by many commentators to be something of a template for other social democratic parties to follow. Indeed, as we shall we see in the remainder of this chapter, similar processes of transformation, occurring in parallel with that in the UK, can also be witnessed in the four other cases under investigation in the present study.

Swedish social democracy

The reproduction of 'traditional' social democratic party relations in the case of the Swedish Social Democratic Party (SAP) is a process that has been characterized by a number of extremes. Thus, the SAP managed to achieve, during its 'traditional' social democratic period, a combination of perhaps the most extensively decommodifying public policies in western Europe, with probably the most extensive active labour market policy which sought to ensure the continued participation of Swedish workers within the national labour market (and therefore ensure their ongoing commodification). Moreover, in doing so, the SAP achieved what was probably the most successful reproduction of 'traditional' social democratic party relations, establishing hegemonic status within Swedish politics throughout the post-war period. Nevertheless, the tensions contained within the structure of 'traditional' social democratic party relations became increasingly problematic for the SAP through the course of the 1970s and 1980s, eventually resulting in a series of reforms that witnessed a move towards the adoption of a 'new' social democratic programme. The 'analytical narrative' that follows seeks to chart these developments and the way in which they resulted in the moves by the 'new' social democratic party elite towards the promotion, and adoption, of a social democratic policy programme.

The SAP and the successful reproduction of 'traditional' social democratic party relations?

The SAP adopted a 'traditional' social democratic structure of party relations in the context of the 1930s depression years. Thus, upon its election to office in 1932, the SAP set about increasing spending on public works programmes. This was a policy particularly developed by Ernst Wigforss, SAP finance minister from 1932–36, who drew on ideas developed by young Swedish economists, Gunnar Myrdal, Erik Lindahl, and Bertil Ohlin. These early 'traditional' social democrats sought to challenge classical liberalism with the claim that public spending could successfully stimulate the national economy and therefore facilitate economic recovery during times of recession. Moreover, during the pre-Second World War period, the SAP engineered a successful class-compromise between business and labour. The government promised preferable tax rates for capital spent on investment, and to maintain low, competitive exchange rates that would facilitate business planning. In exchange, Swedish labour was given four guarantees: that the state would be committed to economic growth and the redistribution of income; that full employment would be the primary goal of the state; that the LO (Swedish trade union confederation) would have autonomy in its negotiation of wages with the Swedish Employers Federation (SAF); and that Swedish business would not employ replacement workers or use lock-outs as a means to defeat labour in industrial conflicts. This agreement, reached in 1938, has since become known as the Saltsjöbaden Accords (Blyth, 2002: 104–15). From the 1930s onwards, therefore, the SAP adopted a 'traditional' social democratic commitment to balance both the need for the commodification of labour under capitalism with the introduction of decommodifying measures including a commitment to full employment and the provision of redistributive public policies.

In keeping with the real definition of 'traditional' social democratic party relations adopted in Chapter 2, therefore, the SAP leadership sought, relatively successfully, during this early period to contain the demands of its working-class-oriented constituency. In particular, the SAP Party elite sought to emphasize the way in which a moderation of workers' demands would ultimately facilitate the development of a Swedish 'People's Home', a term popularized by SAP leader, Per Albin Hansson in a frequently-cited 1928 parliamentary speech, when he claimed,

> [T]he basis of the home is community and the feeling of togetherness. The good home knows no privileged or disadvantaged, no favourites and no stepchildren. There, one does not look down upon the other, there, nobody tries to get himself an advantage at the cost of the other, the strong one does not hold

down and plunder the weak. In the good home there prevails equality, consideration, cooperation, helpfulness. Applied to the great people and citizens' home this would mean the breaking down of all social and economic barriers, which now divide the citizens into privileged and disadvantaged, into rulers and dependents, into rich and poor, propertied and miserable, plunderers and plundered.

(quoted in Olsen, 1992: 98)

By the time the Second World War had finished, therefore, the SAP had already maintained a 'traditional' social democratic structure of party relations for over a decade. Prior to the end of the war, however, the LO and SAP drafted, and formally adopted in 1944, a post-war programme that sought to significantly reform the structure of Swedish capitalist relations, and as such more closely resembled the 'reformist' model of social democratic parties discussed in the first chapter. Thus, the 1944 programme included a commitment to full employment, stable economic growth, increased public control over investment and the allocation of credit, an extensive planning programme, and the nationalization of insurance, credit institutions, transport, communications and natural resources (provided nationalization was necessary for full employment and economic efficiency). The SAP faced, however, an extremely hostile reaction to its 'reformist' programme, from both employers' associations and non-socialist parties. Partly as a result of this opposition, the SAP lost the 1948 general election (although the inability of the non-socialist parties to form a viable coalition prevented them from entering office). In response, the 1944 programme was effectively jettisoned in favour of a more 'traditional' social democratic agenda similar to the one that had been adopted during the inter-war period (Olsen, 1992: 56–7).

New SAP leader, Tage Erlander, was appointed prime minister in 1946. Upon his accession to office, however, the Erlander Government was unexpectedly faced with a growing risk of inflationary growth. Thus, in the immediate post-war climate of full employment, expansionary welfare provisions,[5] and rapid economic growth, the risk of inflation became a major concern. In seeking to ensure the successful reproduction of the national capitalist economy, therefore, the government initially responded by advocating wage restraint, and, in 1949, by adopting a total wage freeze. This placed great strain on the union movement, which in turn produced tensions across the wider structure of 'traditional' social democratic party relations (Tilton, 1991: 194). Thus, when the wage freeze expired in 1951, 'the LO flatly rejected the SAP's plan for another round of wage restraint the following year', claiming it would 'further undermine the solidarity of the union movement and its relationship to the SAP' (Olsen, 1992: 58). As an alternative, the LO proposed what came to be known as the Rehn-Meidner model: a means to maintain growth and welfare expansion in an open economy, in a form that would avoid stimulating inflation.

The Rehn-Meidner model therefore represented another plank (to complement the Saltsjöbaden Accords) in the development of Swedish 'traditional' social democratic party policy and was finally adopted as official policy by Erlander in 1955

(Ryner, 2002: 81–4). It contained four central elements. First, fiscal policy would seek to keep profit rates down and thereby avoid inflation. Second, the adoption of the practice of centralized wage negotiation, in which the principle of equal pay for equal work would be stressed, aimed to create a redistribution of resources to the most productive firms in the Swedish economy, whilst simultaneously creating a more egalitarian pay structure. Third, an active labour market policy would be used to increase labour market flexibility and ensure that workers moved to productive firms rather than remain unemployed. This was a process coordinated by the National Labour Market Board (AMS), which actively sought to assist and direct the unemployed in their attempt to identify and (if necessary) re-locate to new employment opportunities (Rothstein, 1996: 108–16). Fourth, the state would make public savings available for productive investment in order that restrictions on profit-making would not translate into lower levels of employment. The Rehn-Meidner plan therefore effectively advocated intervention in the labour market as a means to ensure more equitable outcomes. Whilst not a straightforward policy of wage restraint, such as we witnessed in the case of the British Labour Party, its purpose was to ensure sufficient restraint in the overall level of wage rises in order to enable the successful reproduction of capital–labour relations in Sweden, whilst simultaneously seeking to avoid both low pay and high income differentials through a policy of centralized wage negotiation. Whilst there were obvious benefits for those who would otherwise be paid at a lower rate, therefore, for those who were required to moderate wage demands the benefits were less obvious. In its attempt to ensure the acquiescence of this latter group, the SAP leadership relied upon reference to the benefits that would accrue, in terms of national economic stability and growth, and, perhaps most importantly, the rise in welfare expenditure that such a programme of growth would facilitate.

The importance placed on labour mobility, and in particular the role of the AMS in encouraging and facilitating that mobility, clearly illustrated the emphasis placed by the Erlander Government upon ensuring that labour was sufficiently commodified. This was largely achieved through the promotion of free labour mobility, which sought to ensure that workers would be free to move to areas where capital was more profitably able to employ it. In 1957, following the appointment of new director-general, Bertil Olsson, therefore, the AMS adopted a specific policy of producing various types of persuasive campaigns that sought to encourage workers to commit themselves to labour mobility. These campaigns included newspaper articles, films, presentations at public exhibitions, and attendance at study groups, and were supported by both the LO, as it promised to produce full employment (and thereby bolster the strength of organized labour), and the SAF, as it sought to increase labour productivity (Rothstein, 1996: 114–5). The SAP Government therefore successfully managed to secure a working balance between the demands of its 'traditional' social democratic constituency and those of Swedish business. In the words of SAF chief economist, K-O Faxén:

> I do not believe that other countries have the same general attitude at all. There you would find a good deal of romantic talk about the local community,

tradition and the importance of soldiering on, of maintaining the culture of a particular area, so that one does not say – in the ruthless way we are doing here in Sweden and that we consider to be morally right – that when an area ceases to have a good economic potential, we should institute a labour market policy for stimulating mobility to make it easier for people to move away.

(quoted in Rothstein, 1996: 114)

In this sense, therefore, the SAP Government successfully contained constituents' demands within the bounds of the necessary level of labour commodification.

An additional important development in the SAP's 'traditional' social democratic programme occurred with the introduction in 1959 of an earnings-related pension (the ATP reform) that would successfully unify the interests of the SAP's working-class-oriented constitutency with the middle-class votes it also courted. Thus, under pressure from the LO during the 1950s, the SAP leadership drew up a plan for a supplementary pension, based on employer contributions, that would provide a pension worth 50 per cent of the income earned by an employee during their 15 best-paid years. The aim of the scheme was both to ensure that public pension provision would reduce poverty amongst the elderly (and therefore act in a redistributive and decommodifying manner), and to create a large financial reserve that could be used for public investment (Olsen, 1992: 63–4). The lasting achievement of this policy, as already noted, however, was its ability to unite the interests of the working class with those of the salaried class. This was due to the cross-class nature of its generosity, which thereby incorporated the salaried classes into a broad 'traditional' social democratic constituency (Esping-Andersen, 1985: 108–10).

In sum, 'traditional' social democratic party relations in Sweden were constructed around decommodifying public policies that included solidaristic wage agreements, fiscal redistribution through the expansion of universal welfare provisions, full employment, and the expansion of welfare and pension provisions, alongside a concern that capital would remain profitable through the containment of wage demands, an active labour market which engendered a commitment to flexibility amongst the workforce, and a fiscal policy focused on controlling inflation. This model was relatively successful throughout the 1950s and 1960s, experiencing an average annual growth in real GDP of 4 per cent between 1951 and 1970 (Olsson, 1987: 40). Unemployment remained between 1 and 2 per cent during the same period (Ryner, 2002: 84) and social expenditure as a percentage of GDP grew from 11.3 per cent in 1950 to 25.9 per cent in 1970 (Olsson, 1987: 42). Social spending focused on 'the expansion and centralization of work-related benefits', including pensions, health insurance, unemployment insurance, a universal child allowance, an expansion of social housing, and a big increase in the role of the welfare state as an employer (between 1965 and 1980 the public payroll doubled from 0.7 to 1.4 million employees) (Benner and Vad, 2000: 404–6). This strong economic record enabled the SAP to fulfil its commitment to the representation of constituents' demands, whilst at the same time ensuring the relatively successful reproduction of the Swedish capitalist economy (Ryner, 2002: 79–98). As a result, the SAP successfully established itself as the 'natural party of government' in Sweden, remaining in office up until 1976. Alongside its successful economic performance, however, the electoral dominance of the SAP was also, in part, due to the success of the SAP in extending its appeal beyond (but nevertheless continuing to include) its core working-class constituency. Thus, 'by 1960, the party program made little if any reference to class conflict and, following in the "folkhem" [People's Home] tradition, appealed to the *national interest*' (Olsen, 1992: 102). 'Traditional' social democratic party relations in Sweden, therefore, appeared to have successfully balanced the commodification and decommodification of Swedish labour, whilst also ensuring the sufficient containment of the demands of an electoral constituency that included both working- and middle-class constituents, such that those demands could be electorally 'represented' in a mutually-compatible form. In these terms, the post-war experience of the SAP appears to reflect a model of 'traditional' social democratic party relations.

The problematic reproduction of 'traditional' social democracy in the case of the Swedish Social Democratic Party

Despite the apparently successful reproduction by the SAP of 'traditional' social democratic party relations during the post-war period, from the late-1960s onwards the Swedish model that the SAP had so successfully promoted underwent what has been described elsewhere as an 'organic crisis' (Ryner, 2002: 123–58). A series of wildcat strikes throughout Sweden in 1969 and 1970 – most famously in the northern mining town of Kiruna – signalled a growing, and unanticipated, militancy in Swedish workers' demands. In particular, workers in sectors not receiving large pay rises were becoming increasingly unhappy with the system of centralized wage negotiations. Moreover, workers were becoming increasingly unhappy about the restraints being placed upon their lifestyles by the requirements of the Swedish economic model. As one of the Kiruna workers put it,

> All these rules for the workers. You are circumscribed. Surrounded by a river that you cannot cross. You do not feel stupid and you do not feel that work is depriving. You know that it has valuable aspects. All people have a need to create something. But in this kind of work place you do not have any possibilities to be creative. How eight hours can be like years.
> (quoted in Heclo and Madsen, 1987: 141)

These strains on the Swedish class compromise were exacerbated further still by the economic crisis that struck the country in the 1970s. Swedish exports, which had been central to the success of the Swedish model up until the 1970s, began to lose their price competitiveness (Ryner, 2002: 126–32). This resulted in a wide range of economic problems for the Swedish model. The annual average real growth rate declined to 2 per cent during the 1970s. Industrial production declined on average by 6.2 per cent annually between 1974 and 1982. The Swedish terms of trade deteriorated sharply, resulting in a foreign debt of 21 per cent of GDP by 1982 (compared to a net credit position of 5.3 per cent in 1974), and price inflation rose dramatically (Ryner, 2002: 233).

In an attempt to resolve this double problem – rising constituents' demands plus slow economic growth – the SAP Government, now led by Olof Palme, adopted a 'traditional' social democratic strategy of Keynesian reflation, with increased redistributive spending in an attempt to appease the demands of its core constituency. Thus, the government increased public spending in areas where political demand amongst its constituents was highest, including regional policy, labour market policy, gender equality and parental insurance. It also introduced a day-care programme and increased replacement rates for health insurance. As a result, social expenditure continued to grow throughout the 1970s, rising from around 20 per cent of GDP in 1967 to 30 per cent in the late 1970s. Similarly, the government made a number of improvements in workers' rights, including in the area of health and safety, protection against unfair dismissal, and the introduction of co-determination (which received a particularly hostile reception from the SAF) in an attempt to further decommodify the lives of its core constituency. The government also introduced what came to be known as the EFO model, whereby wages would be agreed between representatives of employers and employees according to the market price in the competitive export-oriented or import-competing sector, and applied to the labour market as a whole. This was an attempt, therefore, to ensure that wage rises would remain competitive, thereby seeking to avoid wage drift, which itself risked eroding the profit incentive in the Swedish economy. Moreover, a state industrial policy was introduced that would use national savings (derived from such funds as the national pension's fund) to invest in industry. And, finally, the SAP adopted an LO proposal for a wage-earner fund, whereby a proportion of pre-tax profits would be invested on behalf of the workers in a particular enterprise, thereby achieving a gradual move towards workers' collective ownership of firms. Indeed, the wage-earner fund initiative represented a significantly more radical attempt by the SAP to reform capital–labour relations than it had until this point advocated. As such, it represented a move away from typical 'traditional' social democratic party policy, although severe opposition from the SAF and bourgeois parties meant that it was only ever implemented in a substantially reduced form (Ryner, 2002: 132–44; on the fortunes of these reforms, see Pontusson, 1992). SAF opposition to the wage-earner funds also prompted wider opposition from the business community to the terms of the Swedish model. As a result, Swedish business increasingly came to view the policy aspirations of the social democratic movement as too great an encumbrance upon their economic activity, leading firms, particularly in the engineering sector, to cease to cooperate with the process of collective wage bargaining and to seek instead to relocate internationally in an attempt to avoid high wage costs in Sweden.

Despite these attempts to resolve the dual problem of rising social demands and declining economic growth faced by the Palme Government, in 1976 the SAP lost the general election, for the first time in the post-war period, to a bourgeois coalition consisting of the Moderates, the Liberal Party and the Centre Party. However, this bourgeois coalition equally failed to resolve some of the key structural problems facing the Swedish economy in the second half of the 1970s, therefore resulting in 1982, when the SAP were elected back into office, in the continued existence of a number of these problems. These included relatively high unemployment, an uncompetitive export industry, lack of investment, a structural budget deficit that had risen from 2 per cent in 1976 to 13 per cent by 1982, and rapidly increasing foreign debt (Benner and Vad, 2000: 418–20; Ryner, 2002: 148; Olsen, 1992: 68). As such, the Swedish economy was increasingly characterized by (what we termed in Chapter 2 as) a crisis of overaccumulation, whereby capital was unable to identify opportunities for profitable investment resulting in a period of economic decline.

The combination of a balance of payments deficit and government budget deficit also compounded the dependency of the Swedish economy on international capital markets, as the government was forced to borrow in order to finance these deficits. This therefore prompted further moves to liberalize the Swedish capital market in an attempt to reduce this dependence (Olsen, 1992: 68–9). The same period also witnessed employers increasingly seek to opt out of peak-level wage negotiations, thereby acting to remove a central element of the Rehn-Meidner model (Pontusson, 1992). By the mid-1980s, therefore, we can witness serious strains in the structure of 'traditional' social democratic party relations. Members of the electoral constituency were becoming both increasingly demanding and less satisfied with the SAP's claim to 'represent' their interests. Further, Swedish capital was finding it increasingly difficult to identify opportunities for profitable investment in the Swedish capitalist economy, thereby seriously undermining economic growth. In response to these trends, moreover, capital based in Sweden sought to circumvent the regulations upon investment, such as centralized wage negotiations, which themselves formed such a central role in the SAP leadership's ability to ensure the decommodification of the lives of its electoral constituency. The attempt by the SAP leadership to resolve these tensions, moreover, through *either* the recommodification *or* decommodification of labour, risked a further destabilization of the structure of 'traditional' social democratic party relations, due to the potentially negative impact they would have upon either constituents' acquiescence to the process of representation, or opportunities for profitable investment, respectively.

In an attempt to resolve these problems, the SAP Government introduced, as early as 1982, a 20 per cent devaluation of the Swedish krona, which it combined with restrictive fiscal and monetary policies. These measures sought to reduce the relative costs of Swedish production, and, therefore, the relative cost of Swedish labour, in an attempt to restore the competitiveness of Swedish goods on the international market and thereby restore opportunities for profitable capitalist production (Arter, 2003: 89). This strategy was extended in 1985 when the government introduced a major deregulation of capital and foreign exchange markets, combined with a new commitment to only fund the government deficit through borrowing on the domestic market (Svensson, 2002). The aim of these strategies was to produce a rise in the Swedish interest rate, which would have to rise in order for the currency to be both sustainable on the international market and able to support government debt. The aim, therefore, was to place market pressures upon the Swedish model in order to reduce government debt, push down inflation and thereby stabilize the krona. Nevertheless, problems of wage determination and inflation remained. Indeed, the liberalization of the Swedish economy created pressures upon the solidaristic wage policy that were ultimately unable to be resolved, as more profitable and competitive companies within the Swedish economy were able to pay more than the standardized national wage, which itself prompted demands within the less competitive sectors for wages to rise above levels of productivity, thereby exacerbating the problem of over-valued Swedish labour. This therefore created increased inflationary pressures within the Swedish economy, which were compounded by continued growth in the public deficit and lower than OECD-average productivity growth (Ryner, 2002: 148–52; Benner and Vad, 2000: 420).

The crisis and transformation of 'traditional' social democratic party relations

Whilst the SAP had struggled to resolve the tensions arising from its 'traditional' social democratic party relations throughout much of the 1970s and 1980s, from 1990 these tensions became increasingly overwhelming, ultimately resulting in significant programmatic reform and another spell out of office. Thus, throughout 1990, inflation and government debt continued to rise to dangerous levels, creating pressure on the stock exchange and leading major financial companies to suspend dividend payments. In turn, currency speculation against the krona began to exert overwhelming downward pressure. In its attempt to restore profitability to the Swedish capitalist economy, the government responded with a policy of business- and investment-friendly tax cuts, attempts to tackle absenteeism at work, and the adoption of an austerity fiscal package in April 1990 (Arter, 2003: 90; Benner and Vad, 2000: 426). However, these policies failed to resolve the crisis, leading the government to propose another emergency package on 2 October and an increase by 5 per cent in short-term interest rates on 12 and 18 October. However, these measures still failed to appease international financial capital markets, resulting in continuing downward pressure on the krona. On 26 October, therefore, the government announced a more substantial package of public spending cuts, amounting to a reduction in public spending of 1.5 per cent. These austerity measures were accompanied by the announcement that full employment would be replaced by price stability as the government's key macroeconomic policy aim (Ryner, 2002: 153), which was an important and symbolic step by the SAP as full employment had until then been an essential part of its 'traditional' social democratic programme. As such, the shift in priority, from employment to inflation, represented a significant move towards the adoption of a 'new' social democratic programme. Indeed, a number of scholars identify this point in 1990 as the most significant turning point in the transformation from 'traditional' to 'new' social democracy in Sweden (Ryner, 2004; Arter, 2003: 89). Thus, whilst most commentators recognize that Sweden has continued to maintain the most generous redistributive public policies in the developed world, there is nevertheless agreement that the scope of this generosity underwent a significant change from 1990 onwards (Cox, 2004; Ryner, 2004).

The 1990 emergency statement therefore represented a symbolic break with one of the core aspects of 'traditional' social democracy in Sweden, and with the Swedish social democratic model. Moreover, having overseen a period of prolonged economic turmoil, the SAP was again defeated by the bourgeois coalition in the general election of 1991. This new government oversaw a period of heavy recession (negative growth in GDP between 1991 and 1993), high unemployment (rising from 2.1 per cent in 1990 to 12.5 per cent in 1993), and (as a result) a steep further rise in the size of the government deficit (reaching 14 per cent – the highest of all the OECD countries at the time – in 1993), all of which were unsuccessfully tackled through cuts in social expenditure, tax increases, and the floating of the krona in late 1992 (Lindbom, 2001: 171; Benner and Vad, 2000: 427).

The SAP stood for re-election in September 1994 on a campaign which promised both to balance the budget and to resolve the country's unemployment problem, although it stressed 'that finances had to be given precedence over the labour market or further tax breaks' (Merkel *et al.*, 2008: 161), thereby reflecting the shift towards 'new' social democratic priorities it had begun in 1990. Upon its re-election in 1994, therefore, the new SAP Government was faced with the need to realize its promise to resolve the Swedish economic crisis. In an attempt to do so, the new government led by Ingvar Carlsson introduced a combination of austerity measures and increased taxation on higher income groups in an attempt to bring the government budget into balance. The austerity measures included attempts to limit entitlements to social welfare provisions for the unemployed, sick and elderly (although many of these were not implemented due to opposition within the SAP and LO) and a new pensions system that shifted the emphasis from the provision of a national minimum income to the provision of pensions based more on individual contributions. By early 1995, however, the government moved towards a greater emphasis on cuts in expenditure, particularly focusing on welfare provisions, a trend which continued once Carlsson was succeeded by Göran Persson as the new SAP prime minster in 1996 (Merkel *et al.*, 2008: 162–3). Between 1995 and 1998, therefore, public expenditure as a percentage of GDP was cut from 67.3 per cent to 62.4 per cent and social expenditure as a percentage of GDP fell from 35.2 per cent to 33.3 per cent (Gould, 2001: 45–51; see also Anderson, 2001). According to Scruggs' (2004) welfare generosity index, benefit generosity declined between 1993 and 2002 by over 13 per cent, falling back to a pre-1973 level. Whilst these austerity cuts were being made, moreover, the dissolution of the institutions of centralized wage negotiations gathered pace, witnessing their replacement by a decentralized system of wage determination (Iversen, 1996). In seeking to stimulate higher levels of employment, moreover, the SAP Government introduced a series of labour market liberalizing measures in January 1997 that would make both the hiring of temporary workers and the dismissal of workers easier (Merkel *et al.*, 2008: 169). As a result, wage differentials (which had declined during the 1960s and 1970s) increased considerably as market forces were increasingly relied upon to determine wages (Vartiainen, 2001: 33). Finally, attempts to reduce the size of the budget deficit witnessed the partial-privatization of state-owned companies and cuts to public sector employment (Arter, 2003: 91; Benner and Vad, 2000: 428,

433). Following these significant moves towards the recommodification of Swedish labour, therefore, the Swedish capitalist economy entered a phase of renewed economic growth (Benner and Vad, 2000: 421). As a result, GDP grew by an average of over 4 per cent per annum between 1998 and 2000 and unemployment rates fell from 9.9 per cent in 1997 to 4.9 per cent by 2001 (OECD.stat).

Throughout this 1994–98 period of welfare retrenchment, however, the measures that the SAP undertook in its attempt to ensure the recommodificaton of labour were consistently presented to its electoral constituency as both the necessary cost of economic revival and necessary in order to ensure the long-term sustainability of Sweden's remaining welfare provisions. Thus, during the 1998 campaign, 'the SAP claimed there was no alternative to its chosen course, arguing that full employment was not feasible without balanced budgets' (Merkel *et al.*, 2008: 165). Similarly, in the campaign for the September 2002 general election, the SAP focused on the importance of maintaining universalism as the principle guiding welfare policy (a key element of the Swedish model), claiming 'welfare policies must cover everyone, must be financed in the spirit of solidarity via taxation and be distributed according to the people's needs not on the basis of how fat their wallets are' (SAP, 2002). The SAP leadership also promised to improve provisions in health care, schools and pensions. Indeed, from around 1998 onwards, the SAP Government was able to cautiously extend subsidies for health care (although it did not repeal the introduction of private contributions by health care recipients) and spending on social services. It also raised parental leave pay and sick pay to previous levels (from 75 per cent to 80 per cent), although this was implemented alongside a tightening of eligibility criteria (Merkel *et al.*, 2008: 177). At the same time the government also made clear its continued commitment to the importance of the continued recommodification of labour, for instance seeking a halving of the number of days workers would be entitled to for sick leave (Persson, 2002). Thus, in its 2002 manifesto, the SAP proclaimed the importance of maintaining the liberalizing reforms it had undertaken since its return to office in 1994, claiming,

> Sweden will continue to enjoy strong growth, low levels of unemployment and healthy finances. This entails that public finances must maintain a surplus running equivalent to 2 per cent of the GNP a year, calculated as an average over the business cycle. The ceiling on public expenditure will be maintained. The tax system must be robust and provide incentives to work and to invest.
>
> (SAP, 2002)

The transformation from 'traditional' to 'new' social democracy, in the case of the SAP, was therefore undertaken over a prolonged period in office. Perhaps the most notable point in this process is the 1990 emergency programme, during which the SAP Government formally renounced the party's historic commitment to full employment, replacing it with a commitment to low inflation. However, following its election to office in 1994, the new SAP Government also undertook a number of reforms to public expenditure, and in particular social benefits, whilst overseeing a *de facto* dissolution of the traditional system of centralized wage negotiation. In doing so, moreover, the SAP Government consistently argued for the importance of maintaining fiscal rectitude and incentives to enter the labour market. As a result, therefore, we might argue that, despite the continued commitment of the SAP to a relatively high level of welfare provisions, the SAP has since the 1990s undertaken a number of steps towards the adoption of a 'new' social democratic programme.

French social democracy

In the case of French 'traditional' social democracy, one of the key obstacles faced by the French Socialists (SFIO) in the post-war period was the presence of a relatively large Communist Party (PCF) to its left. Most significantly for the purposes of the present study, the PCF was able to attract much of the electoral support of working-class voters in France throughout much of the post-war period. This factor, combined with the presence of an authoritarian Gaullist party, created a context in which the socialists were, for much of the *Trente Glorieuses*, faced with a choice between a leftist strategy that sought to compete with the PCF for working-class votes, and a centrist one that sought to prevent the Gaullists' accession to office. The existence of a serious competitor on the left of the French party system therefore affected the ability of the socialists to assume a 'traditional' social democratic structure of party relations. In the following account of the adoption by the 'traditional' social democratic French socialists of a 'new' social democratic programme, therefore, more attention is paid than has been in previous studies to the role of the rival, PCF, party to the left of the social democratic party under investigation.

Constructing 'traditional' social democratic party relations

The PCF had been more successful than the SFIO in attracting working-class support throughout the inter-war years. As a result, under the Fourth Republic, the SFIO, led by Guy Mollet between 1946 and 1969, was forced to draw largely upon the support of the petty bourgeoisie and a rural and small-town electorate, whilst the PCF continued to draw far more successfully on French working-class support. The SFIO's centrist position was also consolidated during this early post-war period as the French socialists formed a coalition government with Radicals, the MRP (progressive Catholics) and independents from 1947 to 1951 and 1955 to 1958. The creation of the Fifth Republic in 1958, however, introduced two major institutional changes which were to have a significant effect upon the fortunes of the French socialists. These were a two-round majoritarian electoral system and, following the 1962 referendum, the direct election of the president, both of which witnessed France move towards the adoption of a presidential executive. As Bell and Criddle (1988) note, this move towards presidentialism created a very real risk of exclusion from the French political system for the PCF, as the two-round system marginalized smaller parties and presidentialism favoured moderate parties that could gain the trust of large sections of the electorate. On both of these counts, therefore, the fortunes of the PCF were seriously threatened by the constitutional changes of the Fifth Republic. This in turn created significant incentives for the PCF to become a junior partner in an alliance with the socialists. As a result, from 1962 onwards, the socialists and the PCF began to form mutually beneficial electoral agreements. Mollet and PCF leader, Maurice Thorez, agreed upon mutual withdrawals for the 1962 general election, and from 1967 the socialists and PCF agreed that the candidate receiving least votes in the first-round ballot for each seat would withdraw from the election. Thus, whilst the PCF was historically the party of the French working class, its electoral cooperation with the French Socialists during the Fifth Republic indirectly added a more substantive working-class constituency to the structure of French 'traditional' social democratic party relations that constituted the SFIO.[6] Moreover, the socialists increasingly targeted a growing demographic of white-collar technical workers that many viewed as having characteristics more similar to a typical working-class constituency (Christofferson, 1991: 45–6; Bell and Criddle, 1988: 14–38).

Following the experience of relatively successful electoral cooperation between the socialists and communists during the 1960s, including the common support for the Mitterrand candidacy in the 1965 presidential election, the SFIO and a number of smaller socialist parties sought to unify within the broader *Parti Socialiste* (PS) and also to seek more formal cooperation with the PCF. Thus, in July 1969, those parties considering membership of the new PS held the Issy-les-Moulineaux congress, at which it was decided both to create the PS and to adopt a resolution committing the new party to 'enter into and pursue a public debate with the Communist Party' (Bell and Criddle, 1988: 55). Following the 1971 Épinay congress, moreover, François Mitterrand became the new PS leader, chosen largely due to his centrist political stance, his desire to form a united strategy with the PCF, and his popularity amongst the French electorate. The following year, the PS adopted its party programme, *Changer la vie*, committing itself to a number of measures that would seek to decommodify the lives of large sections of the French electorate. Thus, the 1972 Programme included a commitment to nationalization, worker's input into decision-making (*autogestion*), planning, and the capacity for workers to request their factory to be nationalized. This was followed in June 1972 by the adoption of a Common Programme between the PS and PCF, which included commitments to expand welfare benefits and raise wages, democratize management within the firm, increase trade union rights, demand the retention of freedom of action from the EEC (European Economic Community) for a French left government, and nationalize nine French holding companies. Despite a relatively strong performance in the 1974 presidential election, however, from 1974 to 1977 the PS-PCF relationship became increasingly fractious as ideological differences, particularly over the PS' support for (what it saw as) necessary budget cuts, divided the two parties. This came to a head at the 1977 Nantes congress, when the PS, led by Mitterrand and Rocard (the leader of the PSU, which had recently joined the PS), adopted an explicitly 'traditional' social democratic agenda in declaring the PS a free-market party, and suggesting the need for recommodifying policies such as an incomes policy, wage restraint and a social contract – each of which were vehemently (but unsuccessfully) opposed by the Marxist-influenced CERES faction within the PS. In this context, therefore, the 'Union of the Left', between the PS and PCF, ruptured in 1977 as divisions over the extent of public expenditure, salary differentials, wealth and capital taxation, and, especially, the number of companies to be nationalized, eventually led to the collapse of negotiations to revise the Common Programme (Ross and Jenson, 1994: 166; Bell and Criddle, 1988: 68–101).

The 'traditional' social democratic strategy adopted by the PS eventually proved to be a success when, in 1981, Mitterrand won the presidential elections on a platform that included commitments to longer paid holidays, earlier retirement, and increased minimum wage and a 35-hour working week, whilst nevertheless failing (or succeeding in avoiding) to present a clear programmatic manifesto (Bell and Criddle, 1988: 110–4). Whilst the PCF stood its own candidate – Georges Marchais – in the first round of the election, in the second round it granted Mitterrand its support (Grunberg, 2008: 227). Shortly after the presidential election, and as promised, Mitterrand dissolved the National Assembly rather than face a period of cohabitation. The PS won the subsequent general election by a landslide, securing nearly 70 per cent of the seats and including four PCF ministers in the new government of Prime Minister Pierre Mauroy, in part in an attempt to ensure the continued support of French working-class PCF voters and (importantly) the PCF-dominated trade union, CGT (Ross and Jenson, 1994: 170).

The PS-led Mauroy Government and the Mitterrand presidency therefore represented the coming to office of a 'traditional' social democratic strategy that had been followed for over a decade. As such, the PS party elite had successfully constructed 'traditional' social democratic party relations, through an appeal to a constituency that included the industrial working class, on the basis of a commitment to decommodifying measures, such as welfare expansion, nationalization, and industrial democracy (albeit presented with a significant lack of clarity). Whilst the working-class focus of the PS had initially been based largely on the 'Union of the Left' (i.e. through the alliance with the PCF), moreover, by the early 1980s the PS had acquired its own working-class base of electoral support. Thus, Bell and Criddle (1988: 136) show how the votes of the manual working class for the PS rose from 27 per cent in 1973 (compared with 37 per cent for the PCF) to 44 per cent in 1981 (compared with 24 per cent in the PCF). In keeping with the real definition of 'traditional' social democratic party relations derived in Chapter 2, however, it should also be noted that the PS electoral constituency consisted of voters beyond the industrial working class. Thus, Mitterrand appealed to the middle classes during the 1981 campaign on the basis of his republicanism and promotion of liberty, downplaying a notion of socialism and equality in the process. In the words of Christofferson:

> Liberty was the key word in Mitterrand's final speech, not equality. Every struggle of the left – for better education, free time, better jobs, Third World rights – was part of the grand scheme to achieve liberty in this world. Class struggle, Marxism, the rupture with capitalism, all of which were part of the standard rhetoric of the *Projet socialiste*, were totally absent from Mitterrand's discourse.
>
> (Christofferson, 1991: 27)

The PS had therefore adopted a typical 'traditional' social democratic structure of party relations, in particular appealing to the industrial working class, but also extending that appeal to large sections of the middle classes in France. In gaining a resounding election to office in 1981, moreover, the 'traditional' social democratic party relations of the PS appeared to have been relatively successfully reproduced.

The problematic reproduction of 'traditional' social democracy in the case of the Parti Socialiste

Once elected to office the PS leadership sought to implement a reflationary economic policy that would introduce a substantial decommodification of workers' lives in France (and which was arguably more substantial than the one it had stood for election on, not least due to the opacity of its 1981 campaign). This included an extensive programme of nationalization (including 12 leading industrial conglomerates and 38 banks), a *dirigiste* industrial policy, economic planning, industrial relations legislation favouring organized labour, redistributive social programmes and Keynesian reflation measures such as public sector job creation, a large boost to subsidies granted to public enterprises, and an increase in the minimum wage by 15 per cent in real terms and in social transfers (including pensions and family allowances) by over 12 per cent (Levy, 2000: 321–2). This was, therefore, a programme of 'redistributive Keynesianism', which focused demand management measures upon the poorer sections of French society (Hall, 1986: 194). The initial measures introduced by the Socialist-led government in its early period in office, therefore, had significant decommodifying effects. Housing allocations for low-paid workers were increased by 25 per cent in 1981, health insurance benefits were made more widely available to part-time employees and the unemployed, the purchasing power of social transfers rose by 4.5 per cent in 1981 and 7.6 per cent in 1982, and the minimum wage was raised by 15 per cent between May 1981 and December 1982 (Hall, 1986: 194). All of these measures therefore acted to significantly reduce the dependence of French workers upon the sale of their labour, and thereby represented significant advances in decommodification. The effect of these measures, however, was also to consolidate a long-term decrease in profitability within the French capitalist economy, and thereby undermine investment and economic growth. Thus, real disposable income rose twice as fast as productivity growth between 1981 and 1983, leading to a large rise in imports, a balance of payments deficit, and inflation, all of which created massive pressure for the devaluation of the franc (Hall, 1986: 198).

In response to this decline in profitability, the PS-led government sought to balance the decommodifying measures that it had introduced with what it saw as the requirements of the French capitalist economy, seeking to stabilize the rise of real wages and maintain the competitiveness of industry. Thus, in November 1981, Mauroy made a speech emphasizing the importance of entrepreneurs, the free market (both domestic and international), and profit. Similarly, in late 1981, Finance Minister, Jacques Delors called for 'a pause in the declaration of reforms', and insisted on the importance of facilitating profit-making in order to create 'a climate which is more stimulating for business' (quoted in Christofferson, 1991: 72). Despite opposition from Delors, however, the budget for 1982 was 'one of the most inflationary state budgets in the postwar period', including a 27.6 per cent increase in public spending, prompting inflation to rise to nearly 12 per cent in 1982 (Christofferson, 1991: 70; OECD.stat). Moreover, in late 1981, government polls indicated that a majority of French firms had decided to neither hire new workers nor invest in French industry. The French capitalist economy was, therefore, beginning to acquire all the signs of a crisis of overaccumulation, as capital was faced with a lack of opportunities for profitable investment, and began to choose instead to exit the capital–labour relation that constituted French capitalism itself. In response, and in terms of the conceptualization adopted in the preceding chapter, the PS-led Government sought to ensure the requisite recommodification of French labour in three key ways. First, it introduced a price and wage freeze in 1982 which sought to 'ease inflation and improve profit margins for industry'. Second, the government made a number of concessions to industry in its nationalization plan, which nationalized six industrial conglomerates, along with 36 banks, accounting for 24 per cent of the employees, 32 per cent of sales, 30 per cent of exports, and 60 per cent of annual investment in the industrial and energy sectors of the French economy (Hall, 1986: 204). These concessions included the promise to retain the autonomy of the company management within the organization of nationalized firms, and for the personnel who made up the management to be qualified businessmen. Moreover, the government promised to aim, 'as its first priority, to modernize and improve the competitive position' of nationalized firms, and for the nationalized companies to remain members of the French business association, CNPF. Third, in April 1982 the government promised to end tax rises upon business and to make up for lost revenue through cuts in public spending and increased indirect taxation (Christofferson, 1991: 96).

Throughout this period, however, the ambivalent performance of the Socialist-led government was resulting in tensions within the wider structure of 'traditional' social democratic party relations of the PS. Thus, the party performed badly in the cantonal elections of March 1982 and criticisms began to emerge amongst the trade unions, as falling membership levels were largely blamed on official union support for the government due to its slow delivery of social and economic reform. In response, the government sought to contain these pressures for decommodification by appealing to the importance of maintaining the French capitalist economy. Thus, in announcing the 1982 wage freeze, Delors 'warned the nation that it would have to make sacrifices in order to get the economy back on its feet, sacrifices that might entail cuts in salaries and reductions in social services' (Christofferson, 1991: 102–3). Similarly, in appealing for the restraint of French labour, Mitterrand announced that,

> [I]t is necessary to produce, to produce more and better products. But this can only be done under three conditions: by moderating social and financial charges, by having all workers recognize their responsibilities, and by inventing, investing, and learning how to sell in order to become competitive.
>
> (quoted in Christofferson, 1991: 113)

Despite these appeals, however, the Socialist's popularity continued to decline, witnessing significant losses in the 1983 municipal elections for both the PS and PCF (Christofferson, 1991: 97–119).

The massive trade deficit faced by the Socialist government also continued to place substantial pressure for devaluation upon the franc. Thus, following the results of the municipal elections, the government was faced with the choice of continued reflation, which would realistically only be viable through an autarkic policy of protectionism and exit from the EMS (a position advocated by CERES leader, Chevènement), or the adoption of a deflationary policy that would bolster the franc and impose the discipline of economic competition upon the French economy (as advocated by Delors) (Ross and Jenson, 1994: 173). Eventually Mitterrand decided to impose a series of deflationary measures, including forced loans imposed upon citizens, increased social security contributions, and increased indirect taxes, all of which were introduced alongside a relatively small devaluation of 2.5 per cent (Bell and Criddle, 1988: 160–1). Thus, whilst Mitterrand did consider the autarkic option, he ultimately decided, with the support of both Delors and Mauroy, that the economic risks of doing so would be too great (interview with Christian Sautter, former advisor to President Mitterrand, 24 April 2008).

The ongoing crisis of 'traditional' social democratic relations?

Following its 1983 U-turn, the Socialist government adopted a policy of *franc fort*, which it maintained throughout the 1980s and into the 1990s. This was a commitment to deflationary growth, whereby inflation would be avoided through a tight monetary policy, which would itself be achieved through the informal anchoring of the franc to the Deutschmark (Lordon, 2001). The budget announced by Delors in March 1983, therefore, comprised deflationary measures amounting to 2 per cent of GNP. Whilst these measures were largely achieved through tax increases focused on the richest third of taxpayers, spending cuts were nonetheless felt across the income spectrum. Indeed, the overall goal was a clear attempt to secure the recommodification of labour. Thus, in Mauroy's own words, 'We want to have wages rise more slowly than prices in order to curb consumer purchasing power and increase profitability' (quoted in Hall, 1986: 202). This therefore prompted severe criticism from both the unions (who feared that the measures would produce job losses), the left of the PS, and the PCF (who sought continued social expenditure). By restricting inflation, the French government sought to enhance the international competitiveness of its commodities through 'competitive disinflation', which meant running a lower rate of inflation than its trading partners, in order to ensure that French commodities could be sold at a lower price. This was therefore a major U-turn for the PS in office:

> Redistributive Keynesianism gave way to austerity budgets, wage indexation was abandoned, and most important, monetary policy was tightened, with real interest rates ranging from 5 per cent to 8 per cent for over a decade. These measures reduced French inflation from 9.6 per cent in 1983 to 2.7 per cent in

1986, but at the price of several years of growth below 2 per cent and an increase in unemployment from 8.3 per cent to 10.4 per cent.

(Levy, 2000: 324)

The 1983 U-turn also resulted in an end to nationalization and a subsequent reversal of state assistance for ailing public enterprises. This was combined with a marked reduction in assistance for private enterprises and a deregulation of financial markets, price controls, capital controls, and restriction upon worker layoffs. These fiscally orthodox policies were continued the following year, including the continuation of the 1 per cent social security tax, and a policy of keeping public sector wage rises to below 5 per cent, all of which created an overall reduction in the standard of living of French citizens (Christofferson, 1991: 129). The net result, in terms of French capital–labour relations, however, was a boost in corporate profitability from 9.8 per cent of value added in 1982 to 17.3 per cent in 1989 (Levy, 2000: 325).

The impact upon nationalization was significant. Thus, Laurent Fabius was appointed to the Ministry of Industry in early 1983 and subsequently opened the way for nationalized firms to operate more similarly to private companies, in particular encouraging borrowing on private capital markets. This revision to the process of nationalization was largely justified in terms of the need to successfully 'modernize' French industry. Thus, nationalized coal, shipbuilding and steel industries witnessed plans for widespread plant closures, redundancies, early retirement, and retraining, all put into effect without union consultation, creating 25,000 redundancies in the coal industry, 20,000 in steel, and 5,000 in shipbuilding and thereby prompting widespread union opposition. In seeking to contain the demands of its constituents, who were essentially being asked to support a series of austerity measures in order to ensure the return to profitability of French capital, however, the PS leadership consistently argued for the long-term benefits of restraint. Thus, following the March 1983 budget announcement, Mauroy claimed the increased 'rigour' was only 'transitory' and that in the long term it would result in the 'industrial renewal' of France that would thereby enable the PS to realize its long-term aims, which 'remain based on the will for social justice and the struggle against inequalities' (quoted in Christofferson, 1991: 125). Despite the attempts of the PS party leadership, however, the reproduction of French 'traditional' social democratic party relations was becoming increasingly problematic, in particular witnessing growing despondency amongst its electoral constituency. Thus, the PS performed extremely badly in the 1984 EP elections, in large part due to the very high abstention rate amongst those who had supported Mitterrand in 1981, only 59 per cent of whom voted at all in 1984. Following these poor election results, Mauroy resigned as prime minister and was replaced by Fabius. This represented a further consolidation of the 'modernization' agenda within the Socialist government, and as such prompted the subsequent resignation of the PCF ministers, marking the end of the 'Union of the Left'. Fabius oversaw two years of further attempts to introduce recommodification measures, including cuts in subsidies for nationalized industries, the introduction of job creation schemes for young unemployed (known as TUCs) who were paid below the minimum wage, the liberalization of the labour market (including the introduction of weekend and part-time work), and further redundancies in nationalized industries (Christofferson, 1991: 146, 90–205). Perhaps predictably, therefore, the 1986 general election witnessed the defeat of the Fabius Government, and its replacement by a Gaullist one, led by Jacques Chirac.

The transformation to 'new' social democracy

From its period out of office between 1986 and 1988, until the presidential election campaign of 1995, the PS underwent a period of turbulence and prolonged factional in-fighting as the party struggled both to embrace the significant programmatic revisions it had already adopted in practice following the 1983 U-turn, and also to identify a suitable presidential candidate to replace Mitterrand (interview with Christian Sautter, 24 April 2008). The first of these sources of internal tension was partly resolved at the *Parti Socialiste's* 1991 Arche congress, which finally accepted in principle that the PS no longer sought the transcendence of capitalism. Moreover, competition between Lionel Jospin, Rocard and Fabius eventually witnessed the elevation of Jospin to a clear position of leadership within the PS following his (relatively) successful campaign for the presidency in 1995 (although he did not do well enough to win the election itself). As a result, Jospin was able to construct a new and more stable majority that included both Rocard and Mauroy's supporters, and to form a recognizable *courant – Socialisme et démocratie* – which included Dominique Strauss-Kahn and Pièrre Moscovici and Bergounioux. Jospin's strategy was therefore to seek to unite the moderate and pro-market Rocardian *deuxième gauche* with the Mitterrandist wing of the party around a policy that was neither *dirigiste* nor anti-market, but which nevertheless espoused a faith in the continued possibilities for state intervention in capitalist economies. Having relied upon emergency policy measures from the 1983 U-turn onwards, therefore, during the early to mid 1990s the PS came increasingly confidently to adopt a recognizably 'new' social democratic strategy (Clift, 2003a: 98–143).

Indeed, the 'new' social democratic programme adopted by the PS under Jospin effectively represented a formal acknowledgement of what the party leadership had, in practice, been required to put into practice since (at least) the 1983 U-turn. This was the recognition that the PS would need to engender the requisite commodification of French labour in order to ensure the necessary reproduction of the French capitalist economy. Nevertheless, the 'new' social democratic programme of Jospin's *Parti Socialiste* sought also to highlight the benefits that the French state could continue to provide for PS constituents. Thus, Jospin's programme for the 1995 presidential election stated, on the one hand, that,

> [W]e must learn the lessons of the past, in order to instigate the reorientations of economic policy which today are necessary and possible without increasing public deficit, nor putting our currency, our external balances, or the competitivity of our firms in peril.
>
> (quoted in Clift, 2003a: 123–4)

On the other hand, however, Jospin's programme also announced that,

> [I] reject the idea that the state is powerless, and believe that it should deploy all its capacities to aid job creation.
>
> (quoted in Clift, 2003a: 123–4)

From 1995 onwards, therefore, the PS began to seek once more to promote a role for the state in tackling 'traditional' social democratic problems. This included a focus on unemployment (albeit with an enhanced recognition of the constraining effects of the new international economic context), and a commitment to the Tobin Tax, greater regulation of offshore and hedge funds, a call for IMF regulation of capital speculation, job creation programmes, a reduction in the working week, and the attempt to stimulate consumption. The PS' 'new' social democratic programme under Jospin, therefore, promised a continuation of decommodifying public policies, whilst nevertheless recognizing, and emphasizing, the significantly greater obstacles, arising from an international economic context, that would be faced by a PS Government (Clift, 2003a: 151–2). A similar programme was also adopted by the PS for the 1997 general election, witnessing a PS-led *gauche plurielle* coalition enter office under Jospin's prime ministerialship, following a PS campaign based on a softening of the austere fiscal policies associated with EMU, the creation of 700,000 new jobs, the reduction of the working week to 35 hours, an end to privatization, and a shift in the tax burden from labour to capital (Bouvet and Michel, 1999; Pennetier, 1997; Merkel et. al, 2008: 104).

During its period in office, following the 1997 election the Jospin Government implemented a number of moderate decommodifying measures, such as the 35 hour week, the introduction of a means-tested scheme to make health care available to low income groups (CMU), and a moderately redistributive fiscal policy. However, in contrast to its election to office in 1981, the PS leadership were far more careful to ensure that these measures were combined with sufficient attention to the requirements of the French capitalist economy, thus seeking from the beginning of its incumbency to reduce corporate taxation, to lower the public deficit, and to seek to increase the flexibility of the French labour force (Levy, 2000: 339–42; Merkel et. al, 2008: 104–12). As such, perhaps the most notable aspect of the PS' 'new' social democratic programme was the extent to which it sought a more stable balance between the redistributive measures and the recommodification of workers within France. It therefore witnessed the pursuit of less radically redistributive policy goals during the 1997 election campaign, resulting in a more moderate programme in office and thereby avoiding the need for the kind of emergency measures to recommodify French labour in response to crises in the French capitalist economy witnessed in 1983.

Italian communism, Eurocommunism, post-communism, and 'new' social democracy

The transformation from 'traditional' to 'new' social democracy in the case of Italy is considerably different to the other cases we have studied thus far. The Italian

Communist Party (PCI) was a major force within Italian politics, gaining the considerable support of large sections of the Italian working class. At the same time, however, it co-existed with a large Italian Socialist Party (PSI), which was itself a member of the Socialist International and therefore more comparable to a typical social democratic party. The period during which the PCI underwent a transformation towards becoming a 'new' social democratic party, however, witnessed both the implosion of the PSI and the rapid transformation of the PCI into a newly-named Party of the Democrats of the Left (PDS). Moreover, according to former DS party leader, Piero Fassino, for much of its post-war period, the PCI 'had only the name of communism. Its policies were more similar to the social democrats than to the communist parties' (interview with author, 6 May 2008). As a result, this section argues that in order to examine the transition from 'traditional' to 'new' social democracy in the case of Italy, we should investigate the development of the PCI and its successor parties (rather than the PSI), as it developed from a third international communist party, through a Eurocommunist strategy that had much in common with 'traditional' social democracy, before undergoing a transition to a post-communist, and essentially a 'new' social democratic political party. This process is outlined further below.

The Italian Communist Party: towards 'traditional' social democratic party relations?

The PCI's post-war strategy was heavily influenced by Gramsci. Indeed, its first post-war Secretary, Palmiro Togliatti, was almost singlehandedly responsible for the publication of Gramsci's prison notebooks. Upon assuming leadership of the PCI at the end of the Second World War, therefore, Togliatti adopted a 'war of position', meaning that the PCI would seek to gradually permeate the influential institutions of Italian political and civil society, thereby putting it in a position to achieve a successful transition to communism. The effect of this was to commit the PCI, throughout the post-war period, to an engagement with the institutions of Italian liberal democracy. Under Togliatti, the PCI was also committed to the promotion of gradual reforms that would benefit its largely working-class constituency (maintained through its *de facto* control of the trade union, General Confederation of Italian Workers (CGIL)) (Weinberg, 1995: 35–7). Thus, whilst the PCI was throughout the post-war period committed to the transcendence of capitalism, it nevertheless in practice adopted many of the key characteristics of 'traditional' social democratic strategy, including representation of a constituency based around the working class but also extending beyond it to become a mass party, the promotion of redistributive reforms, and an acceptance of the need to co-exist with capitalism (at least in the short term) (Gray, 1980: 24–30). Thus, according to Gray, 'Togliatti opted for a gradualist approach in the conquest of state power through the integration of the working class into the Italian political system'. This meant, therefore, that 'extremist tendencies among the rank-and-file were quickly smothered, while ideological fervor was tempered in favour of pragmatic political goals' (Gray, 1980: 23). Indeed, in heralding *il nuovo corso* (the new course), adopted in the early post-war period, Togliatti stated early in the post-war history of the Italian Communist Party that it would seek to successfully manage the Italian capitalist economy. Thus, he declared:

> We are accused, when we speak of a 'new course', of wanting to suppress private initiative. This is not so. We want to leave a large area to the development of private initiative, particularly to that of the small- and medium-sized entrepreneur. At the same time we maintain that the state must intervene in order to direct the whole work of reconstruction, in order to co-ordinate private firms, to guide them, to tie them organically to each other according to national needs, and ensuring that healthy private initiative is not suffocated and eventually destroyed by the prevailing of plutocratic groups and by speculation.
>
> (quoted in Sassoon, 1981: 41)

The PCI also sought, from its early post-war period onwards, to promote public policies that would have a decommodifying effect upon its working-class constituency, including the extension of the public sector within the national economy, well-run and generous public services (including public transport, and child care), a low rents policy, and the promotion of 'Red cooperatives of production and distribution' within Communist-run municipalities (Pasquino, 1980: 93–5). During its early period in opposition, therefore, the PCI placed strong emphasis on the need for 'public investment and public direction of the economy' (Sassoon, 1981: 77). It also supported the CGIL's proposed 'Labour Plan', which included nationalization of electricity, National Boards for land reclamation and public housing, and large-scale public works programmes (Sassoon, 1981: 78–80).

The PCI's transition towards a more typical 'traditional' social democratic party progressed further following Krushchev's 1956 CPSU congress speech recognizing the possibility of different national roads to socialism. This enabled the PCI to adopt the principle of 'progressive democracy', including a commitment to party plurality of a recognizably (but nevertheless qualified) liberal democratic nature. Thus, in 1958, Togliatti announced,

> one can solve *through parliament* the problem of enabling the working class not only to express their will but also to participate in the direction of political and economic activities, while maintaining firmly that the coming to power of the workers must inevitably entail an extension of the forms of direct democracy.
>
> (quoted in Sassoon, 1981: 128, emphasis added)

The PCI formally accepted, therefore, (albeit in a somewhat qualified form) the benefits that could accrue to its working-class constituency through the promotion of policies within the Italian liberal democratic state. From 1956, moreover, the PCI adopted a strategy that sought to promote 'structural reforms', which 'represent the demands around which the working class can fight at the present time' (Sassoon, 1981: 141). In the terms of our present study, therefore, the PCI was committed to the promotion of decommodifying reforms to the Italian capitalist economy. On the one hand, these reforms were viewed as part of a strategy for the transition to socialism, and therefore not in keeping with a 'traditional' social democratic strategy that typically accepted co-existence with capitalist relations. On the other hand, however, the implication of the strategy was that even demands made by 'traditional' social democratic parties such as the PSI, provided they were made on behalf of the working class, and even if they were without an accompanying longer-term strategy seeking the transcendence of capitalism, could be supported by the PCI. This was, therefore, 'tantamount to putting the party, if not on a reformist road at least not against it' (Sassoon, 1981: 144). There was in practice, therefore, little difference between the 'structural reforms' of the PCI and the reforms being advocated by the DC-PSI Government (Fouskas, 1998: 25). The PCI was, however, excluded from office throughout the entire period of the Italian First Republic (which ended in 1993). Contrary to more typical 'traditional' social democratic parties, therefore, the PCI had less incentive to contain the demands of its working-class constituents. This gave the PCI an opportunity to challenge rival parties on the social democratic left of the Italian party system (especially the PSI, its main contender for popular working-class electoral support) for their (implicit or explicit) support for measures that would act to recommodify the Italian working class. For instance, the PCI opposed the incomes policy of the centre-left DS-PSI Moro Government of 1963–4 on such grounds (Sassoon, 1981: 157–60).

By the mid-1970s, however, the PCI had achieved large gains in electoral support, moving to within reach of the majority of the vote in the 1976 general election. At the same time, the PCI underwent a moderation in party strategy, with new first secretary, Enrico Berlinguer, arguing that the experience of the Chilean Allende Government illustrated the importance of cross-party cooperation. As a result, he proposed a 'historic compromise' with the DC and the PSI, the first step towards which was to be the parliamentary support of the PCI for the DC Government between 1976 and 1979 (Weinberg, 1995: 38–9). This period of moderation also witnessed an attempt by the PCI to further extend its electoral appeal beyond the working class. Thus, Berlinguer announced in 1974 that the PCI sought to appeal to 'entire groups, social forces not classified as classes, such as women, young people, the popular masses of the South, cultural forces, movements of opinion, etc.' (quoted in Sassoon, 1981: 224). Further, in seeking to become a party of government, the PCI also increasingly sought to contain workers' demands in line with the need to reproduce capital–labour relations. For instance, at the end of 1975, senior PCI figure, Giorgio Napolitano launched a medium-term programme, 'which tended to justify the governmental deflationary policies, and asked for the understanding of the workers, since any economic recovery would be linked with the *long-term* goal of an advance towards democratic socialism' (Fouskas, 1998: 41–2). Similarly, in 1977 Berlinguer began to speak of 'austerity [which] means rigour, efficiency, seriousness, and it means justice' (quoted in Fouskas, 1998: 42).

The crisis of the PCI's 'traditional' social democratic party relations?

A wave of left-wing terrorism, and especially the Moro killing by the Red Brigades in 1978, effectively ended the prospect of a historic compromise and also prompted a long electoral decline for the PCI that began with the 1979 general election. In response, the PCI adopted a strategy it called the 'democratic alternative'. This sought, first, to replace the personnel of the current ruling elite once the (anticipated) failure of Keynesianism had left them without a founding ideology, and, second, to adopt a more concrete programme for government (Fouskas, 1998: 74–6). However, the electoral fortunes of the PCI fared badly during the 1980s, and a poor performance in the 1987 general election strengthened the position of Deputy Party Secretary, Achille Occhetto, who was a keen supporter of attempts to further 'social democratize' the PCI.[7] Thus, whilst electoral support for the PCI had risen to 34 per cent of the national vote in 1976, by 1987 it had consistently fallen at each national election from 1979 onwards to 27 per cent. These electoral problems were compounded by falling membership, an identity crisis caused by the incomplete rejection of Eurocommunism and the strategic dilemma posed by the seeming failure of both Soviet communism and social democratic Keynesianism.[8]

Occhetto's succession to the party leadership in June 1988, therefore, presented him with the necessity of renewing the party programme. In doing so, he sought to steer the PCI in a social democratic direction, criticizing Togliatti for his role in the Third International and calling for the PCI to follow such 'great' leaders as Willy Brandt and Olof Palme (Weinberg, 1995: 55). In launching his *nuovo corso* (new course) 18 days before gaining the party secretaryship, therefore, Occhetto confirmed that he sought a social democratization of the PCI. This 'new course' included cooperation with the PSI, a commitment to 'civilized growth'[9] and a 'programmatic alternative'.[10] The 'new course' strategy was, however, opposed by Armando Cossutta, who presented an alternative proposal, *Un nuovo corso per il socialismo*, which sought to resist what it saw as an abandonment of communism and Marxism, although the tradition within the PCI of supporting the party leadership ensured that Cossutta was only able to gain 4 per cent of the vote (compared with 95 per cent for Occhetto) (Weinberg, 1995: 56). At the 18th party congress in March 1989 the *nuovo corso* was further complemented by *riformismo forte* (strong reformism), which sought to appeal to some of the post-materialist values and new social movements that arose during the 1980s. 'Strong reformism', therefore, committed the party to workers' rights, environmentalism, feminism, and democratic rights. In contrast, some of the more traditional communist concerns were played down – for instance, mention of the proletariat or working class were conspicuously absent from Occhetto's opening speech to the congress. There were also reforms to the internal decision-making process of the PCI, in an attempt to democratize the party and to end the Leninist practice of 'democratic centralism' (Fouskas, 1998: 110–8; Weinberg, 1995: 58). By the late 1980s, therefore, the PCI had made significant moves towards the adoption of typical 'traditional' social democratic party relations. Its electoral appeal was focused on, but nevertheless (increasingly) extended beyond a core working-class constituency. It sought to promote decommodifying policies within the machinery of the Italian state that would benefit its constituency, and it sought to present itself as a viable party of government that would be able to successfully manage the Italian capitalist economy.

The transformation to 'new' social democracy

Following the fall of the Berlin Wall, Occhetto moved successfully to change the party's name and to drop the hammer and sickle symbol, therefore transforming the party between 1989 and 1991 into a post-communist party, the Party of the Democrats of the Left (PDS). This also prompted those who sought to retain a communist party presence within Italy, led by Cossutta, to leave the newly named PDS and form instead the *Rifondazione Comunista*, or Refoundation Communists (RC) (Weinberg, 1995: 63–89). The birth of the PDS also coincided with the transformation of the Italian polity, from the 'first' to the 'second' republic, witnessing both the collapse of the PSI and the DC in the light of ongoing corruption revelations, and a change in the electoral system from proportional representation to a three-quarters plurality system (Cotta and Verzichelli, 2007: ch. 3). The year 1994 therefore witnessed the first opportunity for the PDS to campaign for election to office following both the transition from the First to Second Republic and the transformation to a post-communist party. In seeking to gain the confidence of the electorate, and to symbolize the reforms that had occurred within the party following its change in name, the PDS 'strove to present itself as the firmest champion of financial orthodoxy, committed above all to cutting public spending and reducing the budget deficit, no matter what the difficulty in a time of crisis' (Abse, 2001: 68). In this sense, the birth of the PDS represented a leap from the PCI's tentative adoption of 'traditional' social democratic party relations during the 1980s, to the outright adoption, under its new PDS name, of a 'new' social democratic programme in the early 1990s (with the RC adopting a stance typical of 'traditional' social democratic parties, particularly committing itself to the maintenance of redistributive public policies). In emphasizing its prioritization of fiscal orthodoxy, therefore, the PDS gave an early signal to both its core electoral constituency, and the wider electorate, that it would not seek to destabilize Italian capital–labour relations through the promotion of excessive demands for the decommodification of labour. Nevertheless, the PDS was defeated by Berlusconi's new *Forza Italia* party in the 1994 elections, although the following year the Berlusconi Government was replaced by another technocratic government, this time led by Lamberto Dini (the treasury minister in the Berlusconi government), which implemented various austerity measures that were supported by the PDS. By April 1996, however, the Dini government was itself forced to resign, prompting another general election, which this time was won by the *Ulivio* (or Olive Tree) coalition, formed in February 1995 as an electoral coalition of the centre-left led by the PDS. The year 1996 therefore witnessed the election of leftist Christian Democrat Romano Prodi to the post of prime minister, and the coming to power for the first time of a governing coalition within which the PDS was the largest party.

The main economic issue facing Italy during the 1990s was slow growth and massive government debt. Average annual growth in GDP was over 1 per cent lower than the OECD average from 1990 to 1996 (own calculations, OECD.stat) and upon its arrival in office in 1996 the *Ulivio* Government was faced with government debt of 128 per cent of GDP and real GDP growth of less than 1 per cent (OECD.stat). Moreover, whilst these problems would certainly have required attention irrespective of the requirements of European integration, Italian governments throughout this period focused heavily on meeting the Maastricht convergence criteria, which in turn necessitated a series of austerity budgets in order to bring the government deficit in line (Quaglia and Radaelli, 2007: 929). Thus, the *Ulivio* Government placed heavy emphasis throughout its period in office both on the need to limit or reduce decommodifying policies, and on the importance of Italian workers moderating, or containing, their demands, especially in the area of wage claims. Under the heading of 'Healthy finances for a healthy state', therefore, the coalition committed itself to 'keeping inflation under control; the independence of the central bank to achieve that end; continuing to reverse public deficits and debts; and to the incomes policy agreements of 1992–93 that saw trade unions limit their wage demands' (Della Sala, 2002: 120). This had a clear recommodifying effect upon the workforce in Italy, with real unit labour costs (i.e. the wage share of GDP) falling by over twice the amount it fell in the rest of the pre-1995 EU 12 member states during the 1993–2000 period, and also witnessing the amount of workers on fixed-term contracts doubling between 1996 and 2004 (Molina and Rhodes, 2007: 816–7, 821).

The Prodi Government lost the parliamentary support of the RC in October 1998, however, leading to Prodi's replacement by (the again renamed) Democrats of the Left (DS) leader Massimo D'Alema. By this time, the DS had consolidated its 'new' social democratic policy commitments. For instance, a motion adopted at its second congress in 1997, agreed that, 'we must be brave enough to think in terms of less guarantees and protections, and more culture, work and expansion of individual opportunities on the basis of equal starting points' (quoted in Abse, 2001: 72). This was also reflected in a commitment to employment-creation that emphasized the importance of reducing labour costs by cutting employer contributions to social programmes and increasing labour market flexibility; a position that had repeatedly led to clashes with the RC over the latter's demands for more 'traditional' social democratic-style public sector employment as a means to create jobs (Della Sala, 2002: 122). The DS therefore entered the 2001 elections on a clearly 'new' social democratic platform. Thus, in the words of Della Sala, providing an overview of the DS position:

> There is a great deal of rhetoric about social solidarity and tempering inequalities that result from economic liberalization, but the reference point to solving collective problems, whether it is unemployment or the welfare state, is to create the right competitive conditions.
>
> (Della Sala, 2002: 124).

The 2001 election, however, witnessed a severe defeat for the *Ulivio* coalition, and an electoral crisis for the DS, whose vote share fell to just 16.6 per cent.

The transformation from 'traditional' to 'new' social democracy in the case of Italy therefore went through a relatively atypical process. Having adopted party relations that increasingly resembled those of 'traditional' social democratic parties, and following the rapid transitions in both the PCI and the Italian Republic around the end of the 1980s and early 1990s, the PDS/DS leadership moved to adopt a clear focus upon the facilitation of the market as the means through which it would seek to meet the demands of its electoral constituency in the 1990s. Thus, in a manner similar to that which we witnessed in the case of the British Labour Party, rather than seek to promote decommodifying public policy measures through the Italian state, the 'new' social democratic DS leadership based its electoral appeal on its ability to oversee the successful recommodification of Italian labour in the light of the economic problems facing the Italian capitalist economy throughout the 1990s. Also similar to the British Labour Party, this followed a period of prolonged electoral decline from the late-1970s onwards. As such, the PDS/DS party leadership adopted a 'new' social democratic programme, in part as an attempt to overcome the declining electoral support experienced by the PCI during its adoption of 'traditional' social democratic party relations, and also in the light of slow growth and large public debt facing the Italian economy, which themselves suggested the need for a move towards the recommodification of labour within Italy. In terms of the tensions engendered by the 'traditional' social democratic party relations of the PCI, therefore, the party leadership's exclusion from office for the duration of its existence in one sense had an ameliorating effect, particularly in contrast to those 'traditional' social democratic party elites in other countries who did gain election to office. As the PCI leadership was never in a position where it was required to manage the Italian capitalist economy, therefore, it was also spared the experience of needing to impose significant recommodifying measures upon its core constituency. Nevertheless, its prolonged exclusion from office also meant that the PCI leadership was unable to achieve, or plausibly promote, significant decommodifying policy outcomes. As a result, the historic basis for the electoral support of the PCI was largely built upon an ideological conviction. As the ideological purity of the PCI was increasingly diluted (as part of the party's 'social democratization') from the 1970s onwards, so the electoral support for the party also began to decline. In the case of the PCI, therefore, the adoption by the 'traditional' social democratic PCI of 'new' social democratic party policies (as part of its more general transformation into the PDS) was in large part prompted by the increased inability of the party leadership to reproduce a stable 'traditional' social democratic constituency as long as it was effectively excluded from office. In its desire to improve its appearance as a serious contender for government, the PDS leadership undertook a commitment to a 'new' social democratic policy programme that would have a significant recommodifying effect upon its traditional electoral constituency.

In this sense, therefore, the transformation from the 'traditional' social democratic PCI to the 'new' social democratic PDS reflected the inability of the party leadership to successfully reproduce the party relations of the former, which prompted the view amongst the PCI/PDS leadership that this could be resolved through a turn towards a more concerted promotion of recommodifying policies that would (and indeed for a period of time did) facilitate the more successful reproduction of capital–labour relations within Italy. As such, the adoption of a 'new' social democratic party programme in the case of Italy can be viewed as an attempt by the PDS/DS leadership to both implement a more significant recommodification of labour within the Italian economy, and secure the consent of their constituents to those recommodifying policies. In this sense, the PDS/DS leadership sought both a more successful 'representation' of its constituents' demands and a more successful reproduction of Italian capitalist relations, and in turn a more successful reproduction of party relations in general, particularly in the light of its increasing inability to reproduce PCI party relations through the pursuit of more 'traditional' social democratic policy aims.

Spanish social democracy

As with the Italian case, the transformation from 'traditional' to 'new' social democracy in the case of Spain follows a relatively atypical pattern. Most notably, the Spanish Socialist Workers Party (PSOE) was outlawed for most of the post-Second World War period. Following the death of Franco on 25 November 1975, however, Spain moved towards a liberal democratic polity, witnessing the legalization of the PSOE and its emergence as the main social democratic party within the new Spanish party system. By the time of the 1982 elections, moreover, the PSOE had become the dominant party within the Spanish party system, gaining 202 seats compared with the second-placed *Coalición Popular*, which won 107 seats.[11] This began a prolonged period, from 1982 to 1996, during which the PSOE leadership was in government, overseeing the political and economic 'normalization' of Spain. By the late 1980s, however, the PSOE had undergone a number of important ideological and policy revisions, in particular witnessing moves towards the adoption of a 'new' social democratic programme. This process it outlined in the following sections.

The post-Franco PSOE: towards 'traditional' social democratic party relations

The PSOE was legalized in 1977. Only a few months earlier, the 1976 party congress officially embraced Marxism for the first time in its history, claiming that 'the economic subjugation of the proletariat is the primary cause of enslavement in all forms of social misery, intellectual degradation and political dependence' (quoted in Smith, 1998: 55n). In a programme agreed at the same congress the party also adopted the principles of self-management, committing itself to nationalization, elimination of private education, abolition of the monarchy, and self-determination for the regions (Smith, 1998: 55). In this early post-Franco period, therefore, the PSOE adopted a programme that sought a considerable transformation of capitalist relations. As such, we might argue that during this period in the PSOE's history it should be considered a 'reformist' social democratic party. Nevertheless, following the legalization of the party, Felipe Gonzalez, the PSOE leader, sought to moderate the PSOE and thereby move the party towards a more 'traditional' social democratic programme. Following the March 1979 election, therefore, Gonzalez staked his leadership on the removal of Marxist principles from the party programme, arguing that the working class did not constitute a majority of the Spanish electorate and that therefore it was foolish to limit the party's electoral appeal to a minority group. Despite Gonzalez's intentions, the May 1979 congress adopted a political resolution stating that, 'we are a Marxist party because we understand that the scientific method of knowing and transforming capitalist society is through the class struggle, as the motor of History' (quoted in Gillespie, 1989: 346), which in turn prompted Gonzalez's resignation. An extraordinary party congress four months later, however, witnessed Gonzalez take a more conciliatory stance. A new motion was agreed committing the party to

> Marxism as a theoretical, critical, and non-dogmatic method for the analysis and transformation of social reality, making use of the various Marxist and non-Marxist contributions that have made socialism the great emancipatory alternative of our age, and fully respecting personal beliefs.
>
> (quoted in Gillespie, 1989: 355)

This resulted in Gonzalez' re-election as party leader with 86 per cent of the vote. From this point on, therefore, we might consider the PSOE a more typical 'traditional' social democratic party. Indeed, in rapidly moderating its ideological ambitions, and also in seeking to appeal to a constituency that included but nevertheless went beyond the working class, the 1979 extraordinary congress is widely viewed as the point at which the PSOE assumed a 'traditional' social democratic structure of party relations (Gillespie, 1989: 337–56; Share, 1989: 56–8).

The PSOE in office: towards 'new' social democracy?

Having adopted a 'traditional' social democratic structure of party relations following the move towards liberal democracy in Spain, the PSOE was quickly able to improve its electoral appeal amongst the Spanish electorate. Thus, following the rapid process of party restructuring during the early period of Spanish democracy, the PSOE was elected to office in 1982 on a 'traditional' social democratic programme. This included a commitment to implement moderate attempts to decommodify Spanish labour, such as social reforms, measures to tackle the growing economic crisis, and a forty hour week (Holman, 1996: 77). Once it entered office, however, the PSOE leadership was confronted with a struggling capitalist economy that showed many of the signs of a crisis of overaccumulation, and particularly a lack of opportunities for profitable investment. Thus, real GDP shrunk in 1981 and grew at only 1.24 per cent in 1982 (OECD.stat). This was linked with a decline in investment levels, which itself witnessed unemployment levels at around 16 per cent. In a climate of low growth, moreover, the government budget and balance of payments were both suffering from deficits, partly causing inflation to rise to around 15 per cent. Moreover, the Spanish economy suffered from not having kept up internationally with innovations in production processes. Thus, the agricultural sector largely depended on old fashioned and inefficient production techniques, and the industrial sector was most fully developed in areas where international demand was low (Recio and Roca, 1998: 139–40). In the light of these problems with the capitalist economy in Spain, the PSOE Government sought to implement a process of economic modernization. This therefore required that the government attempt to create a more flexible, more efficient and more technologically advanced economy, geared towards the production of goods and services with higher levels of demand in the international market. A number of the measures pursued in order to achieve greater efficiency, moreover, effectively sought the recommodification of workers' lives within Spain. Thus, the PSOE leadership's strategy included attempts to prioritize low inflation over low unemployment, to reduce the fiscal deficit in order to remove subsidization of inefficient activity, to extend the use of temporary employment contracts, and to encourage wage moderation in order to facilitate high profit incentives and productivity (Smith, 1998: 92; Rueda, 2007: 114). Each of these measures therefore represented a significant move away from the PSOE's manifesto commitments, witnessing a clear attempt to recommodify Spanish labour in order to improve opportunities for profitable investment in the Spanish economy. Thus, the government announced an austerity budget in April 1983 that made clear the government's commitment to reducing public expenditure in order to achieve fiscal rectitude (and thereby ease inflationary pressures) (Rueda, 2007: 183). At an early point in its post-Franco history, therefore, the PSOE began to prioritize the reproduction of the Spanish capitalist economy over the attempt to promote measures that would decommodify the lives of its working-class constituency.

For much of this period wage restraint was sought through a policy of centralized *concertation*, whereby either tripartite or government-sponsored bilateral accords between business and labour would link wage rises with productivity increases. This produced agreements in 1983 and 1986 which sought to limit wage increases in line with inflation. These agreements benefited organized labour in Spain as they committed the government to tackle unemployment, to reduce annual working hours and the retirement age, and to facilitate a greater unionization of the labour force. However, the 1986 accord also controversially agreed to reform Spanish industrial employment laws so that mass dismissals would no longer require administrative authorization, in line with practices elsewhere in Europe. Moreover, in 1984, the PSOE Government failed to reach any agreement with business and labour, as the government sought to impose a wage rise limit of 5–6 per cent (2 per cent below expected inflation), which the unions opposed. This thereby produced one of the earliest signs of tension within PSOE party relations, as the party leadership's attempt to achieve a significant recommodification of labour within Spain was opposed by organized labour. Similarly, the government's plan in 1984 to implement social security reforms was strongly opposed by the Workers' General Union (*Unión General de Trabajadores*, UGT), which traditionally had close ties with the PSOE, on the grounds that the plan would reduce existing coverage of welfare provisions (Royo, 2000: 82–7). Indeed, these concerns were well founded as both the 1984 social security reforms and 1985 Pension Law acted to *decrease* the level of protection provided by the Spanish state (Rueda, 2007: 183).

The attempt by the PSOE Government to negotiate a subsequent tripartite agreement in 1986, however, proved unsuccessful. This was in part due to the impact that previous agreements had had upon labour in Spain. Thus, by 1986, in large part as a result of the government's incomes policy (which sought to limit wage rises at least in line with productivity), there had been a fall in real wages every year during which the PSOE had been in office. This, combined with the attempts by the government to reduce social security provisions and introduce labour market liberalization, resulted in growing union opposition to government attempts at wage restraint. This opposition was most obviously apparent in the increased frequency with which trade unions demanded wage rises above inflation, irrespective of productivity gains. Further reflecting tensions within the wider 'traditional' social democratic party relations of the PSOE this increased militancy by the trade unions was in part the result of increased opposition amongst individual union members to the UGT's participation in the government's policy of tripartite wage bargaining (Rueda, 2007: 118). Despite its inability to secure a subsequent agreement in 1986, however, the PSOE Government did impose a 5 per cent limit on public sector wage rises (compared with an average rise of 6.82 per cent in the private sector), prompting a wave of industrial unrest. Thus, 1986 witnessed a breakdown in the government's *concertation* strategy and also marked a significant breakdown in 'traditional' social democratic party relations. In particular, the PSOE leadership in office was no longer able to ensure the consent of its 'traditional' constituency to what it viewed as the necessary level of labour commodification. Thus, according to Royo:

> The government was adamant about the need to develop a restrictive budget to control inflation and foster an environment where business profits would flourish – which in turn would result in higher investment and more jobs. The UGT and CCOO, on the contrary, demanded the fulfilment of previous commitments (such as the compromise included in the AES [an earlier tripartite agreement] to increase unemployment benefits to 48 per cent of the unemployed), and the implementation of an expansive policy ... to stimulate domestic demand.
>
> (Royo, 2000: 90)

The government was therefore far less concerned with implementing macroeconomic policy goals that would have a decommodifying effect upon labour within Spain.

Indeed, the Gonzalez Government actively sought to avoid any policies that would have a decommodifying effect, and also to present them as ineffective. The key focus of the PSOE Government, therefore, was its attempt to recreate the conditions necessary for profitable investment within Spain, and thereby facilitate a more smooth reproduction of the capital–labour relations that constituted the Spanish economy. Thus, through its macroeconomic policy, the PSOE Government sought to implement restrictive measures that would reduce inflation. In this way, the PSOE leadership sought to present policies that would have a dampening effect upon its electorates' demands as necessary for their longer term realization. For instance, in the words of Carlos Solchaga, Socialist minister for industry from 1982 to 1985 and minister for the economy from 1985 to 1993:

The problem of macroeconomic policy, and in particular monetary policy, was not unemployment, since this did not depend on the direction and content of economic policy, but inflation. Once this had been corrected, all the advantages which come from economic stability, including perhaps an increase in employment and reduction in unemployment, could be obtained.

(quoted in Recio and Roca, 1998: 140)

The PSOE therefore began, from entering office onwards, to seek the modernization of the Spanish capitalist economy, and thereby achieve a more successful reproduction of the capital–labour relations that constituted that economy. This was sought, in particular, through an attempt to recommodify labour within Spain by implementing restrictive wage, welfare and macroeconomic policies that would restrict the realization of popular demands. Such policies were presented, moreover, as necessary in order to avoid further economic crisis, thereby seeking to limit the expression of those popular demands, and hence ensure the maintenance of a relationship of 'representation'.

The initial effect of these reforms was considerable. Although price rises were brought somewhat under control (from an annual rise in consumer prices of 14.4 per cent in 1982 to an annual rise of 8.8 per cent in 1985), unemployment increased from over 16 per cent to over 21 per cent between 1982 and 1985 and economic growth only grew by an average of 1.8 per cent per annum (Smith, 1998: 93; Recio and Roca, 1998: 141–4; OECD.stat). Whilst the government was successful in its attempt to restrict demand, therefore, there was no immediate recovery within the Spanish capitalist economy. Nevertheless, perhaps of most importance, in terms of attempting to ensure a recommodification of labour within Spain in order to create increased opportunities for profitable investment, labour productivity did increase. Indeed, this early period in office witnessed productivity gains of 3 per cent (Royo, 2000: 105). This appeared eventually to pay off in the second half of the 1980s as Spain entered an economic boom. Labour costs in production had been reduced, thereby enabling an increase in profits. Indeed, as Royo (2000) points out, this was crucial to the recovery of the Spanish economy, as, on the one hand, increased profits 'increased the capacity of business to reinvest'. Further still, on the other hand, 'higher profits also increased the profitability of business investment, which expanded 7.5 per cent between 1985 and 1988, and made investing in business more attractive' (Royo, 2000: 103–4). This obviously also had a parallel effect upon the extent to which labour experienced exploitation within the Spanish economy. Thus, the wage share of national income fell by over 10 per cent throughout the PSOE's entire period in office between 1982 and 1996 (Recio and Roca, 2001: 182–3), and profits (measured as the return on assets) increased from 5.4 per cent in 1983 to 21.3 per cent in 1988 (Royo, 2000: 169). In one sense, therefore, the considerable recommodification of labour within Spain ensured a more smooth reproduction of capital–labour relations. Thus, the Spanish economy experienced 4.7 per cent average annual growth in GDP between 1986 and 1989 (compared with an EC average of 3.3 per cent) (Smith, 1998: 94). However, in implementing such considerable recommodifying measures, the PSOE leadership placed significant strains upon the 'traditional' social democratic party relations it sought to reproduce.

In seeking to implement policies which would have a recommodifying effect upon labour within Spain, therefore, the PSOE undermined the electoral support of its core constituency. Thus, as noted earlier, the PSOE began in the early stage of its period in office to liberalize the Spanish labour market. In 1984 the government introduced new temporary employment contracts, which meant that as employment began to increase in 1985, 'almost all of the new jobs took one of these new [temporary] forms, so the percentage of temporary jobs increased dramatically, especially in the private sector' (Recio and Roca, 1998: 146). By 1988, therefore, 25.1 per cent of the working population in Spain was under temporary contract, rising to one third in 1992 (a trend that would continue to the extent that, in 1996, 97 per cent of the contracts signed that year were temporary) (Royo, 2000: 105; Rueda, 2007: 121). This led to growing tensions between the UGT and the PSOE Government throughout the second half of the 1980s. This included clashes over continued attempts by the government to implement a number of further recommodifying policies, such as a freeze in real wage levels, the introduction of temporary work contracts for the young, and the government's failure to increase public sector pay in line with inflation in 1988 (Recio and Roca, 1998: 149; Smith, 1998: 95–8). These tensions culminated on 14 December 1988 with a general strike that involved 80 per cent of the workforce, thereby marking a major and dramatic breakdown in the cohesion of the PSOE's 'traditional' social democratic party relations. Indeed, in witnessing such a direct confrontation between the PSOE in office and the Spanish labour force, we might argue that in 1988 the 'traditional' social democratic party relations of the PSOE had entered a crisis whereby the obstacles to successfully reproducing those relations were becoming increasingly insurmountable. Whilst this growing unpopularity was in part offset, in terms of electoral support, by concerns that the Popular Party (PP) opposition would impose even more draconian measures if elected to office, the growing tensions within the 'traditional' social democratic party relations of the PSOE did manifest themselves in the form of a fall in the party's share of the vote in the 1989 general election. This left the PSOE with 175 seats in the Cortes, but nevertheless a slim majority which enabled it to maintain its place in office.

Having experienced a prolonged period of tension and mounting crisis, particularly in the form of the 1988 general strike, in 1990 the PSOE launched its *Manifesto of the Programme 2000* at the 32nd party congress. This document sought to rejuvenate PSOE policy, consolidate (or, arguably, re-establish) its dominance over the Spanish party system, and attempt to re-inject 'traditional' social democratic values into the PSOE policy programme (interview with Juan Fernando López Aguilar, 21 May 2008; Gillespie, 1993: 82–5). Nevertheless, this was not entirely successful. Thus, the manifesto was relatively free of original content as the debate was closely controlled by the party leadership, and especially by the Deputy Prime Minister, Alfonso Guerra. As a result, the manifesto had only limited impact upon both the party and the electorate. Perhaps the most important innovation announced by the manifesto, particularly for our attempt in the present study to understand the nature of the PSOE party relations, was the abandonment of an exclusively working-class identity and electoral strategy (Gillespie, 1993: 90–4). Thus, having increasingly moved from a platform committed to decommodifying outcomes in the early 1980s to the implementation of policies with clear recommodifying aims throughout the rest of the1980s, in 1990 the PSOE leadership sought to reposition itself in terms of the electoral constituency that made up internal party relations. In this sense, therefore, we might consider the changes undertaken by the PSOE leadership throughout the 1980s as being characterized by a gradual move towards a 'new' social democratic programme, particularly in terms of the focus upon inflation, welfare retrenchment, the end to tripartite wage negotiations from 1986 onwards, and the move away from a focus upon the working class.

However, this gradual transformation, which occurred throughout the 1980s, also underwent something of a reversal at the end of the decade. Thus, following the experience of the 1988 general strike, the PSOE sought to respond to the growing antipathy of its 'traditional' constituency by increasing pensions and unemployment benefits in the 'so-called' *Acuerdos del 25 de Enero*, introduced in 1990. At the same time, the government passed a number of laws allowing the unions to monitor the temporary work contracts to which they had been so opposed, in an additional attempt to pacify union opposition[12] (Smith, 1998: 99; Royo, 2000: 91). This turn to the implementation of ameliorative measures that would ease relations between the PSOE leadership and its constituency was, however, short-lived. From 1989 onwards, a combination of increased social security benefits and a global economic downturn resulted in increased public debt, inflation and downward pressure on the peseta. As a result, the government implemented three currency devaluations between September 1992 and May 1993, devaluing the currency by 19 per cent in total, and thereby significantly curbing domestic consumption in an attempt to further improve the profitability of the Spanish capitalist economy (Boix, 2000: 175–8; Royo, 2000: 91). Further still, in 1991 the PSOE Government sought (unsuccessfully) to convince the unions 'of the need for a Competitiveness Pact that would promote further labor market flexibility and a commitment to wage moderation' (Rueda, 2007: 122). In December of the same year, the Spanish government announced its *plan de convergencia* for the period 1992–96. This outlined cuts in public expenditure and social spending, deregulation and flexibilization of capital and labour markets, and also an accelerated partial privatization of public enterprises. The plan therefore marked another shift in emphasis, from decommodification to recommodification, and prompted another (albeit less well supported) general strike (Holman, 1996: 155; Smith, 1998: 101). The inability of the government to reach agreement with the unions on the Competitiveness Pact, alongside the holding of another general strike the following year, illustrated the continuing tensions in the PSOE party relations. These moves were accompanied by further reductions in social spending, including the 'decretazo', introduced between 1992 and 1993, which both raised the minimum period of previous work required to be eligible for unemployment benefits and lowered the amount of those benefits (Rueda, 2007: 185–6). Perhaps the clearest impact of this new turn to welfare retrenchment was the rise in government spending on the main social expenses (pensions, unemployment, health and education). Thus, whereas the government's social expenditure had risen by 3.4 per cent of GDP between 1982 and 1991, and by another 2.8 per cent whilst the government was under pressure to increase expenditure between 1991 and 1993, it went on to fall by 1.3 per cent between 1993 and 1995. This was a particularly severe period of retrenchment for unemployment benefit, which fell back in 1995 to its 1982 level (Recio and Roca, 2001: 193).

The unpopularity that arose from the latest wave of welfare retrenchment measures in the early 1990s, combined with a growing spate of scandals which also harmed the government, resulted in a further fall in support for the PSOE in the 1993 elections. The party gained 39 per cent of the votes and 159 of the 350 seats in the Cortes, requiring it to form a coalition with the small party, *Convergència I Unio*, in order to form the next Socialist government (Smith, 1998: 101). The remainder of the Spanish socialist's period in office, however, was heavily focused on preparing the Spanish economy for entry into the single currency, including further privatization and restrictive fiscal and monetary policies. It also witnessed a further shift towards the implementation of restrictive labour market policies, including an (unsuccessful) attempt to get the unions to agree to below-inflation wage rises for three years, and the introduction of more short-term and part-time employment contracts. Nevertheless, unemployment remained extremely high, reaching 24.3 per cent of the active labour force by 1994, and in the 1996 election support for the PSOE was exhausted, witnessing its replacement in office by the *Partido Popular* (PP) (Royo, 2000: 93–5, 215).

During its prolonged period in office from 1982 to 1996, therefore, the PSOE consistently promoted the intensification of Spanish labour's productivity, in order to engender the successful reproduction of the Spanish capitalist economy. Whilst the party leadership sought throughout this period to argue that the measures it was promoting would enable more generous welfare provisions, and therefore greater social security protection, in its attempt to achieve these aims the party relied almost exclusively upon policies that focused on low inflation, supply-side reforms of the labour market, and fiscal rectitude. From 1986 onwards, moreover, this produced a dramatic schism between the leadership of the PSOE and the organized labour movement in Spain. The government was repeatedly unable to agree to the tripartite wage pacts with which it sought to underpin its macroeconomic policy, and the experience of three general strikes (1988, 1992 and 1994) were further evidence of the strains experienced by the 'traditional' social democratic relations of the PSOE. Indeed, from 1986 onwards, notwithstanding a brief hiatus following the 1988 general strike, the PSOE leadership sought increasingly to focus upon the introduction of labour market liberalizing measures, and to reduce welfare generosity, in an attempt to balance the government budget and to stimulate economic growth. Moreover, as we witnessed in discussing the *Manifesto of the Programme 2000*, the PSOE leadership sought to significantly scale down its commitment to the representation of the working class in Spain. We might consider, therefore, the PSOE to have undergone a transition towards a 'new' social democratic programme from the second half of the 1980s. Whilst, in contrast to some of the other parties we have studied thus far, there was no clear break from 'traditional' to 'new' social democracy for the PSOE, there was, nevertheless, a consistent move away from labour market regulation, tripartite wage negotiations, and 'passive' welfare provisions throughout this period. Thus, the period following the 1986 breakdown in tripartism, and the period following the adoption of the Maastricht convergence criteria, both witnessed clear moves away from a 'traditional' social democratic party programme.

Reconceptualizing 'new' social democracy

The foregoing analytical narratives of transition, from 'traditional' to 'new' social democracy, have attempted to employ the real definition of 'traditional' social democratic party relations provided in Chapter 2 in order to account for the adoption by 'traditional' social democratic party actors of 'new' social democratic policies. In focusing on the tensions arising from the structure of 'traditional' social democratic party relations, therefore, we have been able to identify some of the key causal processes which led to this policy change. In each case we have witnessed some important commonalities. First, the tension between the attempt to represent the interests of an electoral constituency that is based upon, but extends beyond, a core working-class constituency has, in each case, witnessed the pursuit, to varying extents, of policies that seek to decommodify the lives of those constituents, but which have themselves prompted tensions in the reproduction of 'traditional' social democratic party relations. Thus, in the case of the British Labour Party, the Swedish SAP, and the French PS we witnessed the introduction of a number of policy commitments, both in opposition and in office, including the extension of welfare provisions, attempts to reduce unemployment, and the attempt to limit the role of the market in resource allocation (through, for instance, labour market regulation, trade protectionism, or demand management) within each national economy. Similarly, both the PCI and the PSOE made commitments to introduce decommodifying measures prior to their entry to (or attempt to enter) office. Thus, in the case of the PCI leadership this took the form of a commitment to the improvement of the lives of their constituents through working-class-oriented reforms. In the case of the PSOE, we witnessed a commitment to overcome the 'enslavement' of the proletariat, to introduce the principle of 'self-management', and the adoption of a programme that included nationalization and a commitment to social reform. However, each of these cases have also resulted in significant tensions in party relations arising from the concomitant attempt of the party leadership to manage (or maintain the appearance of the ability to manage) the national capitalist economy they sought to govern over. Thus, during its periods in office in the 1940s, 1960s and 1970s, the leadership of the British Labour Party experienced significant opposition from the labour movement that formed its core constituency (this was especially the case towards the end of the 1964–70 government and of the 1974–79 government). Similarly, from the late 1960s onwards the SAP leadership struggled to balance its constituents' demands for greater decommodification with the experience of slow economic growth and a declining currency. In the case of the French PS in office in the 1980s, we witnessed rising opposition from the French labour movement, and declining electoral support, in response to the heavily restrictive measures it sought to implement. This was matched in Spain, where the PSOE Government found it increasingly difficult to reach desired corporatist agreements with organized labour, eventually resulting in a succession of general strikes from 1988 onwards. Finally, the PCI leadership sought, from the early 1970s onwards, to locate itself within the mainstream of the party system, increasingly moderating its demands for decommodification, as part of a general process of ideological moderation, whilst at the same time witnessing a continual decline in electoral support from 1979 onwards. The reproduction of 'traditional' social democratic party relations has, therefore, been problematic and tension-ridden throughout the period under investigation.

Second, in seeking to use the real definition of 'traditional' social democratic parties derived in Chapter 2, the present study has viewed the move by 'traditional' social democratic parties to adopt 'new' social democratic policies, in each case, as a significant reprioritization by the party leadership of the promotion of recommodifying public policies. In each case, moreover, this reprioritization has been presented to the party constituency in terms of it being the most appropriate way in which the party leadership is able to meet the policy demands of those constituents. Thus, in the case of the British Labour Party, we witnessed an attempt to portray the move to 'New' Labour as the best possible means to ensure both economic growth and to unseat the Conservative opposition. In the case of the Swedish SAP we witnessed the promotion of the 1990s structural reforms as necessary in order to ensure the continuation of (remaining) welfare provisions. In the case of the French PS, the reforms of the 1980s were consistently promoted as necessary for the continued viability of the French economy within a wider European economy. For the PDS/DS, the economic problems of low growth and a high budget deficit of the 1990s were portrayed as necessitating the move towards budget and wage retrenchment, in particular in the light of the forthcoming need to meet the Maastricht convergence criteria. Finally, in the case of the PSOE, the structural reforms undertaken were presented as necessary in order to re-integrate the Spanish economy into the wider European economy and international community, and by doing so achieve similar levels of welfare provision to that experienced in the rest of western Europe. In each case, therefore, we witness the adoption of 'new' social democratic policies as part of a shift by the social democratic party leadership towards the placing of greater emphasis upon the recommodification of the lives of workers (who themselves form a central constituency within 'traditional' social democratic party relations), whilst at the same time presenting this move as being necessitated by either the economic or political contexts within which each party is located.

Third, and finally, in each of the cases that we have observed above, a key problem facing the 'traditional' social democratic party leadership, and therefore prompting moves towards the adoption of 'new' social democratic policies, was the inability of the capital–labour relation to reproduce itself without a concomitant recommodification of labour. Thus, in the case of Sweden, France and Spain, we witnessed a struggling capitalist economy that was able to return to acceptable (and functioning) levels of growth following the recommodifying measures put in place by the 'traditional' social democratic party in office. Similarly, in Italy, we witnessed a coincidence of stagnating economic growth alongside a burgeoning public sector debt, the partial resolution of which contributed to economic recovery by the late 1990s. Finally, the British Labour Party faced ongoing economic problems throughout the 1960s and 1970s; low productivity and wage drift undermined the profitability of the British economy and the value of sterling, and therefore economic growth. Despite consistent efforts to stimulate greater profitability within the British capitalist economy, the Labour Party leadership proved unable to sufficiently limit wage growth to the level necessary to avoid the economic crisis of the 1976–9 period, producing the subsequent political fallout that followed.

Based on the preceding analytical narratives, therefore, we can summarize the process by which 'traditional' social democratic party leaders came to adopt 'new' social democratic policies as a result of the following three processes (see table 3.1):

1. The tensions arising from the attempt by party elites to contain the demands of 'traditional' social democratic constituents – either due to the inability to sufficiently contain demands, or the decline in support resulting from the attempt to do so – acted increasingly to problematize the reproduction of 'traditional' social democratic party relations;
2. This ultimately resulted in a crisis point (or series of crisis points), during which 'traditional' social democratic party elites were no longer able to reconcile the conflicting tendencies contained within 'traditional' social democratic party relations;
3. This was therefore followed by a turning point, during which the 'traditional' social democratic party leadership sought to reprioritize social democratic party values, witnessing a shift away from the promotion of the decommodification of labour and towards an emphasis upon recommodification.

This account therefore characterizes the process whereby 'traditional' social democratic parties came to adopt 'new' social democratic policies. In keeping with the critical realist approach outlined in Chapter 2, however, we should also seek to outline the way in which, if at all, this transition has also witnessed change within the structure of social democratic party relations. We are particularly interested, therefore, in whether, and how, the relationship between the party leadership and the social democratic party constituency has changed as a result of these policy revisions. Thus, based on the foregoing discussion, the most important change observed has been a shift by the party leadership from a focus upon decommodification as a policy goal towards that of recommodification. Moreover, in seeking to undertake such a policy revision, the social democratic party leadership in each case has sought to acquire the consent of (at least sections of) its 'traditional' constituency, whilst nevertheless accepting that it may need to broaden its electoral appeal further than the traditional focus on the working class (albeit one that extended beyond that class) under 'traditional' social democratic party relations. Moreover, in experiencing opposition from its traditional constituency, the social

Table 3.1 The transformation from 'traditional' to 'new' social democracy

Country	Increasingly problematic reproduction	Crisis point(s)	The re-prioritization of recommodification ('new' social democracy)
UK	AEU/NUR refusal to support TUC-backed wage freeze (1950) Late 1960s strike wave + defeat of *In Place of Strife* 1976 IMF crisis 1978–9 winter of discontent	1979–83 ideological schism 1983 election disaster Prolonged period in opposition between 1979 and 1997	1988–91 policy review programme 1995 Clause IV revision
Sweden	LO refusal to adhere to further wage restraint (1951) 1969–70 wildcat strikes 1970s slowdown in economic growth 1976–82 period in opposition Breakdown in centralized wage negotiations from early 1980s Mid-1980s budget and balance of payments deficits	1990 Currency Crisis	1990 emergency programme 1994–8 austerity measures 1997 labour market liberalization
France	1981–3 balance of payments deficit and heightened currency speculation Decline in electoral support for the PS in 1982 and 1983	1982–3 economic crisis Poor electoral performance in 1984 EP election, and defeat in the 1986 general election 1986–95 ideological vacuum and internal elite-level in-fighting	1983 U-turn, *franc fort* and disinflation competitive 1991 Arche Congress 1997 Jospin Programme
Italy	Prolonged period in opposition	Prolonged electoral decline from 1979–1987	The transformation from the PCI to the PDS (and exit of the RC) 1996–2001 *Ulivio* Government Programme
Spain	Spanish crisis of overaccumulation upon entering office Inability to reach 1984 tripartite agreement UGT opposition to 1984 social security reforms Failed 1986 Accord	1988 general strike 1992 general strike	Post-1986 austerity and labour market liberalization measures 1991 attempt to agree 'Competitiveness Pact' *Manifesto of the Programme 2000* 1992 plan de convergencia

democratic party leadership has consistently sought to argue that the policy programme it is presenting represents the best possible alternative available to that constituency. As such, we might provide a real definition of 'new' social democratic party relations in the following terms:

'New' Social Democracy (real definition): *'New' social democratic parties are constituted by a party elite seeking to suppress the demands for decommodification of an electoral constituency which has been historically constructed around the pursuit of such demands in order that these demands might be* both *(a) 'representable' within the institutions of the representative-democratic state, and (b) compatible with the successful reproduction of the capital–labour relations that constitute the national capitalist economy, through the promotion of the recommodification of labour in response to recurrent crises of overaccumulation.*

One of the central arguments of the present chapter, therefore, is that in using the real definition of 'traditional' social democratic party relations derived in Chapter 2 to inform a series of analytical narratives mapping the adoption, by 'traditional' social democratic party elites, of 'new' social democratic policies, we have been able to derive a real definition of 'new' social democratic party relations. The following chapter attempts to use this in order to inform analytical narratives of the 'new' social democratic parties' turn to 'Social Europe', and thereby hopefully resolve the paradox that underpins the present study.

4 'New' social democratic party relations and the turn to 'Social Europe'

The aim of this chapter is to examine the turn towards 'Social Europe' by the social democratic parties that form our present study. As with Chapter 3, the aim here is to draw upon a real definition of the parties under investigation in order to provide an insight into the motives underpinning the actions and reactions of the constitutive actors with regard to the contextual changes they find themselves confronted with. The chapter therefore seeks to examine the way in which 'new' social democratic party relations were constructed, and subsequently reproduced, paying particular attention to the role of a 'Social Europe' agenda within this process. The chapter therefore provides an analytical narrative tracing the development of the European policy of the five parties under investigation, focusing particularly on the way in which this policy changed as social democratic parties shifted from 'traditional' to 'new' structures of social democratic party relations, as conceptualized in Chapters 2 and 3.

The British Labour Party and the turn to 'Social Europe'

The British Labour Party held an ambivalent position on European integration throughout much of the post-war period. Indeed, for much of the Labour Party's period as a 'traditional' social democratic party, there was no clear Labour Party position. As such, the more interesting developments in the Labour Party's European policy occurred during the transition from 'traditional' to 'new' social democratic party relations. What follows, therefore, is a brief overview highlighting the ambiguity of the Labour Party's position during much of its period as a 'traditional' social democratic party, before a more detailed discussion of how that position developed in parallel with the transformation from 'traditional' to 'new' social democratic party relations.

The first Labour Government refused to support the Schuman Plan, and once in opposition the Labour Party leadership was also against the European Defence Community and European Political Community. It was nevertheless supportive of EFTA (European Free Trade Association). Similarly, whilst Labour Party leader, Hugh Gaitskell, famously declared at the 1962 party conference that EC membership would mean 'the end of a thousand years of history' (Labour Party, 1962), the Labour Party's National Executive Committee (NEC) announced in the same year that it would support UK accession provided there were sufficient safeguards on national sovereignty. In its 1964 election campaign, moreover, the Labour Party favoured the Commonwealth over EC membership, but by 1966 it supported membership (although this was again conditional upon safeguards for national and Commonwealth interests). This move away from an initial Euroscepticism was, however, opposed by a significant section of the Labour Party, particularly by those on the left. Thus, in 1967, 74 Labour MPs signed an article in the *Tribune* opposing EC membership and 36 Labour MPs voted against the Wilson Government's application for EC membership (with 51 MPs abstaining). These divisions were also reflected in the party conference of the same year, with 2.7 million delegate votes registered against the resolution welcoming the application to join the EC and 3.36 million in support. Further still, in the 1970 general election campaign the Labour Party stood on a pro-accession platform. Yet, during the 1970–74 period in opposition, Wilson adopted a position of opposition to the *terms of entry* negotiated by the Conservative Government, seeking a referendum on a renegotiated package for membership. Thus, in neither fully supporting nor fully rejecting EC membership, Wilson hoped to reconcile the two conflicting positions on Europe within his party (Featherstone, 1988).

Upon its election to office in 1974, the Labour Party stuck to its commitment to renegotiate the terms of the UK's entry to the EC (although the reforms achieved were of only marginal significance), and the following year the promised referendum on continued membership was held. The EC issue continued to divide the party, however, with both the NEC and Conference opposing membership, and the majority of the cabinet supporting a yes vote. These divisions were repeated in 1976 when the Labour Government agreed to direct elections to the European Parliament, a decision opposed by the Labour Party conference by 4 to 2.2 million votes. Similarly, in 1978 the Labour Party conference voted to reform both the Treaty of Rome and the accession agreement between the UK and the EC, aiming to re-assert the supremacy of British sovereignty, and thereby threatening to undo the careful compromise Wilson had sought to create with his referendum on the renegotiated terms of membership (Featherstone, 1988:61–2). Throughout much of the post-war period, and for most of the time that the Labour Party was characterized by 'traditional' social democratic party relations, the Labour Party was highly ambivalent on the European question. Whilst much of the party leadership shifted towards a pro-European position from the 1960s onwards, a large anti-European constituency remained both within the parliamentary party and within the wider party membership. As the 'traditional' social democratic party relations of the Labour Party moved into crisis from 1979, however, the position of significant party actors, and the official position of the party as a whole, began to shift more dramatically.

The European question and 'traditional' social democratic party crisis

Perhaps most noteworthy of the 1979–83 period for the Labour Party, in terms of the relationship between its position on European integration and the more general transformation affecting the structure of party relations, was the way in which the ascendance of the left was, in part, mobilized around fierce opposition to EC membership. The left versus right split within the party therefore correlated closely with an anti- versus pro-EC divide. The left opposed EC membership on the grounds that it obstructed national economic sovereignty, which it viewed as necessary for the reflationary and socialist goals it pursued within the British nation-state. The right of the party, however, viewed both the reflationary measures, and withdrawal from the EC, as economically, and therefore also electorally, impractical (Callaghan, 2000b). As we witnessed in Chapter 3, during this 1979 to 1983 period, the left was largely successful in its attempt to promote its agenda within the Labour Party. This was also the case in terms of the Labour Party's European policy.

The 1979 post-election Labour Party conference unanimously adopted a resolution stating that Britain's position within the EC was detrimental to the British people and the Labour movement, and that 'should changes not be made by the early 1980s the question of Britain's continuing membership of the European Economic Community (EEC) should be reconsidered' (Labour Party, 1979: 327–8). This Eurosceptic position was more firmly adopted by the Labour Party the following year when the conference agreed by 5 million to 2 million votes that,

> Conference does not believe that the demands to which we are committed [reform of the Treaty of Rome and of the UK accession agreements] are capable of being fulfilled and urges the Labour Party to include the withdrawal of the United Kingdom from the European Economic Community as a priority in the next general election manifesto; to disengage Britain from the European Economic Community institutions and in place of our European Economic Community membership to work for peaceful and equitable relations between Britain and all the nations in Europe and the rest of the world.
>
> (Labour Party, 1980: 125–6)

Withdrawal was advocated on the basis of a combination of reasons relating to national interest and ideological aims. Thus, the list of criticisms of European integration voiced at the conference included the claim that membership of the EC had exacerbated the imbalance of trade, that the UK was a net contributor to the EC budget despite being one of the poorer countries, that the CAP was wasteful and inefficient, that the EC was undemocratic, that it restricted global trade and therefore represented a 'club for capitalism', and that it prevented the implementation of the AES (Labour Party, 1980: 125–32). In opposition to the resolution, David Owen, representing the position of many on the right of the party, argued that the Labour Party needed to accept that economic and political reality were such that the policy of withdrawal was impractical. Thus, he claimed that it was necessary,

> to face certain realities. The Community is now our dominant trading partner. Seven out of ten of our biggest export markets are in the European Community. Since 1975 UK exports to the Community have expanded faster than imports. In the first six months of this year exports covered 94 per cent of

imports. Forty-three per cent of our exports went to the EEC ... In 1984 jobs are going to be the massive issue that faces this country after the devastation of Thatcherism, and it will be a very serious decision as to whether this movement feels that we should withdraw from the European Community.

(Labour Party, 1980: 128)

As we saw in Chapter 3, these divisions, and the clear ascendance of the Labour left in the early 1980s, eventually resulted in the decision by the Gang of Three to leave the Labour Party and form the Social Democratic Party (SDP). This therefore ensured that the remaining left wing within the Labour Party had even less opponents, and thereby became even more influential within the party,[2] resulting in the further consolidation of anti-EC sentiment. Thus, the 1981 conference overwhelmingly supported a motion for withdrawal from the EC, by 6.21 million to 782,000 votes, and went on to declare in its 1983 general election campaign that,

[T]he next Labour government, committed to radical socialist policies for reviving the British economy, is bound to find continued membership [of the EC] a most serious obstacle to the fulfilment of those policies. In particular the rules of the Treaty of Rome are bound to conflict with our strategy for economic growth and full employment, our proposals on industrial policy and for increasing trade, preventing us from buying food from the best sources of world supply, they would run counter to our plans to control prices and inflation.

For all these reasons, British withdrawal from the Community is the right policy for Britain – to be completed well within the lifetime of the parliament.

(Labour Party, 1983)

As we have already seen, however, the extremely poor performance of the Labour Party in the 1983 election meant that it would undergo a series of significant changes that ultimately resulted in its transformation into a 'new' social democratic party. We seek, therefore, to investigate this transformation to 'new' social democratic party relations, and the way in which the party position on Europe changed in the process.

The transition to 'new' social democracy: turning to 'Social Europe'?

As noted in Chapter 3, it was between 1983 and 1995 that we witnessed the Labour Party begin its transformation from 'traditional' social democratic to 'new' social democratic party relations in the light of the continued experience of party crisis. This transformation included a concerted attempt to further contain the demands of those members of the Labour Party constituency who typically demanded the pursuit of decommodifying public policies from the Labour Party leadership. It also witnessed a clear move towards the adoption of a 'Social Europe' agenda. Thus, following the 1983 general election defeat, the new incoming leadership around Neil Kinnock sought to steer Labour Party policy away from its policy of EC withdrawal. In an article published in 1984, for instance, Kinnock argued that the EC had the potential to be helpful for both the Labour Party and the UK if it were able to be reformed in such a way that it would facilitate cooperation and coordination between member states along the lines of a 'Euro Bretton Woods' (Kinnock, 1984). Thus, Kinnock claimed, 'a new Euro Bretton Woods should take initiatives to harness multinational finance capital. It should aim to achieve the conditions for modern full employment policies in Europe and positive policies for the rest of the world' (Kinnock, 1984: 232). Interestingly, however, this was not an argument made only by those on the right of the party. Indeed, as early as 1982, a number of articles appeared in the party's journal, *New Socialist*, which argued that the EC should be considered a means to promote Keynesianism or the AES on a European scale. Barbara Castle, who had campaigned for a no-vote in the 1975 referendum, also made a similar argument in an article she published in the *New Statesman* in September 1982 (Broad, 2001: 145–54). Following the 1983 electoral defeat, therefore, and in the light of the growing acceptance by some of the Labour Party that its national-level Keynesian reflation agenda was perceived by many as unfeasible, this argument began to be adopted by others broadly on the left of the Labour Party. Thus, in the same edited collection as the Kinnock article mentioned earlier, Stuart Holland, a left-wing economist and supporter of the AES, made the case for a European-wide programme that would include reflation, planning, investment and redistribution. According to Holland, this 'Eurokeynesian' programme should be promoted by a unified left at the EC-level. Indeed, he saw coordinated European action as the only means to achieve a social democratic programme of economic stimulation. Thus, he asked, 'How can the European left hope to succeed where the French government failed in gaining sustained recovery?' To which he answered:

> Precisely, in part, by being a European left rather than a left within one country, or a minor Atlantic partner offering capital with a human face. Precisely by being a left open to all of Europe and a wider world rather than confined by the Common Market. Precisely by arguing for the maxi budget which will help the world spend its way out of slump rather than only for mini budget rebates on a food-price policy. If even some like-minded left governments can jointly face this global challenge on the lines of the recovery programme spelled out in the 1984 manifesto of the Confederation of Socialist Parties, then not only Europe but also the world would have a chance of surmounting the current crisis.
>
> (Holland, 1984: 263–4)

This shift in perspective, by an influential thinker on the Labour left, from an initial focus on the nation-state to a new focus on the European level, was an important recognition of the limitations of a nationally-oriented 'traditional' social democracy. Moreover, this position developed through collaboration between members of the executives of the socialist parties of the UK, Portugal, Spain, Italy, Greece, France, Belgium, the Netherlands and Sweden, published under the editorship of Stuart Holland himself, entitled the *Out of Crisis* project (Holland, 1982). There was, therefore, a view gaining ground amongst both the Labour left and the party leadership that the EC-level had important opportunities to offer. For the left, there was increasing optimism that key elements of their programme would actually be *more* feasible at the European level (see, for instance, Teague, 1985). For the party leadership, also, there was a recognition that the Labour Party's commitment to withdraw from the EC made it appear impractical and unfit to govern (interview with Neil Kinnock, 3 December 2002).

Despite these tentative moves towards a pro-EC position, we should nevertheless note that opposition towards the EC remained strong within the Labour Party and as a result no changes in official policy were immediately forthcoming. This was in part due to the reluctance of the Labour Party leadership to discuss the issue at the formal level due to its potential to divide the party. Indeed, the issue of European integration was not discussed at all at the Labour Party conferences held between 1983 and 1987. Similarly, official party statements on the EC sought to avoid any clear statement of either pro- or anti- European sentiment. The 1984 EP manifesto, for instance, accepted that the UK would be a member of the EC until at least 1989, whilst simultaneously advocating attempts to tackle unemployment through the EC and retaining the option of withdrawal. On the Single European Act, the Labour Party opposed the Conservative's opposition to EC-level social policy, and in the 1987 General Election manifesto the Labour Party was committed to working within the EC on the economy and unemployment (Broad, 2001:156–68).

Regardless of this ambiguity within the Labour Party's official statements, however, there was a more consistent undercurrent of increasingly positive opinion within the party as the EC came to be viewed as a means to achieve reflationary measures that might be able to circumvent the Conservative Government's opposition to state-led intervention. This was a view increasingly propagated by the party leadership. Thus, Kinnock argued in an article published in the *New Statesman* in 1986 that sterling should enter the EMS, provided it was part of a wider programme that included macroeconomic management, fiscal reflation, and the avoidance of regional inequality, all to be achieved through a coordinated supranational strategy (*New Statesman*, 7 November 1986). Similarly, Frances Morrell, a one-time leading advocate of the AES and at the time leader of the Inner London Education Authority, argued that,

> the only course of action open to us, if we wish to protect the interests of working people in this country, is to devise joint strategies with other European countries who share the same objectives and face the same problems.
> (Frances Morrell, in *New Statesman*, 6 March 1987)

There was a clear attempt, therefore, by a number of proponents across the ideological spectrum of the party leadership, during a period that we have described above as one of crisis for the Labour Party, to portray European integration as an important opportunity for 'traditional' social democratic party actors, particularly in the light of those crisis conditions.

Following defeat in the 1987 general election, moreover, the opportunities for EC-level policy-making were identified by a larger number still within the Labour Party. Thus, 1988 saw the publication of David Martin MEP's Fabian pamphlet, *Bringing Commonsense to the Common Market – a left agenda for Europe*, in which it was argued that the Left needed to tackle the political agenda within the EC in order to retain political relevance (Martin, 1988). The year 1988 also witnessed Jacques Delors give what was to become a highly influential speech to the Trades Union Congress (TUC). Indeed, this has subsequently come to be viewed as one of the most important points in the Labour Party's adoption of a pro-European position, or in the terms of the present study, of its turn towards 'Social Europe'. Thus, Delors argued that the Common Market would help with attempts to tackle uneven development across Europe, bolster social protection and enhance provisions for collective bargaining. This contrasted with the vehement antipathy of the Conservative Government to British trade unionism in such a way that Delors' speech was immediately attractive to the British labour movement (George and Rosamond, 1992). It thereby prompted the rapid adoption of a 'Social Europe' agenda, whereby the opportunities for pursuing redistributive and decommodifying policies at the EC-level were increasingly embraced across the Labour Party. Thus, the TUC in 1988 responded to Delors' speech by voting to accept its Report on '1992' (TUC, 1988), in which the trade union movement committed itself to campaigning to build the 'social dimension' at the EC level.

Some of the speeches made during the 1988 congress also provide an important illustration of the reasoning that British trade unionists gave for their support for further European integration. They thereby illustrate the way in which the European Community was coming to be viewed by core members of the Labour Party's electoral constituency. Thus, Roy Grantham, delegate for the Association of Professional, Executive, Clerical and Computer Staff, and mover of the composition motion welcoming the TUC report and advocating a campaign for more social rights at the EC level, claimed,

> [T]he Prime Minister may be able to drive the whole of Whitehall into the narrow fundamentalist doctrines of Thatcherism but there is no way that she can stop us reaching agreement in Brussels.
>
> (TUC 1988: 576)

He thereby clearly expressed a view, increasingly held with the Labour Party, that the EC-level offered the opportunity to overcome the drive towards neoliberalism being undertaken in the British national-level context. Further, in the same debate the Union of Communication Workers delegate argued that,

> [W]e call for a major programme. We need to establish common European-wide bargaining so that we can combat the power of the multi-national. We need to plan an informative programme for members on the effects of 1992. We need to draw up a European workers' charter with positive, not negative, rights. We need to use the opportunities under Article 118a of the Single

European Act for extending workers' rights, through directives from the Council of Ministers aimed at upward harmonisation across the European Community.

(TUC 1988: 577)

Thus, British trade unionists were becoming increasingly aware of the nascent institutional and policy opportunities emerging at the EC-level as a result of increased integration, and the way in which this provided opportunities for decommodifying measures that were, at the same time, under attack at the national level.

Following Thatcher's now infamous anti-EC Bruges speech in September 1988, the Labour Party conference two weeks later offered the ideal context within which the leadership of the party could re-launch Labour as the party of Europe. Thus, one of the policy review groups, Britain in the World, made its first report back to the 1988 party conference, in which it stated, 'Our membership of the European Community puts us at the heart of the world's largest trading bloc, and presents opportunities to secure co-ordinated European action to tackle problems at home and abroad' (Labour Party, 1988b: 45). The conference also witnessed the Labour Party adopt a clear 'Social Europe' agenda, when it agreed to a resolution calling for the EC-level to produce an 'upward harmonisation of standards at work', 'industrial and economic democracy', social protection and training, and endorsing the 'new social agenda of Commission President Jacques Delors'. Thus, the resolution agreed that 'the Labour Party, in conjunction with the other socialist parties of the EC, must seek to use and adapt Community institutions to promote democratic socialism' (Labour Party, 1988b: 180).

This new pro-Europeanism was further consolidated in the final report of Labour's policy review, published the following year in 1989, which stated,

> 1992 and the Single Market create great opportunities and great challenges for Britain. We believe that Europe must be a *Community* as well as a Market. We want a Community that modernises industry, protects the environment, generates jobs, advances women's rights and helps the regions. We want the British people to get the best from the European Community.
>
> (Labour Party, 1989a: 79)

This report was also adopted by the 1989 conference, whilst a composite resolution condemning the undemocratic nature of the EC was rejected by the same conference (Labour Party, 1989b: 156–7), thereby providing clear confirmation of the Labour Party's turn to 'Social Europe'. In a telling rhetorical twist, therefore, whereas during the 1960s the Labour Party had promised to maintain *national* safeguards from European integration, in the 1992 election manifesto Labour proclaimed its support for *European* safeguards, promising to,

> promote Britain out of the European second division into which our country has been relegated by the Tories. ... to end the Tories' opt-out from the Social Chapter, so that *the British people can benefit from European safeguards*. ...

fight for Britain's interests, working for Europe-wide policies to fight unemployment and to enhance regional and structural industrial policy. The elected finance ministers of the different countries must become the effective political counterpart to the central bank whose headquarters should be in Britain.

(Labour Party, 1992, emphasis added)

By the time of the 1992 general election, therefore, and towards the end of the crisis period in the Labour Party's 'traditional' social democratic party relations, the party leadership and the grassroots of the party appeared united in their endorsement of European integration, viewing it as a clear opportunity for 'traditional' social democratic aims in the light of the ongoing obstacles presented by the British national context.

Following the Labour Party's defeat in the 1992 election, moreover, two further developments illustrated the strength of its conversion towards the 'Social Europe' agenda. First, the leadership election campaign that followed Kinnock's resignation saw EC-friendly John Smith gain 90.9 per cent of the vote in a contest against the Eurosceptic candidate, Bryan Gould (George and Haythorne, 1996: 119). Second, a survey published in the same year showed that 89 per cent of Labour Party members believed Britain should continue as a member of the EC and that 72 per cent disagreed with a statement that Labour should resist further EC integration (Seyd and Whiteley, 1992: 125–6). Whilst Holden (2002: 132) comments that 'between 1994 and 1997, Labour under Blair chose not to address the European issue in any form of strategic fashion' (for fear of antagonizing a Eurosceptic electorate), therefore the argument presented here is that 'Social Europe' agenda did play an important role in uniting the Labour Party during the period of its internal policy review.

By the early 1990s, therefore, the goal of 'Social Europe' had become a clear focal point within the Labour Party's programme. The party had not, however, by this point undergone the qualitative shift that would lead to its recognition as a 'new' social democratic party. Indeed, as noted in Chapter 3, this shift did not really occur until Blair's assumption of the leadership in 1994, and was marked by his successful revision of the party's constitution in the following year. Thus, the Labour Party's move from Eurosceptic to Europhile party had largely been undertaken in the period during which the Labour Party leadership was undergoing a prolonged crisis in its attempt to reproduce a 'traditional' structure of social democratic party relations. Upon the election of Blair as party leader, however, the subsequent attempt by the new party leadership to achieve a transformation of party relations, from a 'traditional' to 'new' social democratic structure, witnessed the 'New Labour' modernizers within the party draw upon the 'Social Europe' agenda that, as we have just witnessed, had become something of a consensus across the leadership and grassroots levels of the party. In doing so, the 'New Labour' leadership acted to maintain both a degree of ideological continuity within the Labour Party (despite the significant ideological and organizational revisions it oversaw) and a commitment to pursuing policies, at the European level, that would have a decommodifying effect upon the lives of its 'traditional' electorate (despite arguing for the impossibility of achieving such aims in the national level context). The Labour Party's support for European integration, therefore, enabled the party leadership to present the party as *both* a viable party of government that accepted the constraints of the international economy *and* a party committed to meeting the demands of its core constituency and their traditional pursuit of decommodifying public policies. In this sense, therefore, it can be understood as an ideal means by which the 'New' Labour Party leadership could seek to meet the contradictory pressures arising from the attempt, inherent to 'new' social democratic party relations as conceptualized in the preceding chapter, to suppress the demands for decommodification of an electoral constituency which has been historically constructed around the pursuit of such demands. For instance, key Labour Party modernizers, Peter Mandelson and Roger Liddle, sought in 1996 to portray New Labour's embrace of the supranational level as an indication of *both* its status as a modern party *and* its continued pursuit of decommodifying measures such as full employment. Thus,

> New Labour recognises the role of the nation-state and its historical significance and responsibilities. But it does not confuse symbols with reality. It knows that *in the modern world it is only through Britain's committed participation in the European Union that we can regain true sovereignty* – in other words, the political ability to tackle problems in the public interest – over many issues which have slipped beyond the nation-state's individual reach, whether the question be global warming, the prevention of future wars in Europe, or international economic cooperation to provide the conditions of stability necessary to boost economic growth in Europe *and restore full employment.*
> (Mandelson and Liddle 1996, 27–8, emphasis added)

In the light of these developments, therefore, it is no surprise that a survey of Labour MPs conducted between 1995 and 1996, at the height of the transformation within the Labour Party from 'traditional' to 'new' social democratic party relations, confirms that the EU-level was increasingly viewed as an opportunity to continue to meet demands typically voiced by 'traditional' social democratic party constituents. Thus, this survey found that 88 per cent of respondents agreed with the statement that 'the globalization of economic activity makes European Union membership more, rather than less necessary for the UK'. Eighty-three per cent disagreed with the idea that 'harmonization of social policies should not be an EU objective', and the same percentage believed that 'the extension of "social dialogue" through the institution of works councils is a necessary component of economic progress in the EU' (Baker and Seawright, 1998).

Having undergone a transformation from 'traditional' to 'new' social democratic party relations, therefore, and in the terms of the real definition derived in Chapter 3, New Labour's embrace of 'Social Europe' enabled the party leadership to *both* consolidate its reprioritization of recommodifying public policy *and* to seek to maintain the continued support of a constituency that had been historically constructed around the pursuit of decommodifying measures. Thus, in stressing its commitment to recommodification, the Labour Party's support for European integration enabled it to state in its 1997 general election manifesto:

> Rapid completion of the single market: a top priority for the British presidency. We will open up markets to competition; pursue tough action against unfair state aids; and ensure proper enforcement of single market rules. This will strengthen Europe's competitiveness and open up new opportunities for British firms.
>
> (Labour Party, 1997)

In this way, the European Union was able to symbolize 'New Labour's' transformation to a 'new' social democratic party programme. At the same time, however, the Labour Party manifesto also made the commitment for 'Britain to sign the Social Chapter', thereby appealing to 'traditional' social democratic constituents who viewed EU-level policy-making as a means by which more substantively decommodifying policies could be implemented. Indeed, in committing itself to opportunities for re-implementing decommodifying policies at the supranational level, particularly through its position on the Social Chapter, the 'New' Labour Party leadership was able to symbolize its continued commitment to more 'traditional' policy aims, *provided the institutional scale was compatible with such aims*. Interestingly, and indicating the extent to which the dual-edged appeal of New Labour's European policy portrayed a message of continued commitment to decommodification, whilst voters felt that the Labour Party had undergone a significant move to the right (relative to their own position) on issues such as nationalization and fiscal policy between 1992 and 1997, during the same period voters perceived a significant move *to the left* on the issue of European integration (Heath et al., 2001:107–13). The electorate continued, therefore, to perceive the Labour Party as a relatively 'left-wing' party *on European integration*, whilst accepting its rightward move on economic questions in general.

In sum, the Labour Party's turn to 'Social Europe' took place largely as a result of an internal party crisis characterized by an inability to reproduce 'traditional' social democratic party relations. Thus, between 1983 and the early 1990s a significant section of the core Labour Party constituency increasingly came to view European integration as a means to promote decommodifying policies in a context in which the national-level pursuit of such goals was proving unsuccessful. This was a view particularly promoted by the party leadership at that time. The moderation of decommodifying aims promoted by the Kinnock leadership in the late 1980s and early 1990s, and the more thoroughgoing rejection of decommodifying policies by the Labour Party under the Blair leadership, each witnessed parallel moves towards the advocacy of the European level as a means through which (admittedly more limited) decommodifying measures could continue to be achieved. This was the case with the internal policy review undertaken at the end of the 1980s and early 1990s, and also occurred with the adoption in 1997 of an explicit commitment to sign the UK up to the Social Charter (which the Conservative Government had explicitly refused to agree to since the Maastricht Treaty). New Labour's turn to 'Social

Europe', therefore, played an important role in consolidating the transformation to a 'new' structure of social democratic party relations. First, it enabled the party leadership to officially recognize that it had accepted the importance of committing itself to the overseeing of recommodifying policies as part of the new programme it proposed would enable the successful management of the British capitalist economy. Second, it allowed the party leadership to nevertheless maintain its commitment to the pursuit of decommodifying public policies through the promise of a supranational strategy with such an aim. From this perspective, therefore, the 'new' social democratic turn to 'Social Europe' should not be viewed as a paradoxical policy strategy due to its apparently internal contradictions, but rather should be viewed as a policy strategy which is consistent with the contradictory nature of 'new' social democratic party relations. Having used our real definitions of 'traditional' and 'new' social democratic party relations to provide an explanation for New Labour's turn to 'Social Europe', we can turn now to consider these processes in the cases of the other parties under investigation.

The SAP and the turn to 'Social Europe'

In the case of the Swedish SAP, as with the British Labour Party, the party's position on European integration is of most interest during the transition from 'traditional' to 'new' social democratic party relations. Thus, what follows is a brief overview of the SAP's position prior to the experience of crisis, and particularly transformation, of the SAP.

Due in part to the importance placed upon Swedish neutrality during the Cold War, Sweden chose to join EFTA in 1960 instead of seeking EC membership. Once it became apparent that the UK and Denmark were to join the EC, however, the Swedish government became concerned that Sweden would be economically isolated. In response to the forthcoming 1973 enlargement, therefore, Sweden supported an EFTA-EC free trade agreement adopted in 1972, which removed tariff barriers to trade in all industrial goods between the two organizations (Aylott, 1999: 46–55). The 1972 agreement therefore enabled Sweden to maintain its Cold War neutrality without the risk of undermining trading opportunities, and as such was an ideal compromise, remaining in place up until the mid-1980s. Having reached such a compromise, the Swedish political elite – both social democratic and non-social democratic – was reluctant to re-open the European question in the 1970s and early 1980s. However, as discussed in Chapter 3, the Swedish economy experienced ongoing problems throughout the 1980s. During this period a number of commentators began increasingly to argue that EC membership could act to resolve some of these problems as it would facilitate an increase in trade, especially as the 1972 agreement did not extend to either non-industrial goods or non-tariff barriers (Kite, 1996: 186–8; Bieler, 2000: 70–4; Ryner, 2002: 152–3). Following the signing of the Single European Act (SEA) in 1986, moreover, the question of EC membership rose further up the political agenda in Sweden (Aylott, 1999: 55–62).

It was not, however, until the announcement of the 1990 emergency statement, in an attempt to stabilize the krona, that the SAP Government announced that it would be applying to join the EC. Thus, in the case of Sweden, there is a direct correlation between what, as we saw in the third chapter, was a key turning point in the transition towards a 'new' social democratic model in the SAP, and the turn towards a pro-EC policy stance (Bieler, 2000: 83). In particular, by associating EC membership with the financial package of the 1990 emergency statement, the government sought to signal to the international economy its commitment to currency stability (interview with Allan Larsson, 10 April 2008). The announcement of the intent to join the EC did not at this point, however, include the pursuit of a 'Social Europe' agenda, but was rather presented as a necessity in order to ensure the stable growth of the Swedish economy. The question of EC membership had been an issue that the SAP had begun to discuss during the late 1980s, especially following the Swedish application for membership of the EEA in 1989. Nevertheless, many within the party felt unprepared for an application for full membership when the government announced it as part of a wider fiscal austerity package (interviews with: Sören Wibe, 8 April 2008; Patrik Björk, 9 April 2008; Tone Tingsgård, 11 April 2008). As a result of this lack of preparedness, there was little reaction – either positive or negative – from the SAP grassroots membership or electoral constituency to the SAP Government's decision to apply for membership. Moreover, as the SAP Government was voted out of office the following year, the issue remained relatively low on the social democratic agenda during the early 1990s (interview with Sören Wibe, 8 April 2008).

It was not, therefore, until 1994 that the European question became a major issue in SAP party relations. Indeed, at this point it became necessary for the SAP to adopt a position on the EU, both because it had been re-elected into office, and because a referendum on accession to the EU was due to take place. The SAP congress therefore decided in 1993 to hold a subsequent extraordinary congress meeting devoted entirely to the question of EU accession. By this stage, moreover, a division had emerged within the SAP, witnessing the creation of both official 'no' and 'yes' groups within the party. On the one hand, the 'no' group feared that EC membership, and especially the economic competition and fiscal rectitude created by the single market and Maastricht convergence criteria, would undermine the Swedish economic model, institutionalize high unemployment and constitute a threat to the Swedish welfare system (Bieler, 2000: 112). On the other hand, Social Democrats For the EC (the 'yes' group) sought to show that 'traditional' social democratic aims could no longer be upheld in the new internationalized economy and that membership of the EC would help to stimulate economic growth in Sweden that would enable the government to afford to maintain its generous welfare provisions. It was at this point, moreover, that a clear 'Social Europe' agenda was developed by those within the SAP advocating EC membership, including most of the party leadership. For instance, in June 1994 Prime Minister Carlsson claimed, 'We must show that issues like social-security, unemployment and the environment will be better solved if we are in the EU than if we stand outside' (*Veckans Affärer*, 13 June 1994, quoted in Aylott, 1999: 138). Similarly, a week before the referendum, Carlsson, and Party Secretary, Mona Sahlin, argued that 'those who trust us and want to give us the best means to take Sweden out of the crisis and halt the dismantling of welfare – should vote Yes to the EU' (quoted in Aylott, 1999: 154). Further still, reflecting sentiment amongst the pro-campaigners at the grassroots level of the party, a pro-accession party member argued that,

> [A] state like Sweden is formally sovereign, but today this sovereignty is in practice redundant... [M]odern society's development has upset the symmetry between influencers and the influenced, between those who take decisions and those affected. This relationship no longer applies within the border of the nation-state. The borders between domestic and foreign policy have, quite simply, been rubbed out.
>
> Thus, I see the EU as an attempt to create a new symmetry – a new order for decision-making in cross-border social questions.
>
> (quoted in Aylott, 1999: 79)

The leadership of the SAP also argued that, following accession to the EU, it would be possible for the party to have greater influence over EU policy-making, and therefore act to increase opportunities for 'traditional' social democratic policy outputs. In particular, the fact that Allan Larsson, former SAP finance minister, was asked by the Party of European Socialists to draft a report on European initiatives to tackle unemployment was heralded by many within the SAP leadership as a sign of the influence the party could hope to achieve within the European Union. Thus, in Larsson's words: 'For employment and social policy, it was not seen as though you had to choose between Sweden and Europe. But seen in a more dynamic way; that we could contribute to Europe in a dynamic process' (interview with Allan Larsson, 10 April 2008).

Whilst the adoption by the SAP leadership of a pro-EU position occurred as part of the wider rapid adoption of a 'new' social democratic policy programme, the initial rationale behind the move was an attempt by the party leadership to shore up, and symbolize, the shift towards recommodifying public policies, which were themselves presented as necessary for the successful reproduction of the Swedish capitalist economy.

It was not until the party's European policy actually needed to be sold to the Swedish (social democratic) electorate, however, that the specifically 'social' virtues of 'Social Europe' were increasingly highlighted. Thus, following the adoption of a 'Social Europe' agenda prior to the 1994 referendum, the SAP leadership went on to consistently utilize such an argument whilst overseeing a more thoroughgoing transformation in the SAP to a 'new' social democratic structure of party relations. In this way, and similarly to what we witnessed in the case of the British Labour Party, the adoption by the 'new' social democratic SAP leadership of a 'Social Europe' agenda was consistently deployed in an attempt to provide a sustained symbol of the party leadership's commitment to (again, albeit more limited) decommodifying measures, as long as the institutional scale allowed it.

Thus, as noted in the third chapter, the 1994–98 period witnessed the SAP Government introduce a number of restrictive measures that acted to recommodify Swedish labour. In doing so, the SAP leadership sought to promote a move, begun in the 1990s, towards the adoption of 'new' social democratic party relations. In parallel with these developments, the SAP leadership also sought to promote EU-level policies that would have a decommodifying effect upon the lives of workers in Sweden who would historically have been expected to comprise the core of the SAP electorate (Johansson and Raunio, 2001: 241). For instance, the Swedish government was one of the key players in proposing the new Employment Chapter in the Amsterdam Treaty (Gould, 2000; Johansson, 1999). Similarly, Alan Larsson was appointed director general of DG Employment and Social Affairs in 1995, and although he resigned from his position within the SAP in order to take up the post, he was nevertheless able to promote an employment-creating agenda within Europe, including the adoption in 1997 of the European Employment Strategy. As such, the supporters within the SAP of Sweden's membership of the EU and EMU were able to point to a clear Swedish social democratic presence within the EU institutions (interview with Allan Larsson, 10 April 2008; Ladrech, 1998). By the end of the 1990s, therefore, the SAP leadership had succeeded in making a case for the promotion of a 'Social Europe' agenda at the EU-level. Thus, in a statement on Development and Equality adopted by the SAP extra party congress in March 2000, the party agreed that,

> [M]embership of the EU has created new opportunities to meet the challenge of globalisation. Membership provides us with a real possibility in co-operation with other countries to create a democratic counterbalance to the unbridled speculation against the currencies of individual countries ...
>
> The EU provides the means to combat unemployment in Europe. The number of unemployed in Europe is falling but nevertheless it remains unacceptably high. The struggle against unemployment remains the most important social task facing the EU.
>
> (SAP, 2000)

The party leadership and grassroots party membership were therefore united by 2000 in their faith that decommodifying goals which were no longer viable at the national level were nevertheless achievable at the supranational level.

However, the SAP remained divided over the European question in general. Whilst opinion at the leadership and parliamentary level is generally supportive of European integration, there remains considerable scepticism amongst the broader electoral constituency and party membership. Thus, in the words of *Riksdag* member, Laila Bjurling,

> There is certainly scepticism across the social democratic party. In fact, I would say that most Swedish social democrats are Eurosceptical. ... The leadership, however, they are really very supportive. They say 'yes, we must go for the EU!'
>
> (interview with Laila Bjurling, 7 April 2008)

This is also reflected in the continued presence of an active EU-Critical Social Democrats group within the SAP (interview with Sören Wibe, 8 April 2008) and is evinced in the conflict experienced within the party over the question of the EMU membership prior to the 2003 referendum. Thus, in (unsuccessfully) campaigning for a yes vote in the 2003 Euro referendum, the SAP's Party Board presented a clear 'Social Europe' argument that,

> well functioning monetary co-operation provides a democratic counterbalance to the growing global market forces. This counterbalance provides room for small countries to pursue an active economic policy. In the interests of furthering welfare and employment we Social Democrats wish to see Sweden becoming a member of the economic and monetary union.
> (quoted in Miller, Taylor and Potton, 2003: 21)

The party leadership therefore continued to make the case that the deeper integration of Sweden within the European Union would enable the country to maintain a more 'traditional' policy agenda, including an economic policy that sought to provide a counterweight to the less regulated international economy and to promote welfare and employment. In contrast, however, a significant Eurosceptic contingent continued to exist within the SAP. This was reflected in the result of the 2003 referendum, where 56 per cent of SAP voters voted against EMU membership, and 41 per cent for it (Eurobarometer, 2003: 13). This therefore suggests that the promise of 'Social Europe' has been less successfully advocated by the 'new' social democratic party leadership in the case of the Swedish SAP (but, as we have witnessed herein, it has been consistently advocated nevertheless).

To summarize, therefore, the first major change to the SAP's European policy came in 1990 in an attempt by the SAP leadership to consolidate the shift to 'new' social democratic party policies whilst in office. Sweden's application for EC membership was therefore viewed as a means by which the Swedish capitalist economy could be more successfully integrated within the international economy. The move towards the adoption of a 'Social Europe' agenda, however, began with the subsequent debate on the referendum on Sweden's accession to the EU. Thus, we witnessed the SAP leadership consistently arguing, from the early 1990s onwards, for the importance of the opportunities to implement decommodifying public policies that existed at the European level. This was presented above as an attempt by the SAP leadership to ensure the continued support of its traditional electoral constituency, both for the SAP Government and, particularly, for what it viewed as the necessary integration of Sweden within the European Union. This occurred at the same time as the SAP Government undertook a number of welfare policy reforms from 1994 onwards, outlined in the third chapter, which sought to ensure the necessary recommodification of Swedish labour in order that the Swedish economy could become more profitable. The SAP leadership's European policy, from the early 1990s onwards, therefore, sought to symbolize, and entrench, its adoption of a 'new' social democratic policy programme through deeper European integration. Whereas, in the case of the British Labour Party, the move towards a 'Social Europe' agenda was portrayed above as an attempt to both entrench and legitimate the transition from 'traditional' to 'new' social democratic party relations, in the case of the SAP we have witnessed the move towards a 'Social Europe' agenda as a means to legitimate a move towards European integration, which itself was viewed as a means to entrench the transformation to 'new' social democratic party policies. Despite the less direct role of a 'Social Europe' agenda in the initial construction of 'new' social democratic party relations, therefore the (sought-after) effect has nevertheless been the same – to ensure both that the SAP party leadership could symbolize, and 'lock in', the party's transformation to 'new' social democratic party relations, and to maintain the support of more 'traditional' social democratic party constituents through reference to the ongoing decommodifying policy opportunities existent at the European level. As with the case of the British Labour Party, therefore, we should view the turn by the 'new' social democratic SAP leadership towards a 'Social Europe' agenda not as a paradoxical policy strategy containing apparently internal contradictions, but rather as a policy strategy which is consistent with the contradictory nature of 'new' social democratic party relations themselves. However, and importantly, whereas in the case of the British Labour Party we witnessed a consensus between both the party leadership and the wider constituency regarding the positive opportunities presented by 'Social Europe', in the case of the SAP we can see continued resistance, predominantly at the grassroots and voter level, to the claim of the party leadership that European integration is likely to produce opportunities for public policies that will have a decommodifying effect. In the case of the SAP, therefore, the 'new' social democratic turn to 'Social Europe' has been a development far more consistently occurring at the level of the party leadership. Indeed, at the level of the grassroots and electorate, the turn to 'Social Europe' has occurred on a far less consistent basis, and has arguably failed to occur at all. We might well explain this development both in terms of the more sustained commitment to 'traditional' social democratic goals of decommodification within the SAP, and/or to the high levels of decommodifying public policies that continue to exist within Sweden. Thus, whilst the SAP party leadership has sought to promote a turn to 'Social Europe' that both, on the one hand, entrenches and symbolizes the transformation to 'new' social democratic party relations, and, on the other hand, provides a continued ideological commitment to decommodifying public policies, we might argue that its failure to successfully do so is in part a reflection of the less than thoroughgoing transformation to 'new' social democratic party relations which the SAP leadership has been able to realize in the light of sustained commitment to 'traditional' social democratic ideas and policies within the Swedish national context.

The Parti Socialiste and the turn to 'Social Europe'

As with the British Labour Party and the Swedish SAP, the position of the French Socialists was ambiguous for much of their 'traditional' social democratic period. Thus, we can observe Euroscepticism within the socialist group in the National Assembly during the 1950s, at the same time as socialist prime minister, Guy

Mollet, was negotiating the Treaty of Rome. We also witness the adoption of a common programme with the Eurosceptic Communists during the 1970s, despite being led by Europhile François Mitterrand. Also similar to the previous cases, however, is that the period of particular interest is that from the experience of crisis in 'traditional' social democratic party relations during the 1980s, and the subsequent transformation to 'new' social democratic party relations. Thus, from the 1983 U-turn onwards, the Socialists adopted a consistently positive position on European integration right up to the 2005 referendum. Moreover, the goal of 'Social Europe' formed a significant aspect of the party programme throughout this period. It is this, therefore, that we shall focus more closely on, following a much briefer overview of the ambiguous nature of the French Socialists' European policy during the pre-1980s period.

As noted, for much of the early post-war period the French Socialists held an ambiguous position on European integration. On the one hand, there existed many on the left of the party who were sceptical about the benefits of integration, and who viewed the economic model espoused by the Treaty of Rome as inherently liberal and therefore having a prohibitive effect upon socialist ambitions. Nevertheless, on the other hand, many SFIO party actors were broadly supportive of European integration, at least in principle, for most of the post-war period. This ambiguity could be witnessed on a number of occasions. For instance, the SFIO supported the Treaty of Paris in the National Assembly and the party congress voted to support the European Defence Community (EDC). Yet, when it came to the vote in the National Assembly on the EDC, 54 SFIO deputies voted against the initiative, thereby contributing to its demise. Shortly afterwards, however, socialist leader Guy Mollet signed the Treaty of Rome, and for much of De Gaulle's period in office the socialists consistently accused the president of reactionary nationalism, seeking to portray themselves as progressive Europeanists better able to represent France's national interests (Featherstone, 1988: 111–8). With the signing of the 'Common Programme of Left Government' in 1972, however, the PS, at least implicitly, adopted a far more Eurosceptic position. This was because it would have been (and, indeed, proved to be) impossible to combine support for deeper European integration with the commitment made in the common programme to implement a series of nationalizations of major French companies and a reflationary public expenditure programme. As such, the Common Programme assumed an element of national protectionism that was antithetical to the process of European integration due to the latter's focus upon the creation of a common *European* market (Ross, 1998a: 5). Nevertheless, the relatively low salience of European integration in French political debate during the 1970s meant that the inherent contradiction between the implicit Euroscepticism of the common programme and the Socialists' formal support for European integration failed to have too great an impact upon the PS' fortunes. Thus, according to Ladrech, 'issues regarding European integration were marginal to the more apparently salient issues of domestic economic policy following the beginning of recession after 1973' (2001: 39) As a result, the ambiguous nature of the PS' European policy proved relatively unproblematic.

Indeed, reflecting the relatively low salience of the European issue, upon its election to office in 1981, the Mitterrand presidency and Socialist government paid little direct attention to the EC. Whilst a number of proposals were made, they were nevertheless treated as low priority. For instance, Mitterrand called for the creation of a 'social European space'. Similarly, Junior Minister for European Affairs, André Chandernagor, introduced a 'memorandum for the economic relaunch of Europe', which proposed a reflationary economic policy similar to the one being implemented by the Mauroy government. However, the short shrift given to these proposals by the other member states, and the rather limited attention devoted to them by the PS in office, meant that each of the initiatives ultimately amounted to little substantively (Cole, 1997: 119–21). As we know from Chapter 3, however, in 1983 the PS was faced with the choice of maintaining its policy of wide ranging national reflationary measures, which would inevitably force the franc out of the EMS, or seeking to maintain the value of the franc through a shift towards restrictive fiscal and monetary policies that would effectively act to recommodify workers within France. As Mitterrand himself had been a supporter of European integration before even his election as PS party leader, moreover, the decision to implement the 1983 policy U-turn was in part connected to his personal desire to maintain France's position within the EC, and especially the EMS. The importance of the U-turn for maintaining a credible economic policy, and in particular maintaining economic relations between France and the other European Community member states, should also be noted (interview with Christian Sautter, 24 April 2008; see also Ross, 1998a: 6–7; Hall, 1990).

The 1983 U-turn, and the prioritization of recommodifying policies, in order to maintain France's competitiveness within the wider European and global economy, that it represented, was also accompanied by an explicit increase in Mitterrand's enthusiasm for European integration (Bell, 1998: 76). Thus, Clift notes how European integration became a far more salient issue for the French Socialists, 'the endgame of which would [according to Mitterrand's vision], eventually, involve the recovery of Keynesian economic sovereignty at the supranational level' (2003b: 181). The 1983 U-turn, therefore, witnessed a clear adoption of a 'Social Europe' agenda, whereby the implementation of policies and realization of policy outcomes that were viewed as impracticable at the national level were sought through a more concerted emphasis on their pursuit at the supranational European level. Indeed, this renewed commitment to European integration took effect almost immediately. Thus, Mitterrand used the opportunity granted by the Council Presidency, which France held in the first half of 1984, to support the European Parliament's Draft Treaty of the European Union. He also used the presidency to negotiate a resolution to the British budgetary question at the Fontainebleau summit and set up the Dooge Committee in an attempt to further European integration. This renewed PS position on Europe was also apparent in the appointment of former French Socialist Finance Minister, Jacques Delors, to the post of Commission president in 1985. This enabled Delors to promote, first, the single market, then the single currency, alongside a 'Social Europe' agenda that included the Social Chapter, large increases in the structural funds, and attempts to improve the representation of the 'social partners' within European decision-making (Ross, 1995). Having undertaken a major policy change in 1983, from a highly decommodifying programme to a sharply recommodifying one, therefore, the PS leadership sought at the same time to promote both European integration and to argue that coordinated European level policy-making would enable a continuation of the decommodifying policies that had been halted at the national level. In doing so, moreover, the party leadership acted to stimulate the view across the party that European integration could enable the implementation of decommodifying policies that would otherwise be unfeasible at the national level. For instance, as socialist National Assembly member, Daniel Goldberg, recalls,

> I remember a poster from the socialist party during the 1989 EP elections. The poster said, 'Europe – The New Land', meaning that what we cannot do within France we can do on a broader scale in Europe. Europe was a good way to be more influential in the world and to argue for a specific economic development model.
> (interview with Daniel Goldberg, 22 April 2008)

Indeed, by the time of the March 1986 general election, the shift in support for European integration had extended across most of the party, with even the Marxist-influenced CERES faction (which had been opposed to a capitalist and Atlanticist EEC since 1979) supporting integration (Featherstone, 1988: 132). Thus, Clift notes how Mitterrand's new leadership within Europe 'was seen by some in the party as a means of filling the "gap" left by the end of transcendental rhetoric and the impact of governing constraints on maximalist programmes' (2003a: 114). European integration could therefore substitute for some of the ambitions that had been abandoned as a result of the 1983 U-turn. Indeed, this pro-Europeanism, existing across the PS, continued to be voiced throughout the 1990s, even as European integration became a more controversial issue within French politics. Thus, even at the time of the 1992 referendum on the Maastricht Treaty, during which Euroscepticism was perhaps most clearly voiced amongst sections of the French electorate, the PS remained strongly supportive of European integration, with the 'no' campaign in France being largely made up of a coalition of the Gaullist and far right, and Communist left.

Whilst the post-1983 PS adopted a strongly pro-European 'Social Europe' agenda, which sought to offset a number of restrictive and recommodifying policies being implemented at the national level, however, the details of this agenda remained relatively undefined. The concrete aims, the possibility of achieving them, and the way in which they were integrated were all, therefore, relatively unclear. Thus, whilst Mitterrand did promote the idea of both an 'economic government' to complement the ECB, and the adoption of a Social Chapter, in the negotiations leading to the adoption of the Maastricht Treaty, the extent to which this represented a specifically socialist agenda, rather than merely an attempt to increase the influence of Mitterrand and his presidential office, has been questioned by a number of commentators (Dyson and Featherstone, 1988: 102). Similarly, those EC-level initiatives that Mitterrand promoted – the resolution of the budgetary question at Fontainebleau, the support for the EP Draft Treaty and the Dooge Committee, and the SEA –were largely of either an institutional nature, or sought to create a European marketplace (Cole, 1997: 124–7). As a result, the actual decommodifying effect of these initiatives was not immediately apparent.

We argued in chapter three that Jospin's accession as the clear leader of the PS from 1995 witnessed the adoption of a more consistent 'new' social democratic policy programme that sought to balance a commitment to moderate decommodifying measures, with an explicit recognition of the need to maintain many of the recommodifying measures that had already been implemented in France since the 1983 U-turn. It was also from this point, moreover, that the 'Social Europe' agenda acquired a more substantive role in the restructuring of PS party relations. Thus, Jospin was faced by a context whereby Alain Juppé, the Gaullist prime minister between 1995 and 1997, had aroused significant popular disapproval through the pursuit of austerity measures that most notably included cuts in pension provisions. Juppé had also explicitly linked these reforms to what he argued was a need to meet the Maastricht convergence criteria. This created an opportunity, which Jospin seized upon, to present the PS as a party that would reverse both the restrictive policy stance of the Gaullist Government, but also, and arguably more importantly, the support of the French government for the restrictive stance of EMU. The PS leadership therefore claimed it would act to promote a more interventionist European Union, which would act to implement redistributive and/or decommodifying measures in areas such as employment or social policy (Howarth, 2007: 1070). Thus, Jospin stood in the 1997 general election on a platform that promised to soften the austere fiscal policies associated with EMU, and to promote instead a 'Social Europe' agenda that pursued not only price stability, but also growth and employment. In doing so, therefore, the PS leadership was able to present a policy programme that committed the party to *both* continue to argue for the necessity of continued recommodifying (or significantly limited decommodifying) measures at the national level, whilst simultaneously proposing the pursuit of more substantive decommodfiying measures at the supranational European level. Thus, the party manifesto stated that,

> [W]e want a political and not a technical vision for Europe. We want a dynamic approach to Europe, not one of accounting ... For Socialists, making the Euro succeed involves building a Europe which is turned towards growth, employment and democracy.
> (PS election manifesto, 1997, quoted in Ross, 1998b: 22)

Jospin therefore sought to juxtapose his own European programme with what many within France, particularly following the experience of the Juppé Government, viewed as a technocratic and restrictive process of European integration. Following his election as prime minister, moreover, Jospin sought from an early stage to give greater substance to his election campaign commitments, for instance witnessing the pursuit of an enhanced European-level social policy at the Amsterdam IGC shortly after the 1997 elections (Clift, 2002: 486–8). Whilst the Jospin Government was unable to significantly change the terms of the convergence criteria or the Stability and Growth Pact (SGP), it was able to, however, secure a commitment at the EU-level to tackle European unemployment, witnessing the adoption of a new Employment Chapter. Further still, Jospin also advocated a European economic government to provide democratic input into the European Central Bank, and a more substantial European social policy to offset the effects of the fiscal constraints implicit in the Convergence Criteria and GSP, although neither of these aims were realized in terms of concrete policy outcomes (Howarth, 2002: 160–71).

As we saw in the third chapter, however, in order to meet the convergence criteria necessary for France to join the single currency, the Jospin Government needed to cut net public expenditure to a level where the annual government deficit would be below 3 per cent of GDP. Whilst seeking to achieve these cuts in a form that would be palatable to PS party relations, tensions did emerge as a result of the contrast between the rhetorical deployment of the 'Social Europe' agenda upon which Jospin was elected and the pressure exerted by European integration upon public expenditure cuts. Nevertheless, Jospin continued to assert the opportunities for the pursuit of decommodifying measures that existed at the European level, to the extent that, according to Howarth (2002: 168), even in instances where EU-level policy agreements were actually focused on price stability rather than the stimulation of economic growth (and therefore the opposite to what the Jospin Government had pledged to achieve at the EU-level), they were nevertheless 'seized on by the Jospin government as a victory of the French perspective' (Howarth, 2002: 168). Thus, Europe was increasingly utilized by the PS leadership as a vehicle through which to pursue initiatives that would appeal to their electoral constituency and its concern to pursue decommodifying measures. A number of speeches made by Jospin in 2001 (published in 2002 as *My vision of Europe and Globalization*) clearly illustrate this tendency. Thus, Jospin claimed that, 'the need for a social Europe manifests itself today through the demand for more European control, to counter the integration of markets' (2002: 37). This was therefore an attempt to focus upon the actions of the PS Government at the European level. In a similar vein, Jospin also claimed that:

> For the last four years the French government has fought to give a new direction to the construction of Europe, focusing it more on growth and employment. Major strides were made with the adoption of the European Social Agenda. These goals must produce concrete results for all categories of workers. Working conditions must be harmonized upwards. We must reduce job insecurity and fight discrimination. Let us set the stage for a social dialogue with the trade unions at European level. A genuine body of social law, establishing ambitious common standards, must be put in place and there must be a special focus on the provision of information to employees and their involvement in the life of companies, as well as on layoffs, the struggle against job insecurity and wage policies. We must aim for a European *social treaty*.
> (Jospin, 2002: 17–8)

As such, we can witness a consistent attempt, throughout the period of the Jospin leadership of the PS, to present the European level as a key opportunity to implement decommodifying policies whilst at the same time recognizing the constraints limiting the implementation of such policies at the national level.

To summarize, therefore, the transformation from 'traditional' to 'new' social democratic party relations, in the case of the PS, witnessed an initial shift in support for European integration amongst both the party leadership and wider party membership. Whilst there existed during this period an underlying attempt to promote policies with a 'Social Europe' element, it was not until the ascendance of Jospin to a clear leadership position within the PS, and the adoption of a consistent 'new' social democratic position which that ascendance marked, that the PS leadership also consistently propounded a 'Social Europe' agenda. Indeed, the 'new' social democratic programme adopted by Jospin both argued for the existence of significant obstacles to the pursuit of public policies which would have a substantive decommodifying effect, whilst also claiming that it would nevertheless be possible for the PS in office to implement measures that would go beyond the mere recommodifying strategies of rival parties and public policies in other developed countries. One of the major means through which Jospin claimed to be able to achieve such aims was through their coordinated promotion at the supranational level. Thus, the opportunities for policy-making at the European Union level offered the PS leadership the opportunity to appeal to its constituency on the grounds of its commitment to a decommodifying public policy agenda, despite the highly limited nature of this agenda. As with the British Labour Party and the Swedish SAP, therefore, in the case of the French *Parti Socialiste* we witness a concerted turn towards a 'Social Europe' agenda by a party leadership seeking to meet the dual pressures arising from the need to maintain a consistent commitment to recommodifying public policies *and* to 'represent' the demands of a constituency historically constructed on the basis of an appeal to decommodifying policies. Also reflecting developments within the Labour Party and SAP, therefore, the turn by the 'new' social democratic PS leadership towards a 'Social Europe' agenda should be viewed less in terms of being a paradoxical policy strategy containing apparently internal contradictions, and more as a policy strategy consistent with the contradictory nature of 'new' social democratic party relations themselves.

From communism to post-communism and the turn to 'Social Europe' in Italy

As argued in Chapter 3, the PCI moved increasingly towards the reproduction of 'traditional' social democratic party relations throughout the history of the Italian 'first' republic. We also noted how the party underwent a rapid transformation, in the 1989–93 period, to 'new' social democratic relations, marked by a subsequent prioritization, particularly whilst in office between 1996 and 2001, of policies that sought a sharp recommodification of labour within the Italian capitalist economy. Throughout this period of party transformation we can also witness a parallel development in the PCI/PDS/DS's policy on European integration. Thus, throughout the 1990s the PDS/DS leadership claimed to be pursuing a decommodifying public policy at the supranational level, whilst simultaneously drawing upon the imperatives of European integration to justify the consolidation of the recommodification of labour at the national level. This process is outlined in more detail below, once again focusing, this time in a study of the PDS/DS, especially on the period of transformation to 'new' social democratic party relations.

For most of the post-war period, the PCI opposed European integration on the grounds that the EC was essentially a capitalist organization (interview with Franco Russo, 6 May 2008). However, from the 1960s and, especially, the 1970s onwards, the PCI began to make increasingly positive statements about Europe (Sassoon, 1981). Rather than embrace European integration in its entirety, however, the position adopted by the PCI is better described as being characterized by the recognition that European economic integration was a fundamental aspect of the contemporary capitalist relations faced by the PCI and therefore required a (critical) response from the *European* working class. According to party leader Enrico Berlinguer, speaking to the party congress in 1972:

> Our attention is particularly concentrated on Europe ... The particular emphasis we want to give to our commitment in Europe and to the role of the democratic and labour movement of Western Europe.
> (quoted in Sassoon, 1981: 213)

This moderation of the PCI stance on European integration, whereby the EC was increasingly viewed as a legitimate focus for political activity, continued throughout the 1980s (Abse, 2001: 61), although it was not until after Berlinguer's death, and his replacement as party secretary by Alessandro Natta in 1984, that real reform within the PCI took place. Thus, at the 17th party congress in February 1986 (the first under Natta), the PCI adopted a strategy seeking to construct a 'Euro Left', meaning that it sought a non-sectarian pan-left association of organizations seeking the implementation of socialist ideals at the national and supranational level. In the words of the resolution adopted by the 1986 congress:

> The PCI is and always wants to be, in the best of ways, a decisive component of the European Left. The PCI draws its own unitary inspiration from socialist ideals aiming, above all, at the Left's unification and its reforming will.
> (quoted in Fouskas, 1998: 64)

This position became more entrenched within the PCI following Natta's succession as party leader by Achille Occhetto, who was especially keen to promote reform within the institutions of the European Community. Speaking at the PCI party congress in 1989, therefore, Occhetto claimed that, 'posing the basis for an alternative policy [...] is the first task of the Italian Left that really wants to be a European Left' (Occhetto, 1989, quoted in Fouskas, 1998: 120).

Thus, by the end of the 1980s, the PCI had clearly embraced a pro-*European* position, although the extent to which this implied support for the process, institutions and policies of European integration remained relatively unclear. Indeed, this lack of clarity was in part due to the PCI's tendency to issue vague statements of political principle, rather than clear policy commitments, which was a tradition that itself stemmed from the party's historic commitment to the transcendence of capitalism (and the ending of this tradition of programmatic vagueness was one of the major reforms that Occhetto sought to oversee as part of the transformation of PCI party relations into the 'new' social democratic Democratic Party of the Left). Already by the time of the 1989 EP election campaign, therefore, '*[w]ithout literally saying it*, the PCI argued in fact for a European Keynesianism, for a new European social contract' (Fouskas, 1998: 140; author's emphasis). Once the PCI became the 'new' social democratic PDS, however, a much clearer position on European integration emerged. Thus, as noted in the third chapter, a key goal of each of the *Ulivio* governments during the 1990s was membership of EMU, and, therefore, the ability to meet the Maastricht convergence criteria. Italy was one of the most indebted member states of the European Union during the 1990s, and as a result it needed a significant reduction in public expenditure and/or an increase in tax revenue in order to meet the convergence criteria. The *Ulivio* coalition, led by the PDS, had been elected to office in 1996 on a platform strongly committed to Italy's membership of the Euro. Indeed, 'Italian entry into the euro was the [Prodi] government's most important task' (Abse, 2001: 71). This task therefore required major budgetary retrenchment, privatization and anti-inflationary fiscal policy. Thus, the government conducted a number of privatizations in 1997 which raised revenues by close to 2 per cent of GDP, nearly two-thirds of which was used to repay debt. The government deficit was cut by 4 per cent in the same year as a result of a series of spending cuts and the introduction of temporary tax measures, including the 'Eurotax', which was designed specifically to ensure Italy's membership of EMU (OECD, 1999: 12, 17). Moreover, each of these measures witnessed regular reference to the 'external constraint' of the Maastricht convergence criteria, which was 'deliberately and strategically deployed [by the Prodi Government] to justify a heavy fiscal retrenchment and other related reforms' (Quaglia and Radaelli, 2007: 929). Whilst the PDS/DS leadership was part of the *Ulivio* governments, therefore, it consistently sought to impose significant recommodifying policies in an attempt to return the Italian capitalist economy to profitability and viability. In its attempt to do so, moreover, the *Ulivio* governments drew upon a wider support for European integration in order to justify the more unpopular policies of recommodification, including welfare retrenchment and labour market liberalization. Thus, the PDS/DS within the *Ulivio* Government was able to consolidate its 'new' social democratic party programme through reference to the necessity of reform in order to join the Euro.

Whilst these Euro-linked austerity measures ultimately led to the decision by the Refoundation Communists to end its parliamentary support for the *Ulivio* Government, both the PDS in parliament and the trade unions maintained their support as in each case the broader goal of EMU membership was viewed as being of greater priority (Della Sala, 2002: 121). As a result, the PDS/DS leadership was largely able to gain the consent of the party membership to the 'new' social democratic policies being implemented. Thus, according to former national secretary, Piero Fassino, 'There was no fracture, no contest, within the PDS over European issues.' (interview with Piero Fassino, 6 May 2008). Similarly, based largely on the fear that Italy would fail to qualify for EMU membership, the three major trade union confederations agreed throughout the 1990s to a series of tripartite agreements that introduced both wage restraint and temporary employment contracts. For instance, in 1997 the Prodi Government introduced, with the support of the trade unions, labour market reforms (*pacchetto Treu*) which extended temporary contracts throughout the public and private sector (Della Sala, 2004: 1051; Molina and Rhodes, 2007: 805–6). Whilst this acquiescence by the Italian labour movement came to an end following the entry of Italy into the EMU (Molina and Rhodes, 2007), the period leading up to the EMU membership illustrated the importance of European integration in acquiring the support of organized labour within Italy for the recommodifying policies being introduced by the *Ulivio* Government.

As with the earlier cases, moreover, whilst the *Ulivio* Government was implementing severe restrictive national economic policies in its attempt to join the EMU, DS party leader Massimo D'Alema sought to promote a 'Social Europe' agenda as a means by which to achieve public policies that would produce decommodifying effects at the supranational European level, and thereby provide the party with a degree of electoral appeal amongst those constituents who had historically demanded such measures. In particular, the party focused upon measures for employment promotion at the EU-level. For instance, in an interview given in 1998, D'Alema claimed:

> The European Left is already discussing this, and possible common objectives are emerging, so there is a certain link. The fact that the June 1997 summit of European governments in Luxembourg finally talked about unemployment and decided to institute Europe-wide monitoring of national policies and to make more resources available is due to pressure by and discussion among European socialists.
>
> (D'Alema, in Bosetti, 1998: 13)

Similarly, in an attempt to revive the fortunes of 'new' social democratic party relations following electoral defeat in the 2001 general election, in 2002 Guiliano Amato and Massimo D'Alema co-authored an open letter to the Party of European Socialists in which they argued that 'reformist politics must put its sights on a supranational horizon – a level at which decisions are now also made that directly affect the lives of citizens', and that 'all European reformists must unite in an enlarged supranational political family' in order to 'meet and design a sufficiently strong and convincing programme' (Amato and D'Alema, 2002).

To summarize, therefore, following a prolonged but gradual transition towards a (critical) engagement with the European level by the PCI, the party underwent a more dramatic and rapid transformation towards a full endorsement of European integration upon its adoption of 'new' social democratic party relations. In developments that reflect a pattern already observed in the preceding cases, the PDS/DS leadership sought at once to entrench their commitment to recommodifying policies that would ensure a more adequate reproduction of capital–labour relations within the Italian capitalist economy (through reference to the necessity of such reforms in order to ensure membership of the Euro), *and* to attempt to ensure the continued support of 'new' social democratic constituents for the PDS/DS programme through reference to the (albeit limited) opportunities for implementing decommodifying policies at the European level. Thus, in a trend that is now appearing across the cases we have studied, the apparently contradictory PDS/DS position on European integration can be more clearly understood as a result of the contradictory pressures arising from the structure of 'new' social democratic party relations. In this sense, therefore, and as with the preceding cases, the turn by the 'new' social democratic PS leadership towards a 'Social Europe' agenda should be viewed less in terms of being a paradoxical policy strategy containing apparently internal contradictions, and more as a policy strategy consistent with the contradictory nature of 'new' social democratic party relations themselves.

Spain

The PSOE's European policy remained remarkably stable throughout the post-Franco period. Accession to, and then membership of, the European Community came to symbolize for many within Spain the country's maturation as a modern and democratic country. As a result, 'the Socialist government that was in power in Spain from 1982 to 1996 was unwavering in its support for European integration' (Marks, 1997: 106). Indeed, the PSOE has been a strong supporter of Spanish membership of the EC from its 1976 congress onwards. Thus, whilst concerns were raised within the party, during the late 1970s and early 1980s, that the EC might act too rapidly to liberalize the Spanish economy (Marks, 1997: 81–2), these concerns were outweighed by the overbearing goal of EC membership held by both Spanish society and its political elite. This was particularly due to the fact that Spanish isolation from the rest of western Europe had come to be associated with Franco, traditionalism and authoritarianism. In contrast, the EC represented a commitment to democracy, freedom and modernization, each of which were benefits that outweighed all other potential costs (Featherstone, 1988: 296; Marks, 1997: 17–9). Stressing this point, Gonzalez claimed in 1975 that,

> [F]or many sectors of the Spanish population, the democratic alternative consists in achieving a system of liberties homologous to the European systems, and in addition to this exists the objective of incorporating Spain within Europe, in whose framework Spain finds itself geographically, politically, economically, and culturally.
> (Gonzalez, speaking at the 1975 SPD congress, quoted in Marks, 1997: 78)

Unlike the other social democratic parties in this study, therefore, there have been no real signs of ambiguity or scepticism towards European integration throughout the PSOE's history. There have, however, been noticeable changes in the emphasis placed upon, and the stance adopted towards, the process of European integration over the course of the party's ideological development. In terms of the changes to party relations discussed in Chapter 3, therefore, we are concerned here with any noticeable shift between the period preceding office, when we argued that the PSOE maintained a 'traditional' social democratic structure of party relations, and its period in office, when it made a number of moves towards a 'new' social democratic structure of party relations, particularly following the breakdown of tripartite negotiations in 1986. As with the previous cases, therefore, it is this period that we shall be focusing most closely on in the discussion that follows.

Whilst the PSOE was consistently positive about the prospects of EC accession prior to its entry into office in 1982, it was nevertheless cautious about particular aspects of European integration. From 1982 onwards, in contrast, this caution was notably absent. Thus, as early as 1977, and in response to criticisms from the left of the PSOE regarding the overly liberal nature of European economic policy, the PSOE announced in 1977 that it would work for a 'democratic, socialist and non-imperialist Europe' (quoted in Pollack and Hunter, 1987: 138). The PSOE leadership claimed that it sought to ensure that membership of the EC would not obstruct its wider attempt to restructure Spanish society following the end of the Franco regime. Thus, according to Marks, 'whereas the PSOE's leaders saw the EC as an expression of European democratic values, they were careful to avoid embracing the capitalist elements of the Community which would impinge on the party's radical economic claims' (1997: 78). Reflecting this hesitancy, the PSOE laid out its strategy for negotiating EC-entry in a book published in 1980 titled *Estrategia Económica del the PSOE*. This set out the PSOE leadership's plan to seek to negotiate transition periods for vulnerable sectors of the Spanish economy, in particular so that workers would not experience hardship as a result of restructuring processes unleashed by accession to the EC (Marks, 1997: 79–80). Thus, during the period that we have argued witnessed the PSOE adopt a 'traditional' social democratic structure of party relations, the party leadership advocated a positive European policy, but one that nevertheless contained a number of caveats relating to the importance of avoiding an overly burdensome impact upon, in particular, the PSOE's working-class constituency.

Following its election to office, however, support for European integration, and the attempt to ensure Spain's successful accession to the European Community, became increasingly unconditional. As noted in Chapter 3, it is during this period that the PSOE increasingly moved towards a 'new' social democratic structure of party relations, witnessing the party leadership seek a prioritization of measures that would produce a recommodification of labour in an attempt to ensure a return to profitability for the Spanish capitalist economy. This shift towards 'new' social democratic party relations therefore witnessed a concomitant rise, or perhaps better put, move towards unconditionality, in the support of the party leadership for European integration. Indeed, as with the preceding cases, this section argues that these two developments were closely related, with the promotion of recommodifying policy measures by the party leadership in office repeatedly defended in terms of their importance in order to successfully accede to membership of the European Community. Thus, Holman argues that 'each part of the government's domestic, social and economic policy was presented and legitimized by reference to the necessity of adjusting Spanish socio-economic and political structures in the light of future membership of the EEC' (1996: 80). As a result, the pursuit of EC membership was increasingly adopted as a reason for revising the PSOE ideology, as 'the relevance of the workerist/Marxist rhetoric that the PSOE had championed since its days of clandestinity no longer conformed with the party leadership's new perception of European economic realities' (Marks, 1997: 96).

As noted in the third chapter, however, following the 1988 general strike, there was a concerted attempt by the PSOE leadership during its period in office to meet some of the demands being made by its traditional constituency. In launching its so-called *Manifesto of the Programme 2000* at the 32nd party congress in 1990, therefore, the PSOE began to make similar arguments to those we have witnessed in the other four cases, regarding the possibility of pursuing policies at the European level that would have a decommodifying effect within Spanish society. As with these previous cases, therefore, the adoption by the PSOE party leadership of this 'Social Europe' agenda contained a double-edged message. Thus, in discussing the opportunities that the EC-level provided, the PSOE leadership was able to *both* insist upon the limits upon its capacity to implement redistributive or decommodifying measures at the national level, whilst at the same time promising to pursue such an agenda within wider European debates. For instance, the PSOE leadership stated in its *Manifesto of the Programme 2000* that

> today Europe is the scene where the game is played between the neo-conservative model of society and the democratic socialist project, and our country is now in a crucial position with respect to both the battle of ideas and the task of the construction of Europe. Therefore the power configuration in a united Europe will partly depend on the orientation of Spain ...
> (*Manifesto del Programa 2000*, 1991; quoted in Holman, 1996: 122)

The document therefore represented a clear attempt by the PSOE leadership to hold up the supranational European level as a means by which to compensate for the (implicitly recognized) inability to achieve substantive decommodifying policy outcomes at the national level. The *Manifesto* therefore went on to outline a plan for the construction of a socialist Europe, through which the PSOE 'explicitly intended to ideologically compensate for the short-term conservative drift of government economic policy' (Holman, 1996: 123). In an attempt to provide substantive evidence of the decommodifying opportunities heralded at the EC-level, moreover, Gonzalez negotiated very hard to achieve both the new Cohesion Fund and the increase in structural funds agreed at the Edinburgh European Council in 1992, in the process gaining Spain an allocation of funds that equalled 1.4 per cent of Spanish GDP for the period 1994–99 (Kennedy, 2001: 53).

The Gonzalez Government's European policy was therefore able to both justify the introduction of strict recommodifying measures at the national level, whilst simultaneously holding out the promise of a reversal of such policies at the supranational level. Thus, PSOE's former Minister of Justice, Juan Fernando López Aguilar, claims that the PSOE Government undertook an important 'pedagogical mission' with regard to the Spanish public,

> by stressing the positive aspects of every sacrifice that we demanded in fulfilling European goals, in fulfilling the European strategy. So in this respect the PSOE has paid a service to Spanish domestic politics. ... the PSOE has paid a service in explaining the social benefits that could be drawn and derived from a collective group behaviour in fulfilling these goals. ... We have somehow sorted a virtuous combination of self-discipline, and a certain capacity to sacrifice, a social sacrifice for fulfilling goals.
> (interview with Juan Fernando López Aguilar, 21 May 2008)

Thus, the party leadership sought to legitimate the attempt to contain the demands of its constituents through reference to the importance of doing so in order to achieve wider benefits resulting from European integration. For instance, the government enacted a series of restrictive fiscal and monetary policies in its attempt to keep the peseta within the EMS in the early 1990s, when both Italy and the UK exited the scheme. Equally, following the Maastricht summit in December 1991, the Spanish government announced in spring 1992 its *plan de convergencia*, which sought to prepare Spain for membership of the EMU through reforms that included cuts in public expenditure and social spending, deregulation and flexibilization of capital and labour markets, and an accelerated partial privatization of public enterprises (Holman, 1996: 155; Smith, 1998: 101). As such, the 'new' social democratic PSOE leadership sought at once to entrench the recommodification of labour within Spain through reference to the requirements of European integration, whilst at the same time proclaiming the importance of the European level in an attempt to symbolize a continued commitment to the kinds of decommodfying measures (albeit in a limited form) that the PSOE had been committed to during the time that it assumed a more 'traditional' social democratic structure of party relations.

In sum, therefore, the European policy of the PSOE went through a number of important changes over the course of the post-Franco period. Whilst the party adopted a critical embrace of European integration from the period of its legalization onwards, this became increasingly uncritical from its period in office onwards. Thus, as we argued in the third chapter, the PSOE began a transition towards the adoption of 'new' social democratic party relations from 1982 onwards, but this became more substantive from 1986, following the break down in PSOE-UGT relations. Throughout this period, the PSOE leadership sought to justify the austerity and recommodifying measures it introduced on the basis of both the need to rejuvenate the Spanish capitalist economy and the importance of meeting, first, the criteria for accession to the EC and, then, the need to meet the Maastricht convergence criteria. Further, following the decline in support for the PSOE, and in particular the antagonistic relationship that arose between the party leadership in office and the trade unions, the PSOE sought to maintain its support amongst a core of its constituency through declarations regarding the benefits that would accrue to those seeking policies that would have a redistributive, welfare enhancing, or egalitarian outcome. As with the four other cases outlined above, therefore, we can witness a clear attempt by the PSOE leadership to adopt a 'Social Europe' agenda, as part of a more general transformation to 'new' social democratic party relations, in an attempt to meet the conflicting pressures arising from those new party relations. Thus, as we have observed in each of the cases studied so far, the 'new' social democratic PSOE leadership sought to simultaneously entrench a shift in policy emphasis towards recommodifying measures and away from decommodifying ones, and at the same time to symbolize the continued commitment to decommodifying measures through supranational activity at the European level, and thereby meet the conflicting pressures generated by 'new' social democratic party relations. Again, therefore, we should view the 'new' social democratic turn towards 'Social Europe', this time in the case of the PSOE, less in terms of being a paradoxical policy strategy containing apparently internal contradictions, and more as a policy strategy consistent with the contradictory nature of the structure of 'new' social democratic party relations.

Conclusion

The conclusion to this chapter argues that, based on the foregoing discussion, which sought to use real definitions of 'traditional' and 'new' social democratic party relations to inform a series of analytical narratives of the 'new' social democratic turn to 'Social Europe', we have been able to 'retrodict' an explanation for the paradox of the 'new' social democratic turn to 'Social Europe' in terms of the social relations that constitute those parties. In particular, the real definition of 'new' social democratic party relations adopted in the present study focuses our attention on the relationship of representation between a party elite that seeks to suppress the demands for decommodification of an electoral constituency that has been historically constructed around the pursuit of such aims. In employing this real definition in the present chapter, we have sought to examine to what extent, if at all, the turn to 'Social Europe' has played a role in the construction and reproduction of these 'new' social democratic party relations. In each case, we have witnessed the transition from 'traditional' to 'new' social democratic party relations including a significant emboldening of the party leadership's position on European integration. Alongside the attempt by the party leadership to restrict, and argue for the necessity of restricting, demands for decommodification, and to prioritize instead the need to oversee policies that will have a recommodifying affect upon their constituents, therefore, we have also observed a consistent appeal to European integration. In each case, European integration has been presented as providing an opportunity for the re-assertion of decommodifying measures through supranational policy-making, thereby acting both to compensate for the purported inability to do so at the national level and seek to secure the continued support of 'new' social democratic party constituents on the basis of a continued commitment to (albeit more moderate) decommodifying policies at the supranational European level. Moreover, particularly (but not exclusively) in the cases of Italy and Spain, we have also witnessed the presentation of European integration as a necessitating, and legitimating, factor in the implementation of recommodifying measures at the national level, with restrictive austerity and recommodifying measures presented as a worthwhile price to pay in exchange for meeting the broader goal of successful integration within the European Union.

It is the claim of this chapter, therefore, that it is the opportunity that the EU-level provides for 'new' social democratic party elite actors seeking to appease the contradictory pressures generated by the structure of 'new' social democratic party relations – comprising both a shift in emphasis from decommodifying public policies to recommodifying public policies *and* the continued electoral support of a constituency historically constructed around the pursuit of decommodifying policy outcomes – that explains the apparently contradictory nature of the 'new' social democratic turn to 'Social Europe'. In this sense, the present chapter has consistently argued that we should view the 'new' social democratic turn to 'Social Europe' as the non-paradoxical attempt by the party leadership to meet contradictory pressures arising from the structure of 'new' social democratic party relations. Indeed, and importantly, it is precisely the institutional limits upon the realization of a 'Social Europe' agenda at the European level which ensures that it is unlikely to be realized. As such, the turn to 'Social Europe' allows 'new' social democratic party elites to explain (and thereby, in part, legitimate) their inability to realize the promised decommodifying outcomes at the supranational level *in terms of those institutional obstacles*. In this way, therefore, the internal contradictions of 'new' social democratic party relations can be (in part) both reconciled *and externalized* through the turn to 'Social Europe'. Thus, the EU-level enables 'new' social democratic party elites to both promote policies that will ensure the decommodification of labour, and therefore appeal to a constituency that has been historically constructed around such aims, *and* to ensure that such attempts at EU-level decommodification will be sufficiently obstructed by the institutional limits to European integration that preclude a return to the implementation of decommodifying policies that would otherwise problematize the reproduction of European capital–labour relations (and therefore the wider relations that 'new' social democratic party elites seek to reproduce).

The EU-level provides an opportunity for decommodification, in principle, due to its ability to represent a response to the problem of scale identified by the 'hyperglobalization' thesis. In other words, European integration promises to be able to facilitate the circumvention of the difficulties associated with the apparent loss of national economic policy autonomy purported to have resulted from the internationalization, or globalization, of economic relations, through the coordination of supranational policy-making and, therefore, increase in institutional scale available to policy-makers. This is therefore presented by many 'new' social democratic party elites as a means to overcome the obstacles to decommodifying policy-making at the national level. Nevertheless, it is argued here, the institutional obstacles experienced by those who actually seek to implement such an agenda at the EU-level severely limit the scope for realizing such declared policy ambitions. The 'new' social democratic turn to 'Social Europe', therefore, facilitates the reproduction of 'new' social democratic party relations due to its ability to enable 'new' social democratic party elites to present a policy programme that promises to both ensure the continued recommodification of labour and symbolize the continued commitment to decommodifying policy ambitions, whilst at the same time ensuring that constraints external to 'new' social democratic party relations are able to ensure that such decommodifying policy ambitions both go unrealized *and* that this non-realization can be explained, or legitimated, in terms of factors external to 'new' social democratic party relations themselves. In order to assess the extent to which this explanation resolves the paradox of the 'new' social democratic turn to 'Social Europe' introduced at the beginning of this book, we turn in Chapter 5 to investigate both the actions and outcomes of 'new' social democratic party actors pursuing policy aims at the supranational level.

5 (The absence of) social democracy at the EU-level

The aim of this chapter is to examine the actions and achievements of social democratic party actors pursuing policy outcomes at the European level. The core claim of Chapter 4 was that 'new' social democratic party elites turned to 'Social Europe' in an attempt to continue to mobilize an electoral constituency historically constructed around the pursuit of labour decommodifying public policies, whilst nevertheless seeking largely to suppress such demands for decommodification at the national level. The argument developed was that the institutional obstacles to policy-making at the European level have a self-limiting effect which ensures that social democratic party elites are able to promote decommodifying measures at the supranational level without any significant risk of those policies being realized, thereby producing an absence of decommodifying measures that is explicable in terms of factors external to social democratic parties themselves. In order to examine this claim, the present chapter studies the development of a 'Social Europe' agenda amongst social democratic actors located at the EU-level. It begins with a consideration of the way in which supranational level opportunities have been perceived and portrayed by *EU-level* social democratic party actors, including a more detailed examination of the specific policy commitments agreed by those actors. The chapter then turns to consider the extent to which the self-limiting nature of EU institutional relations has (as claimed earlier) acted to preclude substantive decommodifying measures from being realized. The purpose of this chapter, therefore, is to examine the claim, developed in the earlier chapters, that 'new' social democratic party elites increasingly utilize the opportunities of EU-level policy-making to seek to reproduce an electoral constituency historically constructed around the pursuit of decommodifying measures, whilst nevertheless encountering significant institutional obstacles that impede the realization of such an agenda (and thereby explain, and in part legitimate, the underdevelopment of 'Social Europe').

The development of a supranational-level 'Social Europe' agenda

A number of studies have sought to identify the policies, aims, actions, and outcomes of coordinated social democratic party behaviour at the European level (Lightfoot, 2005; Hix, 2002; Ladrech, 2000; 2003). Rather than replicate this research, the aim in the present chapter is instead to examine the development of the Party of European Socialists' (PES) social and economic policy aims, with particular attention to the extent to which (if at all) these aims have been portrayed as a means by which to circumvent national-level constraints and thereby compensate for the lack of decommodifying policies at the national level. This section therefore seeks to examine the extent to which a concrete 'Social Europe' agenda has been adopted by social democratic party actors operating at the supranational level, which in turn informs a subsequent assessment of the extent to which those actors have been successful in their attempt to promote the agenda which they have adopted.

Developing a supranational agenda

Social democratic activity at the EU-level is predominantly centred around the PES group in the European Parliament and the PES Party federation[1] (Hix and Lord, 1997). Moreover, the origins of this European-level social democratic cooperation can be traced back to the early developments in European integration, with the creation of a socialist group in the Common Assembly of the European Coal and Steel Community in September 1952, which was formed by representatives of member parties of the Socialist International (SI). Social democratic cooperation was further formalized in a Liaison Bureau created by the six SI parties of the EEC member states following the agreement of the Treaty of Rome. These six parties agreed to hold biannual congresses, which were to be attended by the bureau, the socialist members of the European Parliamentary Assembly (EPA), and representatives of the national parties. The Congress, Bureau and Socialist group in the EPA were each committed to discussing, agreeing, coordinating and promoting a cohesive socialist/social democratic agenda with regard to the process and institutions of European integration. Thus, by the time of the fourth Socialist Congress, in May 1960, the social democratic parties that collectively formed the Socialist Group could agree on an admittedly vague commitment to work together, stating that,

> in the present stage of European integration, it is necessary that the socialist parties...work out a common European programme; that this programme should define the principles that must serve as a guiding line to the socialist parties and to the Socialist Group in the European Parliamentary Assembly in the formulation of their opinions regarding the problems of European integration.
>
> (quoted in Hix, 2002: 13)

Having agreed in principle to cooperate with each other, social democratic parties continued to work together, although on something of a loose basis. In 1973 this cooperation was institutionalized further when the Liaison Bureau changed its name to the Office of the Socialist Parties of the European Community, also producing a new document, *Towards a Social Europe*, adopted by the ninth congress in Bonn. This therefore signalled the birth of the concept of 'Social Europe' at the supranational level, marking the point from which European-level social democratic actors would explicitly pursue such an agenda. *Towards a Social Europe*, therefore, outlined a 'traditional' social democratic agenda of labour decommodification, to be promoted within the EC. It included a commitment to European-level social policy, full employment, equality of opportunity, an EC industrial policy, environmental regulation, the pan-EC standardization of social benefits, worker participation and an EC incomes policy[2] (Hix, 2002: 21). As such, it represented an important stage in the development of a social democratic 'Social Europe' agenda at the supranational level.

In 1974 another new step in the development of supranational social democratic cooperation took place with the inauguration of the Confederation of the Socialist Parties of the European Community (CSPEC), in part in anticipation of the forthcoming direct elections to the European Parliament (Lightfoot, 2005: 29). The CSPEC replaced the preceding Office and Congress, and became the main organizational forum through which cooperation between social democratic parties and party actors would now take place. Whilst this development produced little in terms of actual institutional change, the new name was symbolic in that it represented a commitment to the deepening of social democratic party cooperation. These developments also showed early signs of the way in which the turn to 'Social Europe' could be portrayed in a way which implied a recognition that constraints arising from changes within the international economy created an incentive for supranational coordination of social democratic party activity. Thus, the Socialist Parties of the European Community agreed that,

> [T]he larger market in Europe is now characterized by mergers giving rise to concentrations of power which escape any form of control by the Member States. What is lacking at the European level is a political body endowed with powers of its own and subject to control by an effective, directly elected Parliament. ...
>
> Because of the scale of the common market and the interdependence of the various States, the task of gearing production to social objectives can only be carried out at the European level, and then only if world-wide solidarity is brought to bear.
>
> (Socialist Parties of the European Community, 1973)

Notably, therefore, at this point in the history of supranational coordination, *European integration* was identified as a greater problem for social democratic interests than global economic interdependence, thereby reflecting the continued caution of social democratic parties towards European integration during the 1970s. This stance began to change, however, during the 1980s. For instance, the 1982 CSPEC Congress witnessed an attempt to agree a move towards European-level currency protection, an initiative that was viewed as particularly important in the light of the problems that social democratic governments in France, Sweden and the UK had experienced in the 1970s and early 1980s. Thus, the congress agreed that, 'the European Monetary System should be used as an instrument for better control on capital movements and for improved mutual assistance whenever one of the members' currencies comes under speculative attack' (CSPEC, 1982).

Social democratic parties began, therefore, to identify coordinated supranational level activity as a means by which the erosion of national autonomy in economic policy-making could be overcome. As such, we witness from the early 1980s onwards the development of a 'Social Europe' agenda at the supranational level which sought explicitly to symbolize the continued possibility of pursuing decommodifying measures despite the increasingly impracticable nature of such measures at the national level.

This approach was elaborated further still in the CSPEC's manifesto for the 1984 EP election, which explicitly outlined the need for a coordinated European-level solution to the ongoing recession of the early 1980s. Thus,

> [A]lthough an entire series of measures should and could be taken on the national level, in Europe, it is difficult to escape the crisis by 'going one's own way'. On the other hand, the fact the economies of the countries of the European Community are highly integrated offers vital conditions for seeking a common solution to the crisis. A limited amount of common action and cooperation would already enable a number of obstacles to be removed which stand in the way of national policies for economic recovery. The possibility for a coordinated European expansion is an excellent example. In brief, cooperation which paves the way for social progress must replace competitive austerity.[3]
>
> (CSPEC, 1984)

From the early 1980s, therefore, we observe an increase in the frequency of references to the need to overcome constraints arising as a result of developments within the international economic environment. What began as a coordinated attempt to affect the political agenda at the European level *per se*, developed from the early 1980s into a more specific attempt to circumvent, through coordinated European-level activity, the obstacles to autonomous economic policy-making at the national level. The passage from the 1984 manifesto cited above, therefore, is particularly instructive in a number of important ways. First, it shows clearly the declaration by social democratic party elites that alternatives to austerity measures cannot be achieved by 'going one's own way'. There is a clear espousing of the view that 'traditional' social democratic attempts to implement decommodifying measures, or in the terms of the quote above, achieve 'social progress', through the nation-state are no longer viable or practicable, thereby necessitating 'competitive austerity' (or, in the terms of the present study, 'recommodification') at the national level. Second, the passage contains a clear and early identification of coordinated supranational-level activity as the most feasible means through which social democratic parties are able to circumvent these national-level obstacles, due to the 'highly integrated' nature of the EC and the 'vital conditions' it creates for a coordinated response. The European level, therefore, was increasingly presented as a viable alternative to the (tacitly recognized as necessary) recommodifying measures being introduced at the national level.

This double-edged message regarding the necessity of national-level recommodification and the possibility of European-level decommodification, which clearly echoed that which we have observed emerging as part of the transformation to 'new' social democratic party relations at the national level, continued throughout the 1980s. Nevertheless, internal divisions within the CSPEC often acted to prevent the more substantive development of such an agenda. For instance, attempts to formulate a joint position on the 1985 IGC were eventually aborted due to the opposition of the British Labour Party and the Danish Social Democrats (Aust, 2004: 182–4; Hix, 2002: 32–50). As a result, it was arguably not until November 1992, when the CSPEC became the Party of European Socialists (itself a response to the inclusion of the party article (138a) in the Maastricht Treaty), that EU-level cooperation between social democratic actors began to acquire greater substance (Ladrech, 2000). Thus, the creation of the PES included the adoption by the member parties of some important changes to the statutes of the old CSPEC, including two new important aims: 'to prepare structures for an ever closer collaboration between European socialists and social-democratic parties', and 'to adopt a common electoral programme for European parliamentary elections'. It also witnessed concrete institutional developments in the adoption of a qualified majority decision-making process to facilitate joint decision-making by the PES member parties (Hix, 2002: 60–1). Whilst these developments represented significant steps towards the supranational-level coordination of social democratic party activity, therefore, the reservations of national party elites nevertheless continued to ensure that 'the pull of the national political context was still very great' (Lightfoot, 2005: 34). Thus, national party positions continued to take priority over supranational agreements, which themselves, therefore, remained relatively vague on a number of issues.

Despite these continuing limits to supranational-level coordination between social democratic party actors, however, the period following the transition to the PES did witness some important and relatively substantial policy developments. Perhaps most importantly, in September 1993, Alan Larsson, the ex-finance minister from the Swedish Social Democratic Government, was requested by the party leaders' summit meeting in Portugal to draft a report on how European social democrats could solve the EU's growing unemployment problem. Following widespread consultation with the party leaders' personal representatives, Larsson drafted a report which was adopted at the party leaders' summit in Brussels in December 1993. The report, entitled *The European Employment Initiative* (later to become *Put Europe to Work*), represented a comprehensive statement of social democratic ambitions at the EU-level, and formed the basis for PES policy throughout the 1990s. Thus, the PES often referred to the Larsson Report as central to its approach to combating unemployment (Lightfoot, 2005). Indeed, the content of the report consisted of a programme to tackle the mass unemployment which had come to characterize Europe (totalling 20 million at the time). It argued (echoing the sentiment of the 1984 manifesto) that through EU-level cooperation, national governments could circumvent the obstacles to national reconstruction, the likes of which had caused French and Swedish national economic plans to founder in the early 1980s and 1990s, respectively (Johansson, 1999: 90). Thus, from the Larsson Report onwards, the European Union increasingly came to be seen as an institutional opportunity to manage and regulate an increasingly globalized capitalism. In the words of former PES General Secretary, Ton Beumer:

> The Larsson Report was a bit of an eye-opener to some who had been bombarded with this idea that nation-states couldn't act anymore. They feel that the EU has a level which enables them to regain some of the political power over the economic and technological process which is lost at national level, if the political will is there. This was a really challenging document, to make it clear that if we make it into European institutions we can use this to actually give some body to politics and be a real help to social democrats at the national level. This was all relatively new.
> (interview with author, 11 September 2001)

This commentary, by a central policy coordinator for social democratic party actors operating at the supranational level during the late 1990s and early 2000s, is of particular interest as it so clearly evinces the dual-edged nature of the 'Social Europe' agenda (initially observed at the national level) within a supranational context. As such, this highlights the way in which key EU-level social democratic actors viewed the Larsson Report as being based on the recognition of both the inability to implement 'traditional' decommodifying policies at the national level, but also the opportunities to overcome such obstacles at the supranational level. A 'Social Europe' agenda, in keeping with that developed at the national level, was therefore clearly also materializing at the supranational level.

Indeed, the policies contained in the Larsson Report represented an attempt by social democratic party elites to reassert the possibility of implementing policies that would produce a decommodification of the lives of their electoral constituents, particularly through a reduction in unemployment. In particular, the Larsson Report sought to use the institutional opportunities at the EU-level to stimulate an economic revival which would improve European citizens' employment prospects. Thus, the report included proposals for increased productivity through low interest rates, generous national fiscal policies for investment, and lending by the European Investment Fund (EIF). It also called for investment in material and social infrastructure (such as childcare, elderly care, urban renewal and social services) in order to stimulate employment and productivity. Further, the Larsson Report declared the PES' aim to achieve new working patterns throughout the EU, seeking to combine a commitment to flexible working arrangements with the possibility of reduced working hours (on a national basis, negotiated by the social partners). Finally, in keeping with ideological revisions undertaken by social democratic party actors at the national level, the report committed the PES to an emphasis on active welfare provisions as opposed to passive ones (PES, 1993). Interestingly, therefore, whilst the PES adopted in the Larsson Report a document that outlined a consistent attempt to promote policy aims at the supranational level that would attempt to tackle issues of relevance to social democratic parties' historic concern with redistributive, interventionist, or 'decommodifying' public policies, a number of the policies actually adopted were quite clearly influenced by the 'new' social democratic agenda developing within national-level social democratic parties. Thus, in proposing the EU-level as a means to circumvent national-level obstacles to national economic autonomy, PES member parties sought to stimulate economic growth, but nevertheless adopted a number of policies in keeping with a 'new' social democratic agenda, including a commitment to labour flexibility and a favouring of 'active' over 'passive' welfare provisions. As such, the extent to which the supranational level would be used to promote decommodifying policy ambitions was clearly limited from the early stages of the development of a substantive supranational 'Social Europe' agenda. Nevertheless, in calling for fiscal policies focused on increasing investment, and especially investment in social infrastructure, and in seeking to reduce unemployment and working hours, all of which was presented as something that could only be achieved through supranational-level coordination, the Larsson Report represented a significant development in the adoption of a supranational 'Social Europe' agenda that sought to espouse (albeit limited) decommodifying initiatives to counteract the inability to pursue such policy aims at the national level.

Indeed, throughout the 1990s, the PES developed a clear argument expressing the view that autonomous national activity was no longer a suitable means by which to achieve 'traditional' social democratic ambitions, thereby necessitating coordinated supranational activity, particularly focusing upon a coordinated supranational attempt to tackle unemployment. For instance, in its 1994 EP election manifesto, the PES stated,

> We want to concentrate all our efforts on a massive reduction in unemployment. Our aim is to create as soon as possible a society in which everyone will have a job or an occupation. We can only achieve this through a coordinated European strategy.
>
> (PES, 1994: 3)

Similarly, the report of the PES working party on the 1996 IGC, chaired by French Socialist Gerard Fuchs, claimed that 'national initiatives are not sufficient in an open world economy that is marked by globalization and rapid technological change' (PES, 1995: 3). However, despite the development of a 'Social Europe' agenda at the supranational level, which (in part) sought to portray the European level as a means by which to tackle issues in keeping with more 'traditional' social democratic concerns relating to decommodification, supranational-level social democratic party actors nevertheless continued to seek to avoid an outright contradiction of the 'new' social democratic policy agenda being developed at the national level. Thus, despite a rhetorical commitment to circumventing, through coordinated supranational-level activity, the obstacles to a substantive interventionist agenda at the national level, the concrete policy commitments actually reached, particularly from the mid-1990s onwards, were actually quite in keeping with a 'new' social democratic programme, irrespective of the fact that they were presented as only being feasible as a result of the advantages achieved through supranational coordination. For instance, in March 1999 the PES congress in Milan adopted the Guterres Report, *A European Employment Pact for a New European Way*, which sought to find a 'European strategy for growth and employment', including the need to, 'at European level, ... define an appropriate mix between the unified monetary policy, the 15 national budget positions and the multitude of wage and income developments in Europe' (PES, 1999a). What this meant in practice was a commitment to the use of Euro interest rates to facilitate non-inflationary growth, the recommendation of wage increases linked to productivity, and public investment restructured towards supply-side measures, particularly focusing on areas such as entrepreneurialism, research and development, education and training, and active labour market policies (PES, 1999a).

Based on this overview of the development of PES policy throughout the 1990s, we can describe the 'Social Europe' agenda of EU-level social democratic party actors during this period as being characterized in the following terms. First, the 'Social Europe' agenda included the view that reduced policy autonomy at the national level meant that 'traditional' social democratic policy tools were no longer feasible. Second, there was a commitment to coordinated European-level activity as a means to compensate for this reduced autonomy, and in particular to provide an alternative agenda to that prevailing within domestic politics. Third, the actual policies agreed by PES member parties operating at the supranational level were characterized by an extension of, rather than divergence from, the policies emerging from 'new' social democratic party relations at the national level.

A number of policy documents adopted at the beginning of the 2000s illustrate these characteristics. For instance, evincing the view that national-level activity was increasingly redundant but that EU-level coordinated action could compensate for this development, the 2001 Berlin PES congress agreed that, 'we want to manage global change for the benefit of human progress, making possible greater solidarity and social cohesion, and using globalization towards creating opportunities for the many and not the few' (PES, 2001a). More concretely, however, and illustrating the more specific content of proposals adopted by the PES, a common position formulated prior to the Laeken European Council meeting of 2001 set out in more detail some of the ways in which the European Union could be used to circumvent the constraints emergent from developments in the international political economy. According to this document, these policy instruments included an opening of markets – 'The more open the European market is to all of its businesses and the easier it is for them to raise capital throughout Europe, the more they will be able to realise the strength of the European economy' – and a recognition of the stabilizing effect of EMU – 'Through recent turbulent weeks the common single currency has provided a stability in the financial markets that would not necessarily have been available to all its members if they had retained their own separate currency' (PES, 2001b). In this sense, therefore, the policies promoted at the European level were far from a radical return to substantively interventionist, counter-market, or decommodifying public policies. Indeed, echoing much of the 'new' social democratic programme being adopted at the national level during this period, these policies relied heavily on the role of the market as a means to approach traditional social democratic concerns. In terms of more concrete attempts to promote 'social justice', therefore, the PES statement prior to Laeken evinced a strong orientation towards access to the labour market as the means through which to achieve this aim. Thus, the PES claimed in its pre-Laeken statement that,

> [O]ur economies are stronger when our societies are just, and no citizen is denied access to the new technology and the skills to use it. Parties of the Left have secured the commitment to a Europe of full employment. We want Europe to deliver on that commitment and to meet the targets for increased participation in the workforce that will widen job opportunities for women.
>
> (PES, 2001b)

In sum, therefore, social democratic actors operating at the supranational level espoused the view that one of the key ways through which a 'Social Europe' agenda could be realized was through market-making measures that would further liberalize the European economy, and in particular through a facilitation of individuals' ability to integrate within the European labour market.

The foregoing provides a general overview of the broad ideological developments of the PES, particularly during the 1990s and early 2000s. A number of more detailed policy documents were also adopted by the party during this period, therefore outlining the more specific social and economic policy ambitions of PES actors. Table 5.1 documents these main policy commitments based on the major policy documents adopted by the PES since 1992. The purpose of the table is to highlight in more detail the type and scope of policy ambitions of social democratic actors operating at the European level, with a specific focus on those policies that are most likely to have a decommodifying effect, which are in bold in the table. This therefore seeks to enable a subsequent assessment of the extent to which these aims have been realized, and/or are realizable, at the European level. Thus, as noted earlier, those policies adopted at the supranational level to a certain degree reflect the move away from substantive decommodifying policy aims by social democratic party elites at the national level. Nevertheless, a number of more substantial decommodifying policy aims can be discerned within PES policy documents, which therefore provide us with an insight into the extent to which an admittedly limited range of such policies have come to be promoted by social democratic party actors operating at the European level, and thereby expressing in more concrete terms the 'Social Europe' agenda we witnessed developing at the national level in Chapter 4. Thus, as table 5.1 highlights, these decommodifying policy measures included, in particular, a commitment to tackle unemployment and/or achieve full employment (which acts to increase the bargaining strength of labour and therefore has a decommodifying effect), reduce working time, improve working conditions, protect against poverty, and promote a redistributive structural funds policy. Thus, since the creation of the PES in 1992, the party federation has witnessed the adoption of a number of important, although admittedly limited, decommodifying

Table 5.1 Key PES policy developments

	Employment	Social policy	Economic policy	Industrial policy	Fiscal policy and structural funds	EMU	Industrial relations
The Hague Declaration (PES, 1992a)	'job creation'		'coordinated growth strategy'	EC-level industrial policy			'industrial democracy', 'social dialogue'
Edinburgh Declaration (PES 1992b)	'European works programme', (incl. EIB loans) 're-organisation & **reduction of working time**'		National economic policy coordination support Delors II	'active industrial policy at the European level' European level R&D policy			
Copenhagen Declaration (PES 1993a)	Cohesion/Structural Funds focus on employment 'active labour market policies', 'a better distribution of available work'	EIB and EIF to promote investment.	EC-level industrial policy National economic policy coordination	'prudent control of public	'control of erratic expenditure'	movements of speculative capital'	
Brussels (1993) – European Employment Initiative (PES, 1993b)	'reemployment strategy' Coordinate human resources/skills policies **Reduce working time (subsidiarity)** Improve national	'reform welfare policy so that it gives good incentives for work and employment' Training programmes and structural funds	Promote entrepreneurs/enterprises 'early establishment of the EIF' coordinate public and public-private investment; consider	'cooperation with other European countries in the field of research and development' – aim to increase	avoid 'damaging tax competition' Regional redistribution via structural funds and	European-level 'action to reduce interest rates' to 'make productive investments more	'unions as the driving forces in creating the positive flexibility and high quality in production …

Table 5.1 (cont.)

	Employment	Social policy	Economic policy	Industrial policy	Fiscal policy and structural funds	EMU	Industrial relations
	employment services	to promote gender equality in work.	European bond Council for Productivity, Competitiveness & Technology	overall R&D spending from 2 to 3 % of GDP.	cohesion funds	profitable' consider 'options for new measures for currency stabilisation'	to ensure competitiveness, growth and new jobs;' social dialogue
1994 EP elections manifesto (PES, 1994a)	**Coordinated EU strategy to tackle unemployment** 'reorganisation of work, agreed' between the social partners and safeguarding competitiveness' – including reduced working time	Support **'guaranteed minimum wage'**, **high minimum social standards, improvement in working conditions, health and safety at the workplace, protection against redundancy, equality for women, part time, temporary and seasonal workers.**	'European agreement on investment in the future and on employment' 'We need a common initiative from the Community's Member States … low interest rates, **measures to build homes and modernise our cities, re-building the weaker regions**, … effective vocational training – all this will help to create jobs'	'joint industrial and research policy'	'avoid a tax cutting competition between Member States.' 'a tax system which penalizes work less and environmental pollution more.' Redistribute to regions via structural funds & cohesion fund, integrate into labour market, and create jobs	EMU 'can prevent currency speculation'	'more democracy in the economy', incl. **works' councils, and consultation of workers, and European sectoral collective agreements.**

Source						
Essen (PES, 1994b)	'a far reaching human investment programme'	Seek expansion of social provision, incl. **care for the elderly, child care and health care, which will also act to stimulate jobs**. Adopt European Poverty Programme	'mobilise private and public investment' Support SMEs (incl. access to financial resources), training, education and technology transfer. Open energy and telecoms markets. Consider Euro bonds		Resources for TENs and EIF	Stimulate social dialogue. Create a tripartite European Innovation Council
Fuchs Report of PES Working Party on 1996 IGC (June 1995) (non binding) (PES, 1995)		EU coordination of employment policies	Implement Delors White Paper. Combine labour market, social and training policies to provide a 'social' complement to EMU and ECB.			
		equal opportunities in the labour market, incl. work/life balance, equal treatment in social security systems, and in political life.	European cooperation to manage international economic forces			
Malmö (June 1997) (PES, 1997)	**Employment Chapter** Invest in human capital Flexible working life, reorganize working hours	Minimum working rights Support effective social policies				Pro-EMU; pro-convergence criteria
PES Ecofin Group—*The New European Way* (1998) (PES Ecofin Group, 1998)	'active labour market policies', incl. training, incentives to work, tax and social security exemptions, new working time	Support those unable to work Improve gender equality in the workplace, incl. via working time arrangements, provision of services	Coordinate economic policies Support SMEs, and entrepreneurs incl. reduction in bureaucratic, fiscal and cultural obstacles liberalize telecoms	TENs (including PPPs and EIB funding)	'a tax system which favours work but penalizes environmental pollution' Prepare for counter-cylical spending during growth periods Monitor/control use of	ECB focus on price stability 'taking into consideration growth and

Table 5.1 (cont.)

	Employment	Social policy	Economic policy	Industrial policy	Fiscal policy and structural funds	EMU	Industrial relations
	arrangements. Share best practice via EES 'integrate excluded and disadvantaged groups into the labour market.'		market. Promote 'Fair rules of competition' 'the allocation of jobs … is best left to markets'		state aid Avoid tax competition between MSs OECD-wide tax harmonization	employment Tripartite social dialogue to coordinate monetary, employment and wage policy	
1999 Guterres Report – A European Employment Pact: For a New European Way (PES, 1999a)	**European Employment Pact** reorganize working time Active employment policies aimed at young, long-term unemployed, low-skilled Reform social protection 'combining general basic rights and positive discrimination with more individual responsibility' Seek to combine part-time jobs,	**Regional development policies to avoid 'social dumping.'** 'equal opportunities for women and men, combating professional discrimination, **expanding social infrastructures for child care and care of the elderly.'** 'active integration policies for disabled people and job-seekers from ethnic minorities'	'appropriate policy mix between the unified monetary policy, the 15 national budget positions and the multitude of wage and income developments in Europe.' improve coordination between BEPGs & employment guidelines consider Euro bonds	EU-level and MS coordination 'in the areas of infrastructure, industrial policy, R&D, education and training' 'A European Initiative for the Information Society should be launched in June 1999, ambitious enough to close the gap with the US and to	**'deficit reductions' 'automatic stabilisers must be fully utilised if necessary.' 'Tax policy must be better co-ordinated to foster employment'** Avoid 'unfair tax competition' European budgetary policy, incl.	'an accommodating monetary policy in a non inflationary environment'	'wage increases relate to productivity' Improve 'the role of social dialogue at all levels but also the social responsibility of companies'

	training opportunities, parental leave, flexible retirement', social protection and life-long learning' EES to focus on human capital, life-long learning, equal opportunities, adaptability, and corporate social responsibility.			create the basic infrastructure of the future.'	structural funds, EIB, EIF, and PPPs, to focus on innovation in SMEs, TENs, knowledge infrastructures, R&D, human capital, pilot employment policy programmes.	
1999 EP elections manifesto (PES, 1999b)	**European pact for employment**	Support Social Chapter	Economic coordination to achieve sustainable growth and employment	TENs in transport and communications	Coordinate to avoid tax competition	Support EMU
	Especially focus on young and long-term unemployed Possible reduction in working time (with social partners' consent)	Equal gender opportunities to be mainstreamed	Support SEMs		**Structural funds focused on job creation & social cohesion**	ECB should engage with EU institutions
Declaration on the Future of Europe (PES, 2001b)	Promote full employment		Pro-market and capital market liberalization		structural policy aimed at deprived regions	Seek **'informed participation of the workforce'**
2003 *Promoting Investment and Policy Change*	Promote skills and lifelong learning	'high standard of welfare protection'	'Improve the internal market, in particular the service market and better conditions	Focus EU budget on investment	re-direct public budgets towards	Distinguish between investment and current
	Motivate 'people to	'Fight against				Support EU-level corporate social responsibility

Table 5.1 (cont.)

	Employment	Social policy	Economic policy	Industrial policy	Fiscal policy and structural funds	EMU	Industrial relations
for Sustainable Growth and Participation in Europe (PES, 2003)	find and take up jobs and participate in society' 'Full employment' Health and safety at work 'adequate level of protection for atypical workers'	**poverty and social exclusion'** Tackle poverty via increased lab. mkt. participation **Minimum income, pension, and wage** Gender equality, incl. childcare targets Identify best-practice in pensions/education	for businesses' Complete SEM Action plan on entrepreneurship Promote high productivity jobs Consider Eurobonds Improve policy coordination at national level	Favourable conditions for PPPs Invest 3% GDP in research; 2% GDP in higher ed.	investment Link SGP with Lisbon Strategy shift tax burden from labour to capital Introduce 'golden rule' for investment during times of high growth Avoid tax competition, pro-labour and SMEs	expenditure in calculating deficits	policy
2004 EP elections manifesto (PES, 2004)	Support full employment, and more and better jobs				Equitable funding of EU budget	Reform SGP 'to promote higher growth and employment'	'strengthen social partnership'
2006 Congress resolution:	'full and high quality	**'Mandatory social impact assessments**	Coordinate economic policies, to avoid	Structural funds, EU	Avoid fiscal competition		Tripartite social dialogue to

New Social Europe: Ten principles for our common future (PES, 2006)	**employment can be realised'** – creates inclusion/ prosperity Investment in education and training	**of proposed EU legislation' to ensure against social exclusion as a result of competition and internal market legislation.** Promote equal gender rights	mutually contradictory policies at the national level	budget, and PPPs to focus on invesmtnet in innovation, and R&D	promote growth and jobs

policy aims, particularly in the areas of employment policy, social policy, and the structural funds. What follows, therefore, is an attempt to assess the extent to which these decommodifying elements of the 'Social Europe' agenda, adopted by social democratic party actors operating at the supranational level, have been realized, and/or are realizable, in terms of concrete policy outcomes.

The limits to EU-level decommodification

To briefly summarize the argument thus far, social democratic party actors operating at the EU-level adopted, particularly from the 1990s onwards, a 'Social Europe' agenda which espoused the dual-edged view that decommodifying measures are no longer feasible at the national level, but could nevertheless, as a result of the advantages of scale resulting from European integration, be achieved through coordinated supranational activity at the European level. Although the PES has been reluctant to adopt policies that digress too far from the policies they have adopted at the national level. Nevertheless, we have observed a particular focus on decommodifying public policies in the areas of employment policy, social policy, and the structural funds. The aim of the present section is therefore to examine the extent to which these limited decommodifying policy ambitions have resulted in concrete EU-level policy outcomes, particularly focusing on the impact of the often-noted institutional obstacles to EU-level policy-making. The section begins with an overview of employment and social policy, as the key policy developments of importance to the 'Social Europe/agenda' adopted by the PES, and a more brief discussion of the structural funds.

Developments in employment and social policy: an overview

EU social and employment policy has undergone considerable development over the past thirty years, although, as we shall see, there have been a number of obstacles and predispositions that have prevented certain forms of policy outcomes from occurring and resulted in a prevalence for what many commentators have described as market-making, rather than market-correcting, policies. This section provides a brief overview of these developments (for more thorough overviews, see Hantrais, 2007; Geyer, 2000; Kleinman, 2002; Leibfried, 2005).

From the inception of European integration, there has been a small, but limited, commitment to European social policy. Thus, the negotiation of the Treaty of Rome witnessed a number of disputes between the original member states over the extent to which social and labour market policies needed to be harmonized in order to create the common market. These disputes ultimately resulted in 'a small number of concessions for the more 'interventionist' delegations' (Falkner, 2000: 186), which, due to the focus of the Treaty of Rome on market-building, were largely focused on the need to avoid disparities within a common European labour market. Thus, the Treaty of Rome included provisions for the improvement of working conditions (art. 117), for closer cooperation in the social field, and on vocational training, working conditions and social security (art. 118), enshrined the principle of equal pay for equal work by men and women (art. 119), and the right to paid holidays (art. 120), and established the European Social Fund (ESF) in order to improve employment opportunities and increase geographical and occupational mobility (arts. 123–8). These measures therefore provided the institutional basis for policies that were deemed necessary in order to avoid too great a discrepancy between the working conditions of the different member states. However, despite having reached agreement in principle on the adoption of a number of social policy measures, agreement over the implementation of these measures, which required the unanimous support of the member states, proved more difficult to achieve. As a result, little progress was made in the area of EU social policy-making in the 1960s (Hantrais, 2007: 3).

From the early 1970s, however, political momentum in support of an EU-level social policy began to increase. Most importantly, in 1974, a year after the Office of the Social Democratic Parties produced its *Towards a Social Europe*, the Council of the European Union agreed a Social Action Programme, which sought to set out a role for the EC-level in the development of European social policy. This was, therefore, a significant development, witnessing a renewed commitment at the supranational level to the construction of a substantive European social policy. Thus, the declared aim of the Programme was to ensure that economic integration and growth would be characterized by a simultaneous improvement in quality of life in the EC. Although it should also be noted that the initiative was also motivated by the more practical recognition that the removal of barriers to the free movement of labour required the introduction of certain further measures to avoid disparities between national labour market and social policies. Despite these developments, however, the 1974 Programme also clearly displayed the caution of those drafting the document in their attempt to respect national autonomy, particularly in an area within which the EC had not been granted formal competence to implement policy. Indeed, as a result of this caution, initiatives were restricted to the promotion of cooperation between member states, rather than more substantive attempts to either impose harmonization upon member states or develop an autonomous EC-level social policy (Hantrais, 2007: 4–5). Despite these concerns, however, the 1970s did witness a significant development in social provision in the area of gender equality. Thus, two important Directives were introduced to implement the commitment in the Treaty of Rome on the equal pay and social security for men and women (Directives 75/117/EEC and 79/7/EEC). As such, gender equality, and particularly equality between male and female *workers*, witnessed a significant advance at the European level during the 1970s. Nevertheless, it is difficult to argue that gender equality in the labour market is a form of decommodification, particularly as it implies an *increase* in participation in the labour market for female workers, with no obvious means by which dependence upon the sale of labour power is ameliorated. Thus, whereas a decline in unemployment (which also involves a rise in participation in the labour market) has a complementary effect upon the bargaining power of the labour force (and can therefore be considered to have something of a decommodifying effect), it is more difficult to argue this for the case of equal opportunities for men and women in the workplace. Thus, throughout the 1970s, whilst the political support behind European social policy began to grow, less was achieved substantively in terms of concrete policy agreements, and particularly in terms of policies which would be expected to have a decommodifying effect upon the lives of workers based within Europe.

Indeed, more substantive development of EC social policy was not to occur until the agreement of the Single European Act in 1986. Of particular importance was a new article 118a, which allowed decisions on workers' health and safety to be made by qualified majority voting (QMV), and a new article 118b, which provided for a social dialogue between the social partners (i.e., representatives of business and workers) to be held at the European level (Kleinman, 2002). Indeed, in introducing QMV for the first time in the area of social policy, article 118a represented a substantial route out of the stalemate that had been experienced by would-be policy makers facing the impasse created by the unanimity requirement (Falkner, 2000: 187). QMV was therefore frequently used during the 1990s to introduce social legislation that (arguably) only tentatively came under the remit of health and safety, including the Atypical Work (health and safety) Directive (91/383/EEC), the Maternity Directive (92/85/EEC), and the Working Time Directive (93/104/EC) (Leibfried and Pierson, 2000: 273; Hantrais, 2007). Also of importance was the introduction of a new section on structural funds (articles 130a–e) which directed the focus of the funds towards deprived and high unemployment regions.

Another important development during the 1980s was the agreement in December 1989, by all member states except the UK, of the Community Charter of the Fundamental Social Rights of Workers (or the 'Social Charter', as it came to be known). This was a non-binding statement committing the member states to introduce a harmonization and improvement of work contracts, the social dialogue, the right to a weekly rest period and annual paid leave, health and safety regulations, training for young people, and to continue to ensure equal pay and work opportunities for men and women (Kleinman, 2002; Hantrais, 2007). It was subsequently incorporated into the treaties in 1993 as a protocol (due to the continued opt out of the UK) to the Treaty on European Union, thereby introducing a number of institutional developments that would subsequently facilitate decision-making in the area of EU social policy. Thus, the Social Protocol both introduced the need for consultation of the social partners in certain legislation, and also created the possibility that agreements reached between them could be adopted as legislation by the member states, which was a method of drafting legislation that was subsequently adopted for the Parental Leave Directive (96/34/EC) and Part-Time Work Directive (97/81/EC). Further, the Protocol also introduced decision-making by QMV, thereby making it easier to reach legislative decisions, in the areas of health and safety at work, working conditions, the information and consultation of workers, equality between men and women, and the integration of persons excluded from the labour market. Unanimity was retained for a number of sensitive areas that member states refused to relinquish national control over, including social security and the social protection of workers, the protection of workers made redundant, representation and collective defence of workers and employers, and conditions of employment for third-country nationals (Threlfall, 2002; Kleinman, 2002; Hantrais, 2007).

The 1990s also witnessed the increased acceptance at the EU-level of the notion that social policy developments were compatible with, rather than contrary to, the goals of economic growth and increased productivity within the European economy. Thus, the 1994 *White Paper on EU Social Policy* declared that social cohesion was necessary for economic growth. The 1998 *Social Action Programme for 1998–2000* reiterated the same sentiments. Each of these publications, however, made it clear that harmonization of EU social policy was not being sought, thereby reflecting a continuing concern to avoid an impingement upon national sovereignty. As a result, EU-level social policy-making continued to be largely confined to the promotion of monitoring, cooperation, and adoption of 'best-practice' measures across the member states (Hantrais, 2007: 32–3).

The adoption of the Amsterdam Treaty in 1997 also witnessed two further important developments in the area of EU social *and* employment policy. Thus, whilst employment policy had been peripheral to European integration up until this point, at the instigation of a number of governments, and particularly, as we have seen, the Swedish Social Democratic Government and the incoming Jospin Government, the Amsterdam Treaty introduced a new Employment Chapter. This provided the treaty base for the monitoring and coordination of employment policies that has, since the extraordinary 'jobs' summit in Luxembourg in November 1997, provided the basis for the European Employment Strategy. In social policy, moreover, as we have seen, the Labour Party leadership was committed, should it win election to office in the 1997 general election, to the reversal of the UK's opt out from the Social Protocol. In winning that election, therefore, the new Labour Government ensured the formal incorporation of social policy as an EU-level competence, thereby witnessing the formal adoption of the Social Protocol as a new EU Social Chapter. Other initiatives introduced by the Amsterdam Treaty included the introduction of monitoring of member states' social policies (art. 143), and a new article 13 enabling action to be taken 'to combat discrimination based on sex, racial or ethnic origin, religion or belief, disability, age or sexual orientation'.

By the time of the end of the 1990s, social democratic parties were in office in 13 of the 15 EU member states, thereby obtaining the strongest centre-left majority in the Council of the European Union witnessed in the history of European integration. In part as a result, two important developments occurred in 2000. First, the 'Lisbon Strategy' was launched at a summit in March, with the stated aim 'to become the most competitive and dynamic knowledge-based economy in the world, capable of sustainable economic growth with more and better jobs and greater social cohesion'. Alongside a number of targets to increase economic growth and productivity within the European Union, the Lisbon Strategy also included a commitment to launch an open method of coordination in social inclusion and social protection (OMC/SISP), which included commitments to develop the supranational coordination of pensions and health care. This committed the EU to further monitoring and coordinating social policy across the member states, and to integrate this policy within the wider Lisbon Strategy. Second, the Nice Treaty, adopted at the end of 2000, incorporated the Charter of Fundamental Rights of the European Union, which, although not legally binding, did extend the prior commitment to focus exclusively on 'workers' rights' to include the rights of non-workers such as children, and older people, and issues beyond employment, such as housing, health care and religion (Hantrais, 2007: 17).

The Lisbon Strategy subsequently became a central focus and reference point for EU-level policy-making. This included an increased focus upon employment and social policy outputs. Thus, in 2003, the Broad Economic Policy Guidelines (used to coordinate member states' economic policies) were combined with the Employment Guidelines, in an attempt to further integrate the policy objectives adopted at Lisbon. In 2005, however, and following the heavily critical internal review of the Lisbon Strategy published in the 'Kok Report' the previous year, and also in part as a result of the inauguration of the incoming Barroso Commission, the Lisbon Strategy was streamlined to focus more explicitly on 'growth and jobs'. This had a particular impact upon EU social policy, as the OMC on social policy and social inclusion was detached from the Lisbon Strategy, in order that the former could be 'streamlined', although a commitment for social policy to 'parallel and interact closely' with the Lisbon strategy was retained.

This brief overview of EU social and employment policy shows the way in which a coherent institutional, legislative and policy framework has developed at the EU-level. Whilst there has been a strong focus throughout the course of this development upon working conditions, itself a consequence of the market-building nature of much of the process of European integration, we have also witnessed a commitment to social rights in general, particularly with the adoption of the Charter of Fundamental Rights, and the adoption of employment policies. Moreover, a development which was not mentioned in the foregoing discussion, in 1988 and 1992 the budget allocated to the structural funds was greatly extended, resulting in structural funds becoming the second largest area (accounting for roughly one third) of expenditure within the EU budget. Thus, potential does exist at the EU-level for the implementation of policies that might have a decommodifying impact upon European citizens. The following section, however, considers the obstacles to this agenda, and the impact they have had upon the more concrete implementation of EU social and economic policies.

Obstacles to EU-level policy-making

Despite the aims and declared ambitions of social democratic party elites regarding the potential for increased opportunities to implement decommodifying public policies through coordinated activity at the supranational-level, and also despite the institutional, legislative and policy developments charted above, it is the claim of this section that a number of significant obstacles have prevented (and will prevent) substantive decommodifying outcomes arising from social and employment policy or from the structural funds allocated at the EU-level. Indeed, a number of commentators have noted both the predominance of 'market-making' policies, and the parallel absence of 'market-correcting', redistributive, or decommodifying policies at the EU-level (Scharpf, 1999; Raveaud, 2007), whilst also noting the unlikelihood of overcoming the obstacles that have resulted in these outcomes within the foreseeable future (Bailey, 2008). These obstacles are discussed below in turn.

EU Budget As has been noted on many occasions, the small size of the budget of the European Union, combined with the treaty obligation to balance revenue and expenditure, ensures that the scope for fiscal redistribution through EU-level spending is slim. Indeed, the entire EU budget was limited to 1.27 per cent of EU GDP between 2000 and 2006, compared with 45.8 per cent of GDP across the EU27 member states in 2007. From this perspective, therefore, there is little scope for EU-level public spending to produce substantive decommodifying outcomes. Whilst it has been argued, particularly by Robinson (2007), that the impact of the EU budget is under-estimated by looking solely at these kinds of figures, even calculated using the method that he suggests this impact would still be relatively small. Thus, Robinson argues that, in order to understand the impact of EU-level expenditure, we should also consider both the 'leverage effect' that EU expenditure has upon national government expenditure and private investment, and the impact of loans by the European Investment Bank. However, considered in this way, the total amount of these combined figures still only amounts to 3.12 per cent of total government expenditure of the EU25 countries in 2004 (Robinson, 2007: 199). This equates to only 1.5 per cent of GDP. Nevertheless, the targeting of the European Union's structural funds in regions with high levels of poverty and unemployment seeks to ensure that EU spending might have a redistributive effect within member states with below average EU income (Beugelsdijk and Eijffinger, 2005). Thus, in 2004, Robinson's measurement of aggregate EU contributions to the Portuguese economy (the poorest of the pre-2004 member states) amounted to 14.72 per cent of Portuguese government expenditure, or 6.84 per cent of national GDP. Whilst this is clearly a more substantive figure, it should be noted that about 23 per cent of this spending, or 1.56 per cent of GDP, was financed by the Portuguese government itself, meaning that *net* EU contributions might be more accurately estimated at 5.28 per cent of national GDP. The corresponding figure for Spain, another large recipient of EU contributions in 2004, was 3.07 per cent of national GDP. Again, these are more substantive figures compared with those identified when we look solely at EU expenditure, but they are still far less than the level of expenditure witnessed at the national level. Moreover, it is also questionable whether both private investment and EIB loans can be considered to have a redistributive or decommodifying effect, particularly if we consider that both of these types of loans need to be repaid. If we remove these loans from the previous calculation, therefore, the amount of EU expenditure within Portugal and Spain might be more accurately calculated at 3.11 per cent and 1.95 per cent of national GDP, respectively (Robinson, 2007; Eurostat). Compared with average national-level spending of 45.8 per cent of GDP, therefore, it is difficult, even in those countries that benefited most from EU spending, to sustain the argument that fiscal transfers allocated at the EU-level are likely to have a *substantially* redistributive effect.

Formal limits to decision-making Significant formal limits to making both policy and legislative decisions have also acted to impede the development of social and employment policy at the European level. Thus, two constraints in particular stand out. First, the requirement of a treaty base provides (and/or has provided) a number of restrictions upon EU-level policy-making. Thus, there was no Social Chapter or Employment Chapter within the EU until the adoption of the Amsterdam Treaty, which either prevented policy-making from occurring altogether or required the Commission to use alternative articles from different sections within the Treaty to obtain that competence. As a result, the first poverty programme, adopted in 1974, was agreed under article 235(EC) (now 308). This is a catch-all article, which enabled unanimous decisions in the Council 'to attain, in the course of the operation of the common market, one of the objectives of the Community' (Art. 308 (TEC)) (Hantrais, 2007: 184). In contrast, the 1993 proposal for a fourth poverty action programme was successfully blocked by German and British opposition, on the grounds that poverty was not an EU-level competence (Hantrais, 2007: 188). Moreover, it remains the case that decisions on social security systems, pay, the right to association, the right to strike, and the right to impose lock-outs are all explicitly denied EU-level competence.

Second, due to a number of the institutional procedures at the EU-level, there exists a high decision-making threshold at the EU-level. These include unanimous decision-making, the higher decision-making threshold represented by qualified majority voting as opposed to a simple majority, and the addition of an extra veto player, in the form of the European Parliament, resulting from the move towards the codecision procedure. This high decision-making threshold therefore creates further obstacles to EU-level decision-making, which in turn hinders the development of social and employment policy. Thus, as König (2008: 155–8) notes, 'all studies find that qualified majority voting in the Council speeds up decision-making [compared with unanimity] ..., and that participation by the European Parliament slows down the process'. Moreover, given that QMV creates a higher decision-making threshold than straightforward majority voting would do, we can presume that it acts to restrict the development of EU-level social and employment policy, in comparison to that which would be possible under a simple majority vote. Thus, QMV creates the possibility that a relatively small blocking minority can block significant legislative developments, for instance we witnessed the UK, Ireland, Denmark and Germany successfully block the agreement of a temporary work directive, between 2002 and 2008, despite the agreement of the remaining eleven (pre-2004) member states (Nedergaard, 2007). Once decisions have been reached between the member states, moreover, they subsequently require the agreement of the European Parliament, thereby risking a further derailment of the legislative course. Finally, it remains the case that some of the more sensitive legislation, where member states are less likely to cede decision-making capacity to the EU-level, and/or to agree to the ending of unanimous decision-making, remain within the area of social policy and employment policy. As such, the sensitivity of these policy areas for member states' political elites has thus far acted to hinder substantive policy developments at the European level (Streeck, 2001; Leibfried, 2005).

The path-dependence of the EU's market-building tradition   European integration has historically been a project characterized primarily by economic integration. As a result, despite the important developments that have been made in areas such as security, defence, justice and home affairs, and environmental policy, it remains the case that a legacy of the initial economic focus on European integration is the predominance of market-building measures as the key EU-level policy instruments existent at present (Wahl, 2005: 89; Leibfried, 2005; Scharpf, 1999). As a result, EU-level policy-making illustrates a path-dependence characterized by a predisposition towards market-making over market-correcting policy outcomes (Bailey, 2008: 234). Perhaps the most apparent way in which this path-dependence affects the scope for EU-level social and employment policy-making is the greater availability at the EU-level of market-making policy tools rather than those that seek to correct or modify the market mechanism. Thus, many of the social and employment policy aims to have developed at the European level – including increased equality, protection from the risk of poverty, pension provision, and the attainment of full employment – are all predominantly pursued through the market-making policy tools that currently prevail at the EU-level. For instance, in the case of the European Employment Strategy (EES) we can observe the way in which the strategy 'favours market mechanisms as a way to promote employment in Europe' (Raveaud, 2007: 423). Thus, the prolonged emphasis in the European Employment Strategy on market-making mechanisms, including the promotion of employee attractiveness to the employer, flexibility within the labour market, and the promotion of part-time and fixed-term contracts, are all presented within the Strategy as means to increase the EU employment rate, thereby clearly illustrating its market-conforming nature (Raveuad, 2007). Indeed, considered in terms of the extent to which such a policy might produce decommodifying outcomes, it would be difficult to claim that increasing the appeal of employees' abilities to their employer's requirements or the liberalization of the labour market would be likely to have a decommodifying effect. Similarly, if we look at the OMC on Social Inclusion and Social Protection, Büchs (2007) observes the primacy placed upon labour market participation as the key means to achieve the policy's goals. Thus, 'the OMC social inclusion assumes that social inclusion and the eradication of poverty is mainly brought about through labour market participation.' Moreover, 'the OMC pensions is primarily concerned with re-designing pensions systems so that they can cope with ageing populations and limited public resources for social security systems. *It therefore supports to strengthen the role of private pension schemes.*' (Büchs, 2007: 52, emphasis added). In areas where we observed EU-level social democratic party actors developing decommodifying policy ambitions, therefore, the actual policy outcomes realized within the European Union focus predominantly on market-conforming, rather than market-correcting, policy measures, and therefore provide limited scope for producing decommodifying effects upon the lives of workers within the European Union. Whilst such policy measures might act to reduce the cost or increase the market availability of certain services, or to facilitate the integration of workers within the labour market, they are unlikely to engender a decomodification of the lives of those workers.

In addition, the market-building path-dependence of European integration has also led to a more general deprioritization of employment and social policy goals in favour of more established EU-level policy commitments, most notably those of economic growth and the operation of the labour market. Thus, as noted in the overview above, social policy has historically been pursued primarily as a means to avoid national disparities in social and labour market conditions which might distort market integration. This was a key factor underpinning the agreement of the principle of equal pay for men and women in the Treaty of Rome, and was equally important in the raft of directives stipulating minimum working conditions in areas such as working time, parental leave, and part-time work that were adopted during the 1990s. As a result, we should note

> the mainly market-making and regulatory nature of existing legally binding EU social policy provisions since they concentrate on providing the conditions for free movement of labour and a 'level playing field' in the areas of work environment and occupational safety.
>
> (Büchs, 2007: 6–7)

Similarly, the targeting of structural funds in the 1990s was increasingly deployed as a means to ensure participation within the labour market, with employment viewed as a means through which to tackle problems of social exclusion (Hantrais, 2007: 192, 207). From 2000 this continued to be the case, with the pursuit of social policy reform, in initiatives such as the 1994 White Paper, consistently presented as a key means to improve economic competitiveness and levels of employment (Hantrais, 2007: 22). This tendency was strengthened further still in 2005, when the re-launch of the Lisbon Strategy, as the new *Partnership for Growth and Jobs*, narrowed Lisbon's focus to economic and employment policy coordination. As a result, Armstrong, Begg and Zeitlin remark, EU social policy coordination 'looked increasingly like a "satellite" process orbiting the core of the Lisbon Strategy'. Moreover, whereas competitiveness and social cohesion began as complementary aims within the Lisbon Strategy, this changed, following the 2005 re-launch, 'towards a view of social progress as the product of economic growth' (Armstrong, Begg and Zeitlin, 2008: 414). Similarly, Büchs notes how, in the 2005–08 Integrated Guidelines, '[Q]uality of jobs is only mentioned together with labour productivity which means that it is primarily seen as a means to increase productivity through job satisfaction rather than a goal in its own' (2007: 51). Those social and employment policies that have been implemented at the European level, therefore, have in large part been viewed as means to achieve more important goals relating to economic productivity and growth. Again, therefore, the extent to which we might consider this a process of decommodification is significantly questionable.

In sum, therefore, the market-building tradition of European integration has created a path-dependence that ensures that the prevailing policy tools available to policy makers are those which act to consolidate, rather than challenge, the operation of the market, and, moreover, that those policies are in general viewed as means to achieve the more important goals of economic productivity and growth. As a result, even in those areas, such as the attempt to tackle poverty and inequality, where we might consider decommodifying policy aims to be realized, we have witnessed market-making policies adopted as the means through which to tackle such issues. In this sense, therefore, the institutional terrain of the European Union has acted to limit the extent to which decommodifying policy outcomes can be expected to be realized at the supranational level, despite the advantages achieved through the changed institutional scale.

The preference for non-binding decision-making   Finally, in part as a result of the obstacles impeding the adoption of substantive decisions at the supranational level that have already been noted, we can observe at the European level an increasing tendency to resort to non-binding, or 'soft', decision-making and cooperation as a means to produce desired policy outcomes. This is particularly the case for employment and social policy. Thus, one of the first major developments in the use of the open method of coordination (itself one of the key developments in 'soft' decision-making) occurred with the introduction of the European Employment Strategy. This was subsequently adopted on a more general level with the introduction of the open method of coordination in the Lisbon Strategy, including the open method of coordination on social inclusion and social protection. Given the difficulties experienced in attempts to develop employment and social policies at the EU-level, therefore, there has been a consistent attempt to compensate for this underdevelopment through recourse to 'soft' policy coordination in this area (Heidenreich and Bischoff, 2008). Thus, Büchs notes that, 'whilst it seemed clear [from the early 1990s onwards] that it was not possible to establish a European welfare state and harmonize social policies, convergence through soft coordination became regarded as a "middle-way solution" to this situation' (2007: 12). According to proponents of the 'soft' method of decision-making, therefore, rather than (seek to) agree decisions at the supranational level that will require strict and binding adherence by member states, decisions are instead adopted which seek to coordinate and monitor national policies in adherence with broad principles agreed at the European level. This has the advantage of retaining policy autonomy in the hands of member state officials, and therefore overcomes a number of the obstacles to decision-making identified above, reducing the extent to which formal decisions need to be taken and by leaving the majority of implementation decisions to the member states.

The downside of the 'soft' coordination approach, however, is that, due to its non-binding nature, it obviously leaves considerable scope for non-implementation, and as a result has been criticized by a number of commentators for its ineffectiveness. The problem faced by 'soft' policy coordination, therefore, is that it risks both a perpetuation of the limited scope of social and employment policy, and of engendering non-compliance with, and therefore ineffectiveness of, those decisions that are made (Ashiagbor, 2005). For instance, Armstrong (2008) describes how, in seeking to promote the idea of a minimum income scheme, whilst noting both the lack of EU-level competence and the unlikelihood that member states will cede competence to the European level on this issue in the future, the Commission has proposed that a new non-binding recommendation be introduced. As Armstrong notes, however, 'this is a familiar story of a lack of legislative competence in the social sphere leading to a "soft" outcome', albeit one that also represents 'novel experimentation with new governance techniques' (2008: 419). Further, Sapir notes that the European Employment Strategy 'is neither a very convincing benchmarking and peer review exercise, nor does it represent an effective method for changing the behaviour of national governments' (2006: 383). Perhaps the most striking criticism of soft coordination, however, came in the form of the 2004 Kok Report on the Lisbon Strategy. This made a number of severe criticisms, which were themselves particularly striking due to the fact that they were being made at an official level by a report commissioned by the European Union itself, focusing in particular upon both the lack of substance and the problem of ineffectiveness associated with non-binding decision-making. Thus, according to Begg:

> Criticisms centred not only on the desultory record of certain Member States, but also on the lack of focus and of embedding in national policy-making procedures. The Kok report was pretty trenchant, noting problems of implementation, an over-loaded yet poorly co-ordinated agenda with incompatible priorities and a lack of political commitment.
>
> (2008: 427)

Perhaps most problematic, in terms of the likelihood of implementing decommodifying public policies at the European level, Begg goes on to note that, 'the Lisbon approach may have emerged because of a lack of alternatives' (2008: 434). Similarly, Zeitlin notes how the Kok Report 'lambasted the OMC for the weakness of benchmarking and peer review as incentives for Member State delivery of policy commitments, while also noting the ineffectiveness of the community method in ensuring timely implementation of directives' (2008: 436).

More concrete evidence of the ineffectiveness of 'soft' coordination in the areas of employment and social policy is provided by Büchs (2007), who also shows how the most important indicators used by the EU to monitor the performance of the OMCs highlight an ongoing inability to reach the targets that have been adopted. Thus, employment rates only rose from 61.2 per cent in 1998 to 63.8 per cent in 2005, thereby failing to reach the target rate of 70 per cent. Similarly, the EES initially set a target of 6 months (for young unemployed) and 12 months (for adult unemployed) as the maximum period before which unemployed workers should receive active labour market policies, although Büchs notes that 'the UK is currently [2006] the only country which claims to fulfil these goals'. On social policy, moreover, 'poverty has not been reduced in the EU since the late 1990s', and the member states are struggling to meet targets in inequality, proportion of early school leavers, income of over-65s as proportion of income of under 64s decreased between 1998 and 2001 (Büchs, 2007: 110–12).

Finally, even in those cases where 'soft' coordination has been effective, the content of the policies that it has led to have been predominantly market-conforming, thereby continuing to reflect the path-dependence of the EU in the light of its traditional focus on market-making provisions. Thus, Heidenreich and Bischoff

(2008) show how one area in which the 'soft' coordination method of the EES was successful in coordinating member states' national-level policy-making was in the case of German labour market reform. Thus, the Schröder Government, in its attempt to implement its Agenda 2010 reforms, sought to increase incentives to participate in the labour market through a reduction in the generosity of unemployment benefits, which was itself a policy initiative influenced by the EES. Similarly, Raveaud shows how the Employment Guidelines adopted by the Council under the EES consistently favour market-conforming measures, to the extent that Sweden was criticized for its high levels of taxation, despite being the most successful country in terms of the targets set by the EES itself (2007: 425). Again, therefore, it is difficult to claim that 'soft' coordination in the areas of social and employment policies is a development that can be highlighted as a move towards the implementation of decommodifying public policies at the European level.

To summarize, whilst a number of institutional, policy and legislative developments have produced a coherent employment and social policy framework at the EU-level, and without denying the significance of the size of the structural funds as a part of the EU budget, the obstacles to substantive policy-making at the EU-level have ensured that those policies that have been agreed have been largely limited to either market-conforming policies, or that their scope is restricted in such a way that they are unlikely to have a significant decommodifying effect. Thus, we witness a severely restricted budget at the EU-level, significant obstacles to formal decision-making, a policy tradition that prioritizes market-making policy tools, and a preference for non-binding decisions in EU social and employment policy-making that has been found significantly lacking in terms of its ability to produce the desired policy outcomes. The impact of these obstacles, therefore, has been to significantly limit both the scope of policy-making to predominantly market-making measures, and to impede the development of more substantive decommodifying public policies at the supranational level. As such, one of the key claims of the present chapter is that, despite the development of an admittedly limited attempt by social democratic party actors operating at the European level to coordinate the promotion of policies that will have a decommodifying effect upon the lives of individuals within the European Union, a series of substantial obstacles exists which have thus far impeded the actual realization of such an agenda (and which show few signs of waning in the foreseeable future).

Conclusion

This chapter has argued that, whilst EU-level social democratic party actors have sought to develop a 'Social Europe' agenda, this has, nevertheless, remained underdeveloped as a result of the significant obstacles to such policies that exist at the European level (see also Bailey, 2008). As a result, social democratic party elite actors developing, and promoting, a 'Social Europe' agenda within the European Union are able to *both* promote policies that will seek to engender the decommodification of European citizens, and therefore appeal to a constituency that has been historically constructed around such aims, *and* experience institutional obstacles preventing the realization of these attempts at EU-level decommodification. As such, the 'Social Europe' agenda enables a (partial) reconciliation of the contradictory pressures generated by the structure of 'new' social democratic party relations. As we witnessed in our survey of PES policy statements, the 'Social Europe' agenda espoused by social democratic actors operating at the supranational level is itself routinely limited to similar policy ambitions to those adopted at the (apparently more constrained) national level. In an institutional environment characterized by obstacles to substantial policy-making, therefore, social democratic party elites are able to draw upon these obstacles in explaining, and thereby in part legitimating, both the need to limit policy ambitions and the limited policy outcomes that have resulted from their policy advocacy.[4] Thus, in the words of Ulpu Iivari (former MEP, Finnish SDP/PES),

> we need some kind of harmonisation of taxation on capital and taxation of environment. It's really very, very difficult. So-called national interests will come always first. And it's very understandable because prime ministers and other ministers are worrying what will happen in the national elections. It's very difficult to tell the people that the European interest can also be a national interest.
>
> (interview with author, 4 December 2002)

As such, European integration enables both the pursuit of decommodifying public policies and the legitimation of unsuccessful attempts to do so. Considering that the real definition of 'new' social democratic party relations presented in chapter three argued that 'new' social democratic parties are characterized by the attempt to suppress the demands for decommodification of a constituency historically constructed around the pursuit of such demands, the opportunity presented by European integration to realize these conflicting pressures appears far less paradoxical than when considered in the opening chapter. As such, the paradox of the 'new' social democratic turn to 'Social Europe' can be viewed as an attempt by social democratic party elites to reconcile the conflicting pressures – to both suppress and represent demands for decommodification – generated by the contradictory structure of 'new' social democratic party relations.

Conclusion

This book has sought to address the paradox of the 'new' social democratic turn to 'Social Europe'. The socio-economic and political changes that occurred across the developed world since the early 1970s include the end of the Bretton Woods system, the demise of the Keynesian consensus, the prolonged economic downturn that followed the end of the *Trente Glorieuses*, the move to post-Fordist production techniques, and the internationalization (or 'globalization') of economic and political institutions. As part of this process of global socio-economic and political transformation we have also witnessed social democratic parties undertake a number of important changes. We have witnessed the adoption (national variations notwithstanding) of a 'new' social democratic policy programme more heavily focused upon fiscal balance, supply-side economic reforms, means-tested welfare provisions, 'active' labour market policies, and the role of the market (rather than the state) in resource allocation. As the first chapter observed, and later chapters confirmed, this shift towards a 'new' social democratic programme also witnessed a heightened enthusiasm within social democratic parties for the opportunities provided by the process of European integration. In particular, social democratic party actors began to argue that, whilst their capacity to implement more 'traditional' redistributive and/or interventionist policies had been undermined at the national level, supranational coordination might enable the overcoming of such obstacles at the European level. In short, the European Union was presented as a means by which social democratic parties might compensate for the pressures they experienced to limit their interventionist, redistributive, or 'decommodifying' policy aims. This book began by problematizing this view of European integration. It argued that the institutions of the European Union are ill-equipped to produce significant redistributive policy outcomes, and that the process of European integration has arguably acted to encourage, or at least consolidate, the move towards the market-conforming policies, institutions and ideologies across Europe, which advocates of the 'new' social democratic turn to 'Social Europe' claim (or at least imply) that they seek to reverse. As such, the 'new' social democratic turn to 'Social Europe' presents something of a paradox.

In seeking to solve this paradox the present study adopted a critical realist approach, which it argued facilitated the making of explanations that consider both contextual changes, and the way in which agents respond to those changes, something that existing explanations have thus far failed to do. In providing a methodological apparatus through which to explain social outcomes in terms of both structures and agents, therefore, the critical realist approach adopted here has enabled an investigation into the way in which particular actors seek to reproduce and/or transform the social structures and social relations within which they are embedded. Moreover, in drawing upon both Marxist and anarchist theories of social democratic parties, the study has sought to conceptualize the social relationships that constituted 'traditional' social democratic parties and which constitute the 'new' social democratic parties they have become. On this basis it has been possible to derive an explanation for the paradox of the 'new' social democratic turn to 'Social Europe'. The particular merit of the critical realist approach, therefore, is that in pointing towards a focus upon the social relationships that have generated particular events, it forces an awareness of both the structures within which actors are located, and the motivations of actors within those structures, whilst nevertheless avoiding a determinism that views one as the linear and invariable cause of the other. Critical realism, therefore, provides us with the methodological apparatus through which to provide explanations for a social reality that by its very nature resists empirical regularity as either a criterion for verification or the basis for falsification.

The merits derived from Marxist and anarchist theory, moreover, are that they provide us with a series of conceptual insights into the particular relations we sought to examine in the present study, focusing in particular on the problems associated with those relations. Thus, not only do both Marxist and anarchist theories seek to conceptualize relevant social relationships, and thereby provide some analytical meat to put on the bones of the critical realist method adopted herein, but they also problematize those relationships, thereby providing important insights into both why they might undergo change, and the motivations of actors acting to produce that change. As such, the methodological and theoretical approaches adopted in the present study have, hopefully, proven mutually complementary.

The key findings of the research are two-fold. First, the transition from 'traditional' to 'new' social democratic parties resulted from the tensions internal to the structure of 'traditional' social democratic party relations. In particular, there existed a tension between, on the one hand, the construction of a political constituency mobilized around the pursuit of decommodifying public policies, and, on the other hand, the need to contain those demands in order that they would avoid the undermining of either the relationship of representation between the party elite and the wider political constituency, or the capital–labour relations which that party elite sought to reproduce. As these tensions became increasingly problematic, so 'traditional' social democratic party leaders sought to combine a move towards a policy programme that more consistently sought the recommodification of labour, with an appeal to their electoral constituents (the core of whom would be most directly affected by this process of recommodification) to limit their demands for decommodification and therefore provide electoral support for a 'new' social democratic policy framework. 'New' social democratic party relations, therefore, can be conceptualized as the attempt by the social democratic party elite to further limit the demands of their constituents, in order that those demands can be 'represented' in a form that is compatible with the reproduction of the capital–labour relations that constitute the national capitalist economy over which they seek to govern. Second, understood in these terms, the promise of 'Social Europe' has a dual-edged advantage for 'new' social democratic party elites. In promoting the idea that a more redistributive, interventionist, or decommodifying agenda can be achieved by 'new' social democratic parties, *provided* these aims are coordinated amongst social democratic parties and party actors operating at the European level, 'new' social democratic party elites are able to convey two important messages. On the one hand, in advancing the argument that supranational-level coordination is necessary in order to resolve contemporary problems within (global) capitalism, 'new' social democratic party elites are able to further propound the view that it is no longer possible for substantial decommodifying measures to be implemented by national governments unilaterally applying *national* economic policy measures. As such, the 'Social Europe' agenda contributes to a general attempt to limit the (domestic level) demands of 'new' social democratic constituents for national-level decommodifying measures. On the other hand, in engendering a faith in the prospect of reasserting decommodifying policy aims at the supranational level, the promise of 'Social Europe' enables 'new' social democratic party elites to continue to appeal to a 'traditional' constituency on the basis that, *if the institutional scale is sufficient*, 'new' social democratic party elites *will* continue to seek the realization of decommodifying public policies, a goal around which social democratic party constituencies have been historically constructed. Moreover, as the institutional obstacles to European level decision-making significantly impede the realization of such an agenda, 'new' social democratic party actors are also able to explain, and legitimate, their inability to produce such outcomes at the EU-level through reference to institutional factors that are external to their own motives, actions and party relations. The 'new' social democratic turn to 'Social Europe', therefore, enables the pursuit, but the non-realization, of decommodifying policies, both of which appease (at least in part) the contradictory pressures generated by the structure of 'new' social democratic party relations.

Implications for contemporary debates on social democracy

These findings have a number of implications for some of the contemporary debates on social democracy introduced at the beginning of this book. Of particular importance are two questions. First, to what extent should we expect more interventionist, redistributive or decommodifying policies to be re-adopted by 'traditional' social democratic parties? Second, to what extent should we expect such policies to be re-introduced at the European level? The analysis contained within the present study clearly adopts a pessimistic response to both questions. Thus, one of the central claims of the present study is that (both 'traditional' and 'new') social democratic parties should be conceptualized as an attempt by social democratic party elites to contain the demands of their constituents. In witnessing the transformation from 'traditional' to 'new' social democracy, therefore, one of the key trends we observe is a shift towards a *greater* emphasis upon constraint, in part due to the problems associated with the extent to which constituents' demands were both expressed and realized within 'traditional' social democratic party relations. As such, whilst we cannot of course rule out entirely the possibility of a re-activation of European workers organizing to demand decommodifying measures from the state, and/or social democratic political elites seeking to reconstruct an electoral constituency on the basis of an appeal to more substantive decommodifying public policies, there are a number of reasons for being sceptical about the possibility of such outcomes occurring. In particular, there is a lack of motivating factors that would stimulate social democratic party elites to pursue party reforms which might re-problematize their attempts to reproduce social democratic party relations. As such, we might expect social democratic party elites to be resistant towards any attempts to reconstruct a party constituency mobilized around decommodifying public policy ambitions. Moreover, given this resistance, we might expect those individuals who continue to seek such decommodifying outcomes to dedicate their energies towards more amenable institutions, movements and types of activities. From this perspective, therefore, in contrast to those accounts which view social democratic parties as continuing to possess the potential for a return to more 'traditional' social democratic aims (see, for instance, Leggett, 2007; Fitzpatrick, 2007), we might instead have observed the end of the period during which social democratic parties have been vehicles through which substantive decommodifying policies are likely and/or able to be sought.

Second, on the question of a social democratization of the European Union, or the assertion of redistributive, interventionist, or decommodifying policies at the European level, the implications of the present study are equally pessimistic. Thus, having argued that the key attraction of the supranational level for social democratic party elites is the prospect that it offers for the pursuit of a decommodifying 'Social Europe' agenda, whilst nevertheless ensuring the continuation of market-conforming policy outcomes, the likelihood of achieving decommodifying outcomes through the institutions of the European Union appears *more* slim than it does at the national level. Thus, in contrast to those scholars who either seek, or anticipate, the achievement of a more substantive supranational social democracy (Albers *et al.*, 2006; Hay, 2002b), this book argues instead that it is precisely at the European level that social democratic public policy measures are *less* likely to be realized. Indeed, at the European level there exists a policy tradition that favours market-conforming over market-correcting policies, a limited budget and institutional capacity, and a tendency to adopt non-binding, apparently ineffective policy commitments. Moreover, the continued elitist nature of policy-making in Brussels, and the much maligned absence of a European 'demos' (Weiler, 1999; Cederman, 2001; Scharpf, 1999), ensure that popular pressure is unlikely in the foreseeable future to exert itself upon the decision-making preferences of a European technocratic elite. Thus, it is the argument of this book that it is precisely *because* of the unsuitability of the EU's institutional terrain for redistributive, interventionist or decommodifying public policy outcomes that Europe's 'new' social democratic party elite seeks to cede decision-making capacity to the European level. As such, the prospect of those party elites subsequently seeking to fundamentally change that institutional terrain would seem unlikely. There would appear, therefore, to be a significant lack of political actors operating at the European level that might act to bring about the move to 'Social Europe' anticipated by a number of observers.

Nevertheless, if a representative political agent promoting 'Social Europe' were to, first, emerge, and, second, overcome the substantial institutional obstacles to the realization of supranational decommodifying public policy aims, once the European capitalist economy underwent another crisis of overaccumulation, those decommodifying measures would of course act once again to problematize the wider relations of representation and/or capitalism that (partly) constituted that hypothetical actor. In co-existing with processes of representative democracy and capitalism, therefore, the concept of 'Social Europe' itself rests upon an unstable structure of (representative-democratic and capitalist) social relations, the transcendence of which might be a more realistic strategy for those seeking to advance the decommodification of European citizens' lives.

Tensions in 'new' social democratic party relations

In this present study both the transformation from 'traditional' to 'new' social democratic party relations, and the 'new' social democratic turn to 'Social Europe', have been conceptualized as attempts by social democratic party elites to overcome the problems experienced in reproducing social democratic party relations. It does not necessarily follow, however, that the reproduction of *'new'* social democratic party relations is itself an unproblematic process, the turn to 'Social Europe' notwithstanding. Indeed, if we conceptualize the transformation from 'traditional' to 'new' social democratic party relations as in part characterized by an increase in the attempt to contain the demands for decommodification of a constituency historically constructed around the pursuit of such demands, we might well expect social democratic party constituents to display signs of disaffection. Moreover, if we argue that the turn to 'Social Europe' is an attempt to pursue, within an unsuitable institutional terrain, decommodifying policies that are unlikely to be realized, we might also expect a withering of support for such an approach over time as its inability to produce the anticipated policy outcomes becomes more apparent. Thus, two tensions in particular stand out as being potentially problematic for contemporary 'new' social democratic party relations. First, we might expect a decline in the ability of social democratic party elites to secure the sustained support of a core electorate as traditional policy commitments, upon which 'traditional' social democratic party identification was based in the past, are dropped from social democratic party programmes. Second, as the prospect of realizing 'Social Europe' appears increasingly unlikely the longer time elapses without it being realized, so we might expect the extent to which support for 'new' social democratic parties can be bolstered on the basis of such a goal to decline. Indeed, given that we have argued that European integration has acted to consolidate some of the recommodifying initiatives introduced in the European capitalist economy over the previous two decades, we might also expect a return to a more Eurosceptic position by (sections of) the social democratic party constituency as the absence of subsequent developments towards more decommodifying policy outcomes at the supranational level becomes increasingly apparent. A brief assessment of the development of 'new' social democratic party relations following the initial turn to 'Social Europe', therefore, has the potential to offer important insights into the current structure of social democratic party relations and the likelihood that these might undergo continuity and/or change in the foreseeable future. In an attempt to provide an initial investigation into these potential tensions in 'new' social democratic party relations, therefore, what follows is an (admittedly brief) overview of the key developments to have affected each of the social democratic parties that comprise our present study, with particular reference to the way in which the potential tensions highlighted above have acted to problematize the reproduction of 'new' social democratic party relations.

UK

During its period in office, from 1997 to the current time of writing (September 2008), 'New Labour' has been widely viewed as one of the more 'new', 'third way', or 'neoliberal' of the 'new' social democratic parties to have emerged over the previous two decades (Hall, 2002; Motta and Bailey, 2007; Merkel *et al.*, 2008). Thus, New Labour in office, under both Blair and Brown, has implemented a programme that sought to place greater emphasis upon the duty to work, and to stimulate growth primarily through an opening of markets and the promotion of a more adaptable labour market. As such, the Labour Party has undergone a significant and substantive transformation from 'traditional' to 'new' social democratic party relations. In this sense, moreover, the Labour Party is also able to provide perhaps the clearest insights into the tensions arising from 'new' social democratic party relations. Indeed, both of the potential problems highlighted above have particularly affected the Labour Party. Thus, in terms of electoral support, whilst the Labour Party experienced a decline in support between the elections of 1997 and 2005, from 43 per cent of the vote in 1997 to 35 per cent in 2005, this might be considered predictable following eight years in office. What was more noteworthy, therefore, was a simultaneous decline in electoral turnout. Taking this into account, the Labour Party's share of the electoral support of the entire electorate (including non-voters) declined from 30.8 per cent in 1997, through 24.18 per cent in 2001, to 21.6 per cent in 2005. Indeed, calculated in these terms, the 2005 general election victory witnessed the Labour Party gain only slightly above the total electoral support that it achieved in 1983 (20.1 per cent), and considerably lower than it did in 1979 (28.1 per cent). The extent to which this decline in total support for the Labour Party was due to the transformation from 'traditional' to 'new' social democracy can be inferred by data examining voters' perceptions. Most notably, the ability of the Labour Party to mobilize voter interest in areas typically associated with decommodifying public policies appears to have declined considerably. For instance, Clarke, *et al.* (2006: 5) show how voter interest in social services, an area on which the Labour Party is traditionally able to out-compete the Conservative Party, has declined from 38 per cent in 2001 to 25 per cent in 2005 (measured in terms of those viewing health and education as the most important issues facing the country). As a result, a number of commentators argued that, rather than being able to appeal to the British electorate on the basis of its policy programme, the Labour Party was only able to win the 2005 general election as a result of the unpopularity and perceived ineffectiveness of the Conservative opposition (Quinn, 2006; Clarke, *et al.*, 2006).

In terms of European integration, moreover, any potential benefit that support for the European Union had offered the Labour Party during both the transformation from 'Old' to 'New' Labour, and during the 1997 general election campaign, had by the time of the 2005 election dwindled significantly. Again, this is arguably due to the reluctance of the Labour Government to promote substantively decommodifying public policies at the EU-level, for instance witnessing the Labour Party repeatedly oppose moves towards the adoption of the Temporary Workers Directive (Nedergaard, 2007). Indeed, for much of the post-1997 period, the Labour Government was actually keen to avoid any high profile mention of European integration at all, thereby seeking to reduce the salience of the European question. This was largely for fear of alienating a relatively Eurosceptic electorate (Oppermann, 2008). This reduced salience manifested itself in two important ways. First, in terms of party competition, by the time of the 2005 general election, 'Europe barely registered as a campaign issue' (Geddes, 2005: 290). Second, at the level of the electorate, the saliency of European integration fell from being an important issue for 43 per cent of the electorate in 1997, through a level of over 20 per cent in 2001, to less than 10 per cent in 2005 (Oppermann, 2008: 164–5). Indeed, European integration fell from being the most important issue for 7 per cent of the electorate in 2001 to being so for just 2 per cent in 2005 (Clarke, *et al.*, 2006: 6). The ability of the Labour Government to draw upon its position on European integration in its attempt to bolster electoral support, therefore, has significantly waned throughout New Labour's period in office.

Sweden

In the case of the Swedish SAP, the transformation from 'traditional' to 'new' social democracy had a similar effect to that witnessed in Britain, in terms of both a reduction in consistent electoral support, and the apparent inability of the SAP party elite to persuade its core constituency of the interventionist, redistributive or decommodifying benefits of European integration. Thus, following the SAP Government's prolonged period of budget consolidation in the 1994–98 legislative period, during which, Chapter 3 argued, the SAP consolidated its 'new' social democratic structure of party relations, the SAP lost 8.8 per cent of its vote share, with most defecting voters moving to the Left Party (which was increasingly advocating a 'traditional' social democratic policy programme) (Möller, 1999; Merkel *et al.*, 2008: 165). After a brief reprise in the 2002 election, when the vote share rose from 36.6 per cent (1998) to 39.9 per cent (although this was still below the share won in the election defeats of 1976 and 1979), the SAP was voted out of office in

2006 for only the third time in Sweden's post-war history, with its vote share falling to 35 per cent. A key factor in this defeat, moreover, was the SAP Government's inability to reduce unemployment, measured by the OECD in 2006 at 8.5 per cent (but arguably higher when training schemes and subsidized temporary jobs were taken into account). Thus, having overseen a shift towards a 'new' social democratic structure of party relations and a concomitant move towards the implementation of a 'new' social democratic policy programme, the SAP leadership left itself without a substantive policy programme (especially on employment) to deliver to its key electorate. This was an omission which was adeptly utilized by the opposition Moderates in their successful appeal for votes on the grounds of their (albeit more neoliberal) employment creation programme, which enabled them to gain votes directly from the SAP and young and new voters (Aylott and Bolin, 2007).

On the question of European integration, moreover, whilst the SAP political elite has largely sought to ensure the continued support of its core constituency through the appeal to a 'Social Europe' agenda, the success with which it has achieved this aim is questionable. Perhaps most notably, in 2003 the Swedish electorate voted against adopting the Euro, with 56 per cent of those identifying with the SAP voting 'no' in the referendum on EMU membership (Eurobarometer, 2003), and thereby rejecting the advice of the SAP Government and especially that of Prime Minister Goran Persson. This reflected a wider malaise within the SAP regarding the question of Europe, and particularly the 'Social Europe' agenda, which extended through to sections of the actual social democratic cabinet (Aylott and Bolin, 2007: 622). Indeed, perhaps most starkly highlighting the tensions present within the 'new' social democratic turn to 'Social Europe', many social democratic critics of European integration view the EU as a threat to the Swedish welfare model, particularly as any move towards 'Social Europe' might represent a *downscaling* of welfare provision within Sweden. Thus, in the words of *Riksdag* member, Leif Jakobsson,

> the question of 'Social Europe' means something else in Sweden because we don't agree on minimum wages, for example, or other things in the welfare system because we think if we harmonize in the social area it will probably go down. That's no option for us. ... So, we are not in favour of harmonizing or European taxation or that kind of thing. ... If you're on the upper part of the standards of the welfare state then of course people are afraid of becoming worse.
> (interview with Leif Jakobsson, 9 April 2008)

In this sense, therefore, given that Sweden has a historically high level of welfare generosity, European integration has come to represent something of a threat for those within Sweden seeking the maintenance of those decommodifying measures which are currently in place. Indeed, this is a fear that was compounded by the December 2007 Laval Ruling of the ECJ, which threatened to further liberalize the Swedish labour market (interview with Tone Tingsgård, 11 April 2008). The turn by the SAP leadership towards 'Social Europe', therefore, has itself given rise to a number of tensions within the structure of 'new' social democratic party relations.

France

As with the Labour Party and the SAP, the French PS has also experienced a number of significant problems arising from tensions generated by the move towards 'new' social democratic party relations, in terms of both electoral support and the electoral appeal of the PS' European policy. In terms of electoral support, therefore, the moves towards the adoption of 'new' social democratic policies by the Jospin Government, including privatization and the flexibility measures that formed part of the 35-hour week legislation, prompted resentment amongst key sections of the PS constituency who viewed these developments as contrary to a more 'traditional' PS agenda. This was compounded in 2002 by an election campaign 'in which the reference to workers was abandoned and which appeared to be more like the American Democrats than social democrats' (Bell, 2003a: 80–1). Indeed, one of the most frequently quoted statements of the election witnessed Jospin declare his 'not being a socialist' (Cole, 2002: 323). The result, as is well known, was the spectacular defeat of Jospin into third place in the first round of the presidential election, at the hands of the far-right National Front, and the defeat at the hands of the newly-formed Union for the Presidential Majority (UMP) in the general election of the same year. The election also witnessed parties on the right gain equal or better vote shares amongst key occupational groups, such as the working class, employees and the intermediate professions, each of which historically provided important electoral support for the PS (Bell, 2003a: 81). Moreover, the fact that one-third of the working-class electorate voted for Le Pen in the first round of the presidential election can be viewed as a clear sign of the disillusion experienced by many within the PS core constituency (Miguet, 2002: 208). Following electoral defeat in 2002, moreover, the PS was left without a clear direction or leadership, with François Hollande, Fabius and Strauss-Kahn each competing for the leadership of the party without clear ideological positions. Rather than ideological conviction, therefore, each of the candidates sought instead to promote a rather vacuous attempt to further 'modernize' the PS party programme and reduce, or make more effective, the role of the state within the market (Bell, 2003b: 33–5). Indeed, this inability, following the move towards 'new' social democratic party relations, to adopt a coherent ideological alternative that would appeal to a core electoral constituency, in part explains both the adoption, and the subsequent defeat, of Ségolène Royal as PS leader and presidential candidate in the 2007 elections in France. Thus, in seeking to unify the PS, party leader Hollande sought agreement around a new party programme at the Le Mans congress of 2005. Nevertheless, this programme 'suffered from its overriding aim of not offending any of the party's factions', therefore ending up being vacuous and unappealing (Knapp and Sawicki, 2008: 53–4). In such a context, Royal was able to draw upon the apparent bankruptcy of the established PS leadership, and an influx of new '20-euro' party members, to gain election as the party's presidential candidate in 2007 on the basis of a platform that appeared unconstrained by the PS' own programme and historical tradition. On more substantive issues relating to traditional PS constituents' concerns, however, 'the overall impression was that she had not worked out her position on the great issues of the day, such as the financing of social protection and pensions, tax, the working week and education' (Knapp and Sawicki, 2008: 55). Thus, whilst Royal did well to achieve 25.9 per cent of the vote in the first round of the presidential elections, this was largely the result of the collapse in support for other left party rivals, which itself could be viewed as an attempt by the electorate to avoid a repeat of the success of the National Front. The problem, however, was that a significant share of Royal's support in the first round was based on a fear of the National Front. This therefore meant that she had less of a positive programme to appeal to the electorate on when it came to the second round of the presidential election once the National Front had been defeated. As a result, Royal lost the 2007 election (gaining 47 per cent of the vote, compared with 53 per cent for Nicolas Sarkozy), and the PS also lost the subsequent general election the following month. This suggested, therefore, that remaining electoral support for the PS was largely based on a negative 'least-bad' calculation, rather than positive support. Indeed, indicative of this trend was a CEVIPOF poll that indicated that those identifying themselves as 'close to' the PS had fallen from 40 per cent of the electorate in 1998 to 23 per cent in 2007 (Cautrès with Cole, 2008).

Whilst, as we saw in Chapter 4, the PS's position on European integration is largely viewed as being a key contributory factor in its election victory of 1997, by 2002 the promise of a 'Social Europe' agenda had largely evaporated as a means by which the PS party elite could bolster electoral support for its 'new' social democratic policy programme. Thus, Cole notes how, in 2002, 'there was no real debate on Europe', in part because 'neither Jospin nor Chirac wanted Europe to become an issue of debate, not least because partisan opinion appeared divided on the issue and neither leader had built a reputation as a respected European statesman' (2002: 324–5). Thus, following election defeat in 2002, some within the party began to express dissatisfaction at the meagre concrete policy outputs that had been achieved at the European level. This fuelled the ascendance of a more Eurosceptic wing within the *Parti Socialiste*, members of which particularly focused upon the 'neoliberal' elements of European integration and the apparently limited prospect of redressing this tendency through the promotion of decommodifying policies and/or legislation in Brussels. Thus, whilst the PS, and particularly the PS leadership, remained generally united around a pro-EU position, a tendency emerged within the wider party membership which was sceptical about the benefits of *further* integration. Indeed, Laurent Fabius sought to mobilize this current in his attempt to lead the socialist 'no' vote in the 2005 referendum on the European Constitutional Treaty (interviews with Bernard Derosier, 23 April 2008, and Christian Sautter, 24 April 2008). As a result, one third of the PS voted for a 'no' vote in the party conference held to adopt a PS position on the 2005 referendum in the party (Knapp and Sawicki, 2008: 53). Furthermore, 61 per cent of PS voters voted against the Constitution and against the official PS line, with the impact of European integration upon employment, the liberalism of European integration, and the lack of a substantive 'social Europe' all cited amongst the top five reasons given by 'no' voters for their decision (Eurobarometer, 2005).

This increased hostility towards European integration therefore represents to a certain degree the failure by the PS leadership to realize the 'Social Europe' agenda it had been actively pursuing for much of the post-1983 period. Thus, in the words of Daniel Goldberg,

> before, with Maastricht, the socialists made a bet, thinking that if we further integrate on the economic side, the social side will be better. However, 15 years later, I felt that we had lost that bet. So I voted 'no' in the 2005 referendum.
>
> (interview with Daniel Goldberg, 22 April 2008)

Thus, comparing the 2005 referendum with the 1992 Maastricht referendum in France, we can witness a large shift towards Euroscepticism amongst PS voters (Evans, 2007: 1102). As a result, the somewhat vague demands for the 'reconstruction of a political Europe', including a government for the eurozone, growth objectives for the ECB, and the introduction of a new 'social protocol', all of which were contained in Royal's 100-point plan (launched as part of her presidential campaign) (Beunderman, 2007), failed to sufficiently resonate with the French electorate. In this respect, therefore, the 'new' social democratic party relations of the PS have generated a number of significant tensions which have problematized the extent to which they can be successfully reproduced.

Italy

In the case of Italy, political developments in the 2000s have also witnessed significant tensions emerge from the attempt to reproduce 'new' social democratic party relations by the party elites of the DS and newly-formed Democratic Party (PD). Thus, in 2001 the Amato-led *Ulivio* coalition Government was voted out of office and replaced by Berlusconi's right-wing House of Freedoms coalition. Whilst Berlusconi's victory in 2001 was largely due to his improved ability to hold together a coalition that included both the National Alliance and, especially, the Northern League, the electoral support for the DS was particularly poor, falling from 21.1 per cent in 1996 (for the PDS) to 16.6 per cent in 2001[1] (Newell and Bull, 2002: 629–32). The ability of the 'new' social democratic DS to attract the support of a coherent electoral constituency, particularly following a period in office during which it had focused heavily on restrictive measures that sought to ensure Italy's membership of the EMU, was, therefore, significantly questioned by the results of the 2001 election. Thus, the fact that the DS lost support in the regions where it traditionally did well, and also that the election witnessed both private sector workers and the unemployed being more likely to vote for Berlusconi's Forza Italia (FI) (19.4 per cent of private sector workers voted for the DS, compared with 28 per cent for FI, and 12 per cent of unemployed workers voted for DS, compared with 42.2 per cent for FI), suggested that the DS had struggled to hold on to the electoral support of large sections of its traditional constituency. This was viewed by many commentators as a result of the incoherence of the PDS/DS party programme. Thus, having successfully adopted a position that favoured economic stability, fiscal orthodoxy and wage restraint, the PDS/DS had nevertheless failed to advocate (or implement) a sufficiently reformist (or decommodifying) agenda that would appeal to a centre-left constituency historically constructed around either decommodifying reforms or a more ideological commitment to the transcendence of capitalism (Bull, 2003: 62–8).

Once out of office, the DS leadership sough to re-engage with, and reconstruct, a coherent electoral constituency. However, this also prompted an internal division within the party leadership, witnessing a divide between a dominant group favouring a 'new' social democratic strategy, led by new party leader, Piero Fassino, and a minority faction, led by Giovanni Berlinguer (brother of former leader, the late Enrico Berlinguer), which sought a move towards a more 'traditional' social democratic strategy that would return to the 'centrality of labour'. The victory of the Fassino faction, therefore, represented a consolidation of 'new' social democratic party relations within the DS, especially as the centrist electoral strategy implied by Fassino's renewed commitment to the *Ulivio* coalition prevented the party from adopting more substantively interventionist economic policies (Bull, 2003). By the time of the 2006 general election, the (newly-named) *Unione* coalition (*L'Unione*) consisting of a very broad coalition of left parties, from the Refoundation Communists through the DS to a number of new parties formed out of previous left-leaning ex-Christian democrat parties and Radicals stood for election. This new alliance won a narrow majority of the vote share but, due to a new electoral system, this translated into a viable majority within the chamber of deputies, enabling Romano Prodi to form his second centre-left government. This victory was on the basis of a platform that included support for further European integration, moderate (and ambiguous) fiscal initiatives that included the reintroduction of inheritance tax and the harmonization of tax rates on financial activities, and the introduction of limits upon the use of temporary labour (which, rather ironically, the *Ulivio* coalition had done much to promote during its 1996–2001 period in office). Whilst the campaign performance of the centre-left coalition was generally viewed as unimpressive, the electorate narrowly opted for the Prodi-led coalition (with vote shares remaining similar to that achieved in 2001) in part due to a desire for change amongst the electorate following five years of Berlusconi in government (Giannetti and De Giorgi, 2006: 509–10; Newell, 2006: 806–11). Once back in office, however, the *Unione* coalition struggled to balance governmental efficacy with the contending demands of the nine parties that made up the coalition (Belluci, 2008: 190). Thus, Finance Minister, Tommaso Padoa-Schioppa, implemented a controversial budget package in 2006 that sought to cut the Italian budget deficit through the introduction of higher income taxes for higher income earners. A series of market liberalizing measures, named the Bersani decree, were also implemented in 2006, despite opposition from a series of vested interests. From early 2007, moreover, the Prodi Government set about implementing more significant liberalizing measures, seeking to introduce a greater degree of competition into the Italian economy. However, the coalition's fragile parliamentary majority was routinely tested, leading the Prodi coalition to resign (and be reinstated) in February 2007 and, by early 2008 the coalition fractured, in part over the rise in tax incidence that the coalition government had introduced, resulting in a new general election. The 2008 election witnessed the new Democratic Party (PD) (formed largely out of the DS and the ex-DC party, *Democrazia è Libertà – La Margherita*), which was itself a further consolidation of the centrist electoral strategy of the PDS/DS leadership, gain 37.5 per cent of the vote for the lower house, compared with 46.8 per cent for Berlusconi's coalition. Whilst the centre-left held its ground electorally, this continued to prove insufficient to deliver a stable centre-left government (Brunazzo and Gilbert, 2008). Thus, the reproduction of 'new' social democratic party relations in the case of Italy has witnessed a consistent move towards the ideological centre and a strategy of coalition-building in an attempt to broaden the electoral base of a centre-right coalition as much as possible. Nevertheless, in doing so, the leadership of the DS and the new PD have been unable to ensure sufficient electoral support to either hold together a stable coalition government (from 2006–08) or, in 2008, to gain election to office.

With regard to Europe, the Italian electorate has been historically pro-European throughout most of its post-war history. As a result, as we witnessed in Chapter 4, the turn to 'Social Europe' by the PDS/DS enabled a significant legitimation of restrictive measures adopted under the remit of EMU membership. This method of legitimation was repeated by the second Prodi Government. Thus, the budget measures introduced by the 2006–8 government sought to ensure that the Italian economy would stay within the 3 per cent budget deficit ceiling of the Stability and Growth Pact. This arguably enabled Berlusconi, in adopting a more populist Eurosceptical position, to tap into a decline in support amongst the Italian electorate for the European Union (Quaglia and Radaelli, 2007: 930–1, 937). Whilst there was no outright Eurosceptic reaction to the PDS/DS/PD position on European integration, the unpopularity of the second Prodi Government and the poor performance, relative to Berlusconi, in the 2008 election suggests that the legitimating effect of support for the European Union may have dwindled in contemporary Italian politics.

Spain

Finally, in the case of Spain, the implementation by the Socialist government of restrictive policy aims throughout much of its 1982–96 period in office, in large part justified in terms of the demands of joining, first, the EC, and then EMU, eventually led to a period in opposition between 1996 and 2004 during which the PSOE leadership was unable to construct a sufficiently distinctive party identity to present to the electorate. Indeed, following its deselection from office in 1996, the PSOE struggled to distinguish itself from the new Popular Party (PP) Government, particularly due to the emphasis on restrictive policies and EMU membership espoused by both parties (Kennedy, 2003). Nevertheless, the PSOE 'new' social democratic party relations have perhaps shown least signs of internal tensions (of the parties that form the present study), particularly since its election to office in 2004. The loss of the 1996 general election did lead to a period of turmoil for the PSOE as the leadership struggled to reconstruct itself as an electorally viable party. Thus, following the resignation of Gonzalez in 1997, the subsequent rivalry for the party leadership, between Joaquín Almunia and José Borrell, created confusion amongst the electorate. This was compounded in the 2000 general election campaign by a hastily contrived alliance between the PSOE and the ex-communist dominated United Left, which created the appearance of both opportunism and ideological uncertainty. The fallout of the 2000 election defeat, in which large numbers of traditional PSOE voters abstained from voting, witnessed the election of José Luis Rodríguez Zapatero as the new PSOE leader. Thus, between 1997 and 2000, the PSOE had four different leaders. Nevertheless, following Zapatero's election as PSOE leader, the party sought to reinvigorate its public image. Yet, 'the PSOE did not question the main elements of the economic policy carried out by the PP Government', but rather opposed the PP on its handling of Iraq, the *Prestige* oil tanker spillage, and the government's 'authoritarian' style of governing. Moreover, 'the PSOE placed greater emphasis on non-economic policies, such as institutional reform and civil rights' (Méndez Lago, 2006: 432). Whilst the PSOE won the 2004 general election, this was in large part a protest against the communication strategy of the PP Government, particularly its infamous handling of the 2004 Madrid bombings immediately prior to the election. Indeed, the PP was leading in the opinion polls for much of the 2004 election campaign, with the Madrid bombings marking a significant turning point. The 2004 victory was therefore built largely upon the foreign and security policies of the PSOE (which it contrasted with those of the PP), rather than upon traditional commitments to redistributive or decommodifying public policies. Whilst the PSOE leadership did seek to criticize the large incidence of temporary job contracts within the Spanish labour market, the fact that the PSOE had consistently implemented legislation to stimulate such employment patterns meant it was poorly placed to present an alternative labour market model (Blakeley, 2006; Kennedy, 2003). The PSOE was also re-elected in 2008, thereby evincing signs of being one of the more successful 'new' social democratic parties in western Europe. Nevertheless, this followed a period of considerable economic growth,[2] which itself appears to have been facilitated by an unsustainable housing market bubble, thereby questioning the extent to which the PSOE will be able to maintain electoral support for its 'new' social democratic programme, with its emphasis on recommodification, under worse economic conditions expected to result from the Spanish housing market crisis.

Similarly, the PSOE's European policy has also been less obviously prone to generating party tensions than with other 'new' social democratic parties. Indeed, the PSOE successfully portrayed itself as the pro-European party within the Spanish party system in 2004, opposing both the PP's hampering of an agreement at the 2003 IGC on the draft European Constitutional Treaty and what it argued was an Atlanticist foreign policy (Blakeley, 2006: 338). Thus, in the 2004 election campaign, the PSOE contrasted itself with the PP Government, which it claimed,

> has altered Spain's fundamental involvement in the EU, moving away from a federal European Union towards an intergovernmental Union, and dependent on the US in foreign affairs and security, limiting the EU to a strictly economic organization, thereby preventing the development of a true political and

economic Union that could serve the interests of its citizens and promote European interests and influence globally.

(PSOE, 2004: 17, own translation)

Moreover, the PSOE continued to highlight the way in which it would promote measures that spoke to the traditional concerns of its constituents, through coordinated European action. Thus, its 2004 general election manifesto claimed that it would seek,

> to build a Europe to promote the welfare and interest and common objectives of its citizens; a Europe capable of exercising its role as an autonomous, global actor, consisting of peace, stability, the eradication of poverty, sustainable development, social and economic progress, equality and respect for human rights.
>
> (PSOE, 2004: 17; own translation)

The success of the 2004 (and subsequent) election campaign(s) would therefore suggest that the PSOE has been able to utilize the (albeit limited) opportunities to appease the demands generated by the historical commitments of the party through European level policy activity. Nevertheless, concern within sections of the PSOE leadership does exist regarding the possibility that the widespread consensus amongst the Spanish electorate regarding the benefits of European integration may be waning as both Spain matures as a European member state and as the focus of EU spending shifts from southern to eastern Europe (interview with Carlos Carnero Gonzalez MEP, 23 May 2008). Rather than leading to a rise of Euroscepticism, however, this trend has largely manifested itself in declining turnout amongst the electorate on European issues. Thus, turnout in the 2005 referendum on the European Constitutional Treaty was only 42.3 per cent, whilst turnout to the 2004 EP elections was only 45.1 per cent. Whilst opposition to European integration remains very low in Spain, therefore, the nature of the support (and the extent to which it can continue to be used to justify otherwise unpopular public policies) is arguably becoming more tenuous.

Final reflections

Thus, whilst it has had a (temporary) ameliorating effect (at least in some cases), the transformation from 'traditional' to 'new' social democracy has failed to resolve some of the central tensions generated by (both 'traditional' and 'new') social democratic party relations. Whilst 'new' social democratic party leaders no longer promise to be able to construct a socialist society, or to oversee a significant decommodification of the lives of their constituents, they also rarely promise to produce a significant redistribution of wealth, power, prestige or life-chances. As a result, for a number of social democratic parties, their programmatic appeal has become both less distinctive and less attractive to the individuals whose electoral support they depend upon. Whilst the promise to improve the operation of labour markets, to more efficiently manage public bureaucracies, or to use market incentives to improve the delivery of public services might (at times) be sufficient to win elections, they nevertheless appear insufficient to enthuse and impassion a stable core constituency. It is this problem which faces social democratic party elites in the present. Whilst, during the transformation to, and the early reproduction of, 'new' social democratic party relations, the turn to 'Social Europe' appeared able to partly compensate (in some cases) for this apparent lack, developments in a number of cases suggest that it might no longer be able to do so. As such, the question facing 'new' social democratic party actors, and particularly those elites that benefit from being at the top of their respective party hierarchies, is how they might re-connect with a citizenry that shows a number of signs of having disconnected from and disengaged with formal politics. Indeed, such a citizenry shows few signs of desiring such a return to a relationship of 'representation'. Perhaps one of the most interesting trends in recent political developments, therefore, is the rise in 'unconventional' or 'informal' politics observed across the developed world, arguably as a direct result of citizens' parallel disaffection with, and disengagement from, 'conventional' or 'formal' politics (Norris, 2004; Rucht, 2006; Li and Marsh, 2008). Thus, a pessimistic reading of the present study might view the argument as somewhat dismal in that it fails to anticipate (and indeed views as highly unlikely) the reconstruction of a more substantive and sustainable social democratic alternative. Considered differently, however, the unlikelihood of social democratic party leaders being able to 'represent' demands for decommodification in the future might not be such a bad thing. Indeed, it might well be viewed as a reason to be optimistic.

Notes

1 The paradox of the 'new' social democratic turn to 'Social Europe'

1 'Social Europe' is considered here the attempt to promote redistributive and regulatory policies with broadly emancipatory aims, producing more egalitarian outcomes than would otherwise occur if left to the market, within the institutions of the EC/EU (for a similar definition, see Bailey, 2008).
2 Whilst public services that facilitate action in the labour market are to be welcomed (i.e. training, education, active labour market policies), those that support the unemployed in a position of 'dependence' (such as unemployment benefit and social insurance) are to be avoided.
3 Thus, 'the possibilities for mitigating deprivation and inequalities are now seen in quite different terms from the 'traditional' emphasis on Keynesian demand management and a universalist welfare state. These are now seen as hampering the capacities of national economies to compete successfully in the global economy. In contrast, supply-side interventions in terms of, for example, developing education and training are seen as the best approach to mitigation since they enhance economic dynamism and competitiveness' (Stammers, 2001: 36–7).
4 This includes a

> shift in the delivery of public services to be more consumer-based, affordable and responsibility-based. These new forms of public-sector service delivery look to the private sector for 'best-practice' techniques and the market may even gain a role in public provision.
>
> (Thomson, 2000: 157)

5 For example, the implementation of an employment policy, under the Employment Chapter, has been predominantly structured around the principles of employability, entrepreneurship, adaptability, and equal opportunities. Thus, three of the four pillars represent market-conforming measures.

2 Analysing party change: a critical realist method

1 The distinction between price/profit and value/surplus value is unnecessary for the purposes of the argument presented herein, and hence the terms are conflated throughout.

3 Decommodification, recommodification, and crisis: the transformation to 'new' social democracy

1 A comment attributed to Gerald Kaufman MP.

2 In contrast with 24 per cent and 19 per cent for rivals John Prescott and Margaret Beckett, respectively.
3 Including Peter Mandelson, Alistair Campbell and Philip Gould, came to form the leadership of the modernizing wing of the party and key proponents of 'New' Labour.
4 The original clause IV had in reality been moribund since at least the 1960s, and arguably since it was written.
5 The total public expenditure as a percentage of GDP grew from around 25 per cent in 1950 to over 60 per cent in 1995, with a significant levelling off in this expansion occurring around 1980 (Vartiainen, 2001: 23–4).
6 It should be noted that for much of this period the French Socialists actually derided the formal label, 'social democracy', on the basis that it inferred an overly moderate ideological stance (Ladrech, 2001: 38).
7 Indeed, Occhetto was a neo-revisionist who had earlier prefaced an Italian translation of German SPD thinker Peter Glotz' *Manifesto for a New European Left*. Occhetto's support for this 'manifesto' was a symbolic association between the PCI and a pro-European social democratic party, representing a significant stage in the 'social democratization' of the PCI (Abse, 2001: 62).
8 Which left the third way, or *terza via*, of Eurocommunism with no two other ways to be in-between.
9 'Civilized growth' was basically a commitment to managed and redistributive capitalist economic growth.
10 In other words, a specific governing policy rather than a vague commitment to overturn capitalism.
11 The UCD's vote collapsed with the result that it only gained 11 seats in the 1982 elections.
12 Although, according to Recio and Roca, 'these measures had practically no effect' on the practice of temporary employment (1998: 148).

4 'New' social democratic party relations and the turn to 'Social Europe'

1 David Owen, Shirley Williams and Bill Rodgers, later to become the Gang of Four when they were joined by Roy Jenkins. Eventually 28 Labour MPs joined the SDP.
2 Although the creation of Solidarity, a faction containing 100 MPs within the PLP, including Roy Hattersley, Peter Shore and Gerald Kaufmann, did counter some of the influence of the hard left within the party.

5 (The absence of) social democracy at the EU-level

1 The PES party federation will be referred to as simply the PES from here onwards.
2 The Italian PSI and French PS opted out of the commitment to worker participation on the grounds that the policy respected the subordination of labour to capital (Hix, 2002: 21).
3 However, the Italian PSI and PSDI both opted to support the Draft Treaty on European Union, which formed an alternative manifesto for their EP election campaign.
4 Indeed, this was a factor frequently cited in a number of field interviews with social democratic actors in Brussels in November and December 2002.

Conclusion

1 These figures are for the proportional section of the vote. Figures for the plurality vote were aggregated for each coalition bloc, therefore precluding an assessment of the vote share for individual parties.
2 Real GDP growth averaged 3.8 per cent in Spain for 2006 and 2007, compared with an average of 2.8 per cent for the EU15 (Eurostat).

List of interviewees

2001–2002

1. Ieke van den Berg MEP (PES, Netherlands), 7 November 2002
2. Maria Berger MEP (PES, Austria), 4 December 2002
3. Ton Beumer (PES General Secretary) and Nick Crook (PES Political Advisor), 11 September 2001
4. Herbert Boesch MEP (PES, Austria), 4 December 2002
5. Paulo Casaca MEP (PES, Portugal), 12 November 2002
6. Michael Cashman MEP (PES, UK), 12 November 2002
7. Richard Corbett MEP (PES, UK), 6 November 2002
8. Dorette Corbey MEP (PES, Netherlands), 27 November 2002
9. Robert Evans MEP (PES, UK), 6 November 2002
10. Goran Farm MEP (PES, Sweden), 4 December 2002
11. Glyn Ford MEP (PES, UK), 28 November 2002
12. Emilio Gabaglio (ETUC General Secretary), 22 November 2002
13. Robert Goebbels MEP (PES, Luxembourg), 25 November 2002
14. Willi Goerlach MEP (PES, Germany), 6 November 2002
15. Ulpu Iivari MEP (PES, Finland), 4 December 2002
16. Neil Kinnock (Vice President, European Commission), 3 December 2002
17. Helmut Kuhne MEP (PES, Germany), 25 November 2002
18. Bill Miller MEP (PES, UK), 11 November 2002
19. Ritta Myller MEP (PES, Finland), 26 November 2002
20. Poul Nielsen (European Commissioner for Development and Humanitarian Aid), 21 November 2002
21. Christa Prets MEP (PES, Austria), 3 December 2002
22. Bernhard Rapkay MEP (PES, Germany), 4 December 2002
23. Karin Scheele MEP (PES, Austria), 27 November 2002
24. Brian Simpson MEP (PES, UK), 5 November 2002
25. Maj Britt Theorin MEP (PES, Sweden), 26 November 2002
26. Nicolas Théry (Chief of Cabinet for Pascal Lamy, European Commissioner for Trade), 3 December 2002
27. Phillip Whitehead MEP (PES, UK), 5 November 2002
28. Terence Wynn MEP (PES, UK), 6 November 2002

April–May 2008

29. Meritxell Batet Lamaña, Member of Congress, Socialists' Party of Catalonia, 21 May 2008
30. Ibrahim Baylan, member of the *Riksdag*, SAP, former Minister for Schools, 11 April 2008
31. Patrik Björk, member of *Riksdag*, SAP, 9 April 2008
32. Laila Bjurling, member of *Riksdag*, SAP, 7 April 2008
33. Carlos Carnero Gonzalez, MEP (PSOE, Spain), 23 May 2008
34. Bernard Derosier, Deputy, National Assembly, *Parti Socialiste*, 23 April 2008
35. Piero Fassino, Member of Congress, Democratic Party, former Minister of Foreign Trade, former Minister of Justice, former National Secretary, Democrats of the Left, 6 May 2008.
36. Juan Fernando López Aguilar, Member of Congress, former Minister of Justice, PSOE, 21 May 2008
37. Daniel Goldberg, Deputy, National Assemly, *Parti Socialiste*, 22 April 2008
38. Jose Ignacio Torreblanca, Head of Madrid Office, European Council on Foreign Relations, 22 May 2008
39. Leif Jakobsson, member of *Riksdag*, SAP, 9 April 2008
40. Allan Larsson, former Minister of Finance, SAP, and former Director-General Employment and Social Affairs, European Commission, 10 April 2008
41. Juan Luis Rascón Ortega, Member of Congress, PSOE, 20 May 2008
42. Juan Moscoso del Prado Hernández, Member of Congress, PSOE, speaker for PSOE of the European Union Committee at Congress, 21 May 2008
43. Jordi Pedret i Grenzner, Member of Congress, Socialists' Party of Catalonia, 20 May 2008
44. Helene Petersson, member of *Riksdag*, SAP, 10 April 2008
45. Leif Pettersson, member of *Riksdag*, SAP, 9 April 2008
46. Franco Russo, former Member of Congress, *Partito Comunista Rifondazione*, 6 May 2008
47. Christian Sautter, Deputy Mayor of Paris, Former Finance and Budget Minister, Former Adviser to President Mitterand, *Parti Socialiste*, 24 April 2008
48. Olle Thorell, member of *Riksdag*, SAP, 16 April 2008, (interview conducted over telephone)
49. Tone Tingsgård, member of *Riksdag*, SAP, 11 April 2008
50. Professor Sören Wibe, former member of *Riksdag*, SAP, and former Chair Social Democratic EU-Critics (1995–2008), 8 April 2008
51. Maryam Yazdanfar, member of *Riksdag*, SAP, 9 April 2008

Bibliography

Abse, T. (2001) 'From PCI to DS: How European Integration Accelerated The "Social Democratization" of the Italian Left', *Journal of Southern Europe and the Balkans*, Vol. 3(1): 61–74.

Aglietta, M. (1979 [2000]) *A Theory of Capitalist Regulation: The US Experience*, London, Verso.

Albers, D., Haseler, S. and Meyer, H. (2006) 'Introduction', in D. Albers, S. Haseler and H. Meyer (eds) *Social Europe: A Continent's Answer to Market Fundamentalism*, London, European Research Forum at London Metropolitan University: 1–8.

Aldcroft, D.H. (2001) *The European Economy 1914–2000*, 4th edition, London, Routledge.

Allan, J.P. and Scruggs, L. (2004) 'Political Partisanship and Welfare State Reform in Advanced Industrial Societies', *American Journal of Political Science*, 48(3): 496–512.

Amato, G. and D'Alema, M. (2002) 'A Home for all European Reformists: An Open Letter to PES', *Italianieuropei. Bimestrale del riformismo italiano*, no. 4 [translated by the Party of European Socialists].

Anderson, K.M. (2001) 'The Politics of Retrenchment in a Social Democratic Welfare State: Reform of Swedish Pensions and Unemployment Insurance', *Comparative Political Studies*, 34(9): 1063–91.

Archer, M.S. (1995) *Realist Social Theory: The Morphogenetic Approach*, Cambridge, Cambridge University Press.

Armstrong, K. (2008) 'JCMS Symposium: EU Governance After Lisbon: Governance and Constitutionalism After Lisbon', *Journal of Common Market Studies*, 46(2): 415–26.

Armstrong, K., Begg, I. and Zeitlin, J. (2008) 'JCMS Symposium: EU Governance After Lisbon: Introduction', *Journal of Common Market Studies*, 46(2): 413–5.

Arter, D. (2003) 'Scandinavia: What's Left is the Social Democratic Welfare Consensus', *Parliamentary Affairs*, 56(1): 75–98.

Arts, W. and Gelissen, J. (2002) 'Three Worlds of Welfare Capitalism or More? A State-of-the-Art Report', *Journal of European Social Policy*: 12(2): 137–58.

Ashiagbor, D. (2005) *The European Employment Strategy: Labour Market Regulation and New Governance*, Oxford, Oxford University Press.

Aust, A. (2004) 'From "Eurokeynesianism" to the "Third Way": The Party of European Socialists (PES) and European employment policies', in G. Bonoli and M. Powell (eds) *Social Democratic Party Policies in Contemporary Europe*, London, Routledge: 180–96.

Aylott, N. (1999) *Swedish Social Democracy and European Integration: The People's Home on the Market*, Aldershot, Ashgate.

Aylott, N. and Bolin, N. (2007) 'Towards a Two Party System? The Swedish Parliamentary Election of September 2006', *West European Politics*, 30(3): 621–33.

Bailey, D.J. (2005) 'Obfuscation through Integration: Legitimating "New" Social Democracy in the European Union', *Journal of Common Market Studies*, 43(1): 13–35.
—— (2008) 'Explaining the Underdevelopment of "Social Europe": A Critical Realization', *Journal of European Social Policy*, 18(3): 232–45.
Baker, D. and Seawright, D. (1998) 'A "Rosy" Map of Europe? Labour Parliamentarians and European Integration', in D. Baker and D. Seawright (eds) *Britain For and Against Europe: British Politics and the Question of European Integration*, Oxford, Clarendon Press: 55–87.
Bakunin, M. (1870 [2002]) 'Representative Government and Universal Suffrage', in S. Dolgoff (ed.) *Bakunin: On Anarchism*, Montreal, Black Rose Books: 218–24.
Bartolini, S. (2000) *The Political Mobilization of the European Left, 1860–1980: The Class Cleavage*, Cambridge, Cambridge University Press.
Bates, S.R. and Jenkins, L. (2007), 'Teaching and Learning Ontology and Epistemology in Political Science', *Politics*, 27(1): 55–63.
Begg, I. (2008) 'JCMS Symposium: EU Governance After Lisbon: Is there a Convincing Rationale for the Lisbon Strategy?', *Journal of Common Market Studies*, 46(2): 427–35.
Bell, D.S. (1998) 'The *Parti Socialiste* after Mitterrand: A Half-Finished Modernization', in M. Maclean (ed.), *The Mitterrand Years: Legacy and Evaluation*, Basingstoke, Macmillan: 66–85.
—— (2003a) 'The French Left after the 2002 Elections', *Journal of Communist Studies and Transition Politics*, 19(2): 77–92.
—— (2003b) 'France: The Left in 2002–The End of the Mitterand Strategy', *Parliamentary Affairs*, 56(1): 24–37.
Bell, D.S. and Criddle, B. (1988) *The French Socialist Party: The Emergence of a Party of Government*, 2nd edition, Oxford, Clarendon Press.
Bellucci, P. (2008) 'The Parliamentary Election in Italy, April 2006', *Electoral Studies*, 27(1): 151–90.
Benner, M. and Vad, T.B. (2000) 'Sweden and Denmark Defending the Welfare State', in F.W. Scharpf and V.A. Schmidt (eds) *Welfare and Work in the Open Economy: Volume II. Diverse Responses to Common Challenges*, Oxford, Oxford University Press: 399–466.
Beramendi, P. and Rueda, D. (2007) 'Social Democracy Constrained: Indirect Taxation in Industrialized Democracies', *British Journal of Political Science*, 37(4): 619–41.
Berman, S. (2006) *The Primacy of Politics: Social Democracy and the Making of Europe's Twentieth Century*, Cambridge, Cambridge University Press.
Beugelsdijk, M. and Eijffinger, S.C.W. (2005) 'The Effectiveness of Structural Policy in the European Union: An Empirical Analysis for the EU-15 in 1995–2001', *Journal of Common Market Studies*, 43(1): 37–51.
Beunderman, M. (2007) 'French Presidential Candidates Fine Tune Ideas for Europe', *EUobserver.com*, 12 February 2007.
Bevir, M. and Rhodes, R.A.W. (2004) 'Interpreting British Governance', *British Journal of Politics and International Relations*, 6(2): 130–6.
Bhaskar, R. (1975 [1997]) *A Realist Theory of Science*, 2nd edition, London, Verso.
—— (1993) *Dialectic: The Pulse of Freedom*, London, Verso.
—— (1998) *The Possibility of Naturalism: A Philosophical Critique of the Contemporary Human Sciences*, 3rd edition, London, Routledge.
Bieler, A. (2000) *Globalization and Enlargement of the European Union*, London, Routledge.
Blair, T. (1998) *The Third Way: New Politics for the New Century*, London, Fabian Society.

Blakeley, G. (2006) '"It's Politics, Stupid!" The Spanish General Election of 2004', *Parliamentary Affairs*, 59(2): 331–49.

Blyth, M. (2002) *Great Transformations: Economic Ideas and Institutional Change in the Twentieth Century*, Cambridge, Cambridge University Press.

Boix, C. (2000) 'Managing the Spanish Economy within Europe', *South European Society and Politics*, 5(2): 165–90.

Bonoli, G. and Powell, M. (2002) 'Third Ways in Europe?', *Social Policy and Society*, 1(1): 59–66.

—— (eds) (2004) *Social Democratic Party Policies in Contemporary Europe*, London, Routledge.

Bosetti, G. (1998) 'Reinventing the Left: Interview with Massimo D'Alema', *Dissent*, Spring 1998: 11–17.

Bouvet, L. and Michel, F. (1999) 'Pluralism and the Future of the French Left', in G. Kelly (ed.) *The New European Left*, London, Fabian Society: 35–46.

Brandon, H. (1966) *In the Red*, London, Andre Deutsch.

Braunthal, G. (1998) 'Opposition in the Kohl Era: The SPD and the Left', *German Politics*, 7(1): 143–62.

Broad, R. (2001) *Labour's European Dilemmas: From Bevin to Blair*, London, Palgrave.

Brunazzo, M. and Gilbert, M. (2008) 'The Right Sweeps the Board', *Journal of Modern Itlaian Studies*, 13(3): 422–30.

Büchs, M. (2007) *New Governance in European Social Policy: The Open Method of Coordination*, Basingstoke, Palgrave.

Bull, M.J. (2003) 'Italy: The Crisis of the Left', *Parliamentary Affairs*, 56(1): 58–74.

Butler, D. (1992) *The British General Election of 1992*, Basingstoke, Macmillan.

Butler, D. and Stokes, D. (1969) *Political Change in Britain*, London, Macmillan.

Cafruny, A.W. (1997) 'Social Democracy in One Continent? Alternatives to a Neoliberal Europe', in A.W. Cafruny and C. Lankowski (eds) *Europe's Ambiguous Unity: Conflict and Consensus in the Post-Maastricht Era*, London, Lynne Rienner: 109–128.

Cafruny, A.W. and Ryner, M. (eds) (2003) *A Ruined Fortress? Neoliberal Hegemony and Transformation in Europe*, Maryland, Rowman and Littlefield.

Cafruny, A.W. and Ryner, J.M. (2007) *Europe at Bay: In the Shadow of US Hegemony*, Boulder, Lynne Rienner.

Callaghan, J. (2000a) *The Retreat of Social Democracy*, Manchester, Manchester University Press.

—— (2000b) 'The Rise and Fall of the Alternative Economic Strategy: From Internationalization of Capital to "Globalization"', *Contemporary British History*, 14(3): 105–30.

Castree, N. (2003) 'Commodifying What Nature?', *Progress in Human Geography*, 27(3): 273–97.

Cautrès, B. with Cole, A. (2008) 'The 2007 French Elections and Beyond', in A. Cole, P. Le Galès, and J.D. Levy (eds) *Developments in French Politics 4*, Basingstoke, Palgrave: 22–41.

Cederman, L.E. (2001) 'Nationalism and Bounded Integration: What it Would Take to Construct a European Demos', *European Journal of International Relations*, 7(2): 139–74.

Cerny, P. (1996) 'International Finance and the Erosion of State Power', in P. Gummett (ed) *Globalization and Public Policy*, Brookfield VT, Edward Elgar.

Christofferson, T.R. (1991) *The French Socialists in Power, 1981–1986*, Newark, University of Delaware Press.

Clark, D., Kinnock, N., Leahy, M., Livingstone, K., Monks, J. and Twigg, S. (2006) 'A Democratic Left Vision for Europe', in D. Albers, S. Haseler and H. Meyer (eds) *Social Europe: A Continent's Answer to Market Fundamentalism*, London, European Research Forum at London Metropolitan University: 85–110.

Clarke, H., Sanders, D., Stewart, M. and Whiteley, P. (2006) 'Taking the Bloom off New Labour's Rose: Party Choice and Voter Turnout in Britain, 2005', *Journal of Elections, Public Opinion and Parties*, 16(1): 3–36.

Clift, B. (2002) 'Social Democracy and Globalization: The Cases of France and the UK', *Government and Opposition*, 37(4): 466–500.

—— (2003a), *French Socialism in a Global Era: The Political Economy of the New Social Democracy in France*, London, Continuum.

—— (2003b) 'The Changing Political Economy of France: Dirigisme under Duress', in Cafruny and Ryner (2003) 173–200.

Coates, D. (1975) *The Labour Party and the Struggle for Socialism*, Cambridge, Cambridge University Press.

—— (1980) *Labour in Power? A Study of the Labour Government, 1974–1979*, London, Longman.

Cole, A. (1997) *François Mitterrand: A Study in Political Leadership*, 2nd edition, London, Routledge.

—— (2002) 'A Strange Affair: The French Presidential and Parliamentary Elections of 2002', *Government and Opposition*, 37(3): 317–42.

Colebrook, C. (2005) *Philosophy and Post-structuralist Theory: From Kant to Deleuze*, Edinburgh, Edinburgh University Press.

Collier, A. (1994) *Critical Realism: An Introduction to Roy Bhaskar's Philosophy*, London, Verso.

—— (2002) 'Dialectic in Marxism and Critical Realism', in A. Brown, S. Fleetwood and J. M. Roberts (eds) *Critical Realism and Marxism*, London, Routledge: 155–67.

Cotta, M. and Verzichelli, L. (2007) *Political Institutions in Italy*, Oxford, Oxford University Press.

Cox, R. (2004) 'The Path-dependency of an Idea: Why Scandinavian Welfare States Remain Distinct', *Social Policy and Administration*, 38(2): 204–19.

Creaven, S. (2002) 'Materialism, Realism and Dialectics', in A. Brown, S. Fleetwood and J. M. Roberts (eds) *Critical Realism and Marxism*, London, Routledge: 131–54.

Crosland, C.A.R. (1956) *The Future of Socialism*, London, Cape.

Cruickshank, J. (2003) *Critical Realism: The Difference It Makes*, London, Routledge.

CSPEC (1982) *The Crisis in Europe and the Socialist Response*, Paris Congress, 12–13 November 1982.

—— (1984) *Manifesto adopted by the 13th Congress of the Confederation of the Socialist Parties of the European Community*, Luxembourg, 9th March 1984.

Deleuze, G. (1994 [2004]) *Difference and Repetition*, translated by Paul Patton, London, Continuum.

Della Sala, V. (2002) 'D'Alema's Dilemmas: Third Way, Italian Style', in Schmidtke (ed.) (2002) 103–30.

—— (2004) 'The Italian Model of Capitalism: On the Road Between Globalization and Europeanization?', *Journal of European Public Policy*, 11(6): 1041–1058.

Dunphy, R. (2004) *Contesting Capitalism? Left Parties and European Integration*, Manchester, Manchester University Press.

Dyson, K. (2005) 'Economic Policy Management: Catastrophic Equilibrium, Tipping Points and Crisis Interventions', in S. Green and W.E. Patterson (eds) *Governance in*

Contemporary Germany: The Semisovereign State Revisited, Cambridge, Cambridge University Press.
Dyson, K. and Featherstone, K. (1998) 'EMU and Presidential Leadership under François Mitterrand', in M. Maclean (ed.) *The Mitterrand Years: Legacy and Evaluation*, Basingstoke, Macmillan: 89–111.
Elder-Vass, D. (2008) 'Integrating Institutional, Relational and Embodied Structure: An Emergentist Perspective', *The British Journal of Sociology*, 59(2): 281–99.
Esping-Andersen, G. (1985) *Politics Against Markets: The Social Democratic Road to Power*, Princeton, Princeton University Press.
—— (1990) *The Three Worlds of Welfare Capitalism*, Cambridge, Polity.
Eurobarometer (2003) *Flash Eurobarometer 149: Post-referendum in Sweden*, Brussels: European Commission.
—— (2005) *The European Constitution: Post-referendum survey in France*, Brussels: European Commission. Online. Available HTTP: <http://www.europa.eu.int/comm/public_opinion/flash/fl171_en.pdf> (accessed 26 September 2008).
Eurostat, various pages. Online. Available HTTP <http://epp.eurostat.ec.europa.eu> (accessed August 2008).
Evans, J.A.J. (2007) 'The European Dimension in French Public Opinion', *Journal of European Public Policy*, 14(7): 1098–1116.
Falkner, G. (2000) 'The Treaty on European Union and its Revision: Sea Change or Empty Shell for European Social Policies?', in S. Kuhnle (ed.) *Survival of the European Welfare State*, London, Routledge: 185–201.
Featherstone, K. (1988) *Socialist Parties and European Integration: A Comparative History*, Manchester, Manchester University Press.
Fitzpatrick, T. (2003) *After the New Social Democracy: Social Welfare for the Twentieth Century*, Manchester, Manchester University Press.
—— (2007) 'Social Democracy Beyond Productivism', *Renewal*, 15(2/3): 74–82.
Fouskas, V. (1998) *Italy, Europe, the Left: The Transformation of Italian Communism and the European Imperative*, Aldershot, Ashgate.
Fung, H.F. (2008) 'Rise of China and the Global Accumulation Crisis', *Review of International Political Economy*, 15(2): 149–79.
Gallagher, M., Laver, M. and Mair, P. (2006) *Representative Government in Modern Europe*, 4th edition, New York, McGraw Hill.
Gamble, A. and Wright, T. (1999) 'Introduction: The New Social Democracy', in A. Gamble and T. Wright (eds) *The New Social Democracy*, Oxford, Blackwell: 1–9.
Geddes, A. (2005) 'Nationalism: Immigration and European Integration at the 2005 General Election', in A. Geddes and J. Tonge (eds) *Britain Decides: The UK General Election 2005*, Basingstoke, Palgrave: 279–93.
George, S. and Haythorne, D. (1996) 'The British Labour Party', in J. Gaffney (ed.) *Political Parties and the European Union*, London, Routledge: 110–21.
George, S. and Rosamond, B. (1992) 'The European Community', in M.J. Smith and J. Spear (eds) *The Changing Labour Party*, London, Routledge: 171–84.
Geyer, R. (2000) *Exploring European Social Policy*, Cambridge, Polity.
Giannetti, D. and De Giorgi, E. (2006) 'The 2006 Italian General Elections: Issues, Dimensions and Policy Positions of Political Parties', *Journal of Modern Italian Studies*, 11(4): 494–515.
Giddens, A. (1998) *The Third Way: The Renewal of Social Democracy*, Cambridge, Polity.
Gillespie, R. (1989) *The Spanish Socialist Party: A History of Factionalism*, Oxford, Clarendon Press.

—— (1993) '"Programa 2000" – the Appearance and Reality of Socialist Renewal in Spain', *West European Politics*, 16(1): 78–96.

Glyn, A. (ed.) (2001) *Social Democracy in Neoliberal Times: The Left and Economic Policy since 1980*, Oxford, Oxford University Press.

Glyn, A. and Sutcliffe, R. (1972) *British Capitalism, Workers and the Profits Squeeze*, Harmondsworth, Penguin.

Gould, A. (2000) 'Swedish Social Policy and the EU Social Dimension', in L. Miles (ed.) *Sweden and the European Union Evaluated*, London, Continuum: 201–14.

—— (2001) *Developments in Swedish Social Policy: Resisting Dionysus*, Basingstoke, Palgrave.

Gray, J. (1996) *After Social Democracy – Politics, Capitalism and the Common Life*, London, Demos.

—— (1980) 'From Gramsci to Togliatti: The *Partito Nuovo* and the Mass Basis of Italian Communism', in S. Serfaty and L. Gray (eds) *The Italian Communist Party: Yesterday, Today, and Tomorrow*, London, Aldwych Press: 21–35.

Green-Pedersen, C. and van Kersbergen, K. (2002) 'The Politics of the "Third Way": The Transformation of Social Democracy in Denmark and the Netherlands', *Party Politics*, 8(5): 507–24.

Grunberg, G. (2008) 'The French Party System and the Crisis of Representation', in P.D. Culpepper, P.A. Hall, and B. Palier (eds) *Changing France: The Politics that Markets Make*, Basingstoke, Palgrave: 223–43.

Habermas, J. (1976) *Legitimation Crisis*, Boston, Beacon Press.

Hall, P. (1986) *Governing the Economy: The Politics of State Intervention in Britain and France*, Cambridge, Polity.

—— (1990) 'The State and the Market', in P. Hall, J. Hayward and H. Machin (eds) *Develoments in French Politics*, London, Macmillan: 171–87.

—— (2002) 'The Comparative Political Economy of the "Third Way"', in Schmidtke (ed.) (2002) 31–58.

Hantrais, L. (2007) *Social Policy in the European Union*, 3rd edition, London, Palgrave.

Harvey, D. (2006) *The Limits to Capital* (New and Fully Updated Edition), London, Verso.

Hay, C. (1997) 'Anticipating Accommodations, Accommodating Anticipations: The Appeasement of Capital in the "Modernization" of the British Labour Party, 1987–1992', *Politics and Society*, 25(2): 234–56.

—— (1999) *The Political Economy of New Labour: Labouring under False Pretences?*, Manchester, Manchester University Press.

—— (2000) 'Globalization, Social Democracy and the Persistence of Partisan Politics: A Commentary on Garrett', *Review of International Political Economy*, 7(1): 138–52.

—— (2002a) *Political Analysis*, Basingstoke, Palgrave.

—— (2002b) 'Globalization, EU-isation and the Space for Social Democratic Alternatives: Pessimism of the Intellect, a Reply to Coates', *British Journal of Politics and International Relations*, 4(3): 452–64.

—— (2004) 'The Normalizing Role of Rationalist Assumptions in the Institutional Embedding of Neoliberalism', *Economy and Society*, 33(4): 500–527.

—— (2006) 'What's Globalization Got to Do with It? Economic Interdependence and the Future of European Welfare States', *Government and Opposition*, 41(1): 1–22.

Heath, A.F., Jowell, R.M. and Curtice, J.K. (2001) *The Rise of New Labour: Party Policies and Voter Choices*, Oxford, Oxford University Press.

Heclo, H. and Madsen, H. (1987) *Policy and Politics in Sweden: Principled Pragmatism*, Philadelphia, Temple University Press.

Heidenreich, M. and Bischoff, G. (2008) 'The Open Method of Co-ordination: A Way to the Europeanization of Social and Employment Policies?', *Journal of Common Market Studies*, 46(3): 497–532.
High Level Group chaired by Wim Kok (2004) 'Facing the challenge: The Lisbon strategy for growth and employment: Report from the High Level Group chaired by Wim Kok', Luxembourg, Office for the Publications of the European Communities.
Hirst, P. (1999) 'Has Globalization Killed Social Democracy?', in A. Gamble and T. Wright (eds) *The New Social Democracy*, Oxford, Blackwell: 85–96.
Hix, S. (2002) '1957–1994', in S.Hix and U. Lesse, *Shaping a Vision: A History of the Party of European Socialists, 1957–2002*, Brussels, Party of European Socialists, European Parliament.
—— (2005) *The Political System of the European Union*, 2nd edition, Basingstoke, Palgrave.
Hix, S. and Lord, C. (1997) *Political Parties in the European Union*, Basingstoke, Macmillan.
Holden, R. (2002) *The Making of New Labour's European Policy*, Basingstoke, Palgrave.
Holland, S., (1980) *Uncommon Market: Capital, Class and Power in the European Community*, London, Macmillan.
—— (ed.) (1982) *Out of Crisis*, Nottingham, Spokesman Books.
—— (1984) 'Out of Crisis – International Economic Recovery', in J. Curran (ed) *The Future of the Left*, Cambridge, Polity: 243–64.
Holman, O. (1996) *Integrating Southern Europe: EC Expansion and the Transnationalization of Spain*, London, Routledge.
Holmes, M. (1985), *The Labour Government, 1974–79: Political Aims Economic Reality*, London, Macmillan.
Holmes, M. and Lightfoot, S. (2007) 'The Europeanisation of Left Political Parties: Limits to Adaptation and Consensus', *Capital and Class*, 93: 141–58.
Hooghe, L. and Marks, G. (2001) *Multi-Level Governance and European Integration*, Oxford, Rowman and Littlefield.
Hooghe, L., Marks, G. and Wilson, C.J. (2002), 'Does Left/Right Structure Party Positions on European Integration?', *Comparative Political Studies*, 35(8): 965–89.
Howarth, D. (2002) 'The French State in the Euro-Zone: "Modernization" and Legitimizing Dirigisme', in K. Dyson (ed) *European States and the Euro: Europeanization, Variation, and Convergence*, Oxford, Oxford University Press: 145–72.
Howarth, D.J. (2007) 'Making and Breaking the Rules: French Policy on EU "Gouvernement Économique"', *Journal of European Public Policy*, 14(7): 1061–78.
Howell, D. (1976) *British Social Democracy: A Study in Development and Decay*, London, Croom Helm.
Huber, E. and Stephens, J.D. (2001) *Development and Crisis of the Welfare State: Parties and Policies in Global Markets*, Chicago, University of Chicago Press.
Huo, J., Nelson, M. and Stephens, J.D. (2008), 'Decommodification and Activation in Social Democratic Policy: Resolving the Paradox', *Journal of European Social Policy*, 18(1): 5–20.
Iversen, T. (1996) 'Power, Flexibility, and the Breakdown of Centralized Wage Bargaining: Denmark and Sweden in Comparative Perspective', *Comparative Politics*, 28(4): 399–436.
Johansson, K.M. (1999), 'Tracing the Employment Title in the Amsterdam Treaty: Uncovering Transnational Coalitions', *Journal of European Public Policy*, 6(1): 85–101.
Johansson, K.M. and Raunio, T. (2001) 'Partisan Responses to Europe: Comparing Finnish

and Swedish Political Parties', *European Journal of Political Research*, 39(2): 225–49.

Jospin, L. (2002) *My Vision of Europe and Globalization*, Cambridge, Polity.

Keman, H. (1993), 'Theoretical Approaches to Social Democracy', *Journal of Theoretical Politics*, 5(3): 291–316.

Kennedy, P. (2001) 'Spain's "Third Way"?: The Spanish Socialist Party's Utilization of European Integration', *Journal of Southern Europe and the Balkans*, 3(1): 49–60.

—— (2003) 'Spain: Exhaustion of the Left Project?', *Parliamentary Affairs*, 56 (1): 99–111.

Kesselman, M. (1982) 'Prospects for Democratic Socialism in Advanced Capitalism: Class Struggle and Compromise in Sweden and France', *Politics and Society*, 11(4): 397–438.

King, G., Keohane, R.O. and Verba, S. (1994) *Designing Social Inquiry: Scientific Inference in Qualitative Research*, Princeton, Princeton University Press.

Kinnock, N. (1984) 'New Deal For Europe', in J. Curran (ed.) *The Future of the Left*, Cambridge, Polity.

Kite, C. (1996) *Scandinavia Faces EU: Debates and Decisions on Membership, 1961–1994*, Umeå, Sweden, Umeå University, Department of Political Science.

Kitschelt, H. (1994) *The Transformation of European Social Democracy*, Cambridge, Cambridge University Press.

Kleinman, M. (2002) *A European Welfare State? European Union Social Policy in Context*, Basingstoke, Palgrave.

Klitgaard, M.B. (2007) 'Why are they doing it? Social Democracy and Market-oriented Welfare State Reforms', *West European Politics*, 30(1): 172–94.

Knapp, A. and Sawicki, F. (2008) 'Political Parties and the Party System', in A. Cole, P. Le Galès, and J.D. Levy, (eds), *Developments in French Politics 4*, Basingstoke, Palgrave: 42–59.

Koelble, T.A. (1992) 'Recasting Social Democracy in Europe: A Nested Games Explanation of Strategic Adjustment in Political Parties', *Politics and Society*, 20 (1): 51–70.

König, T. (2008) 'Analysing the Process of EU Legislative Decision-Making: To Make a Long Story Short ...', *European Union Politics*, 9(1): 145–65.

Kotz, D.M. (2008) 'Contradictions of Economic Growth in the Neoliberal Era: Accumulation and Crisis in the Contemporary U.S. Economy', *Review of Radical Political Economics*, 40(2): 174–88.

Kropotkin, P. (1897 [1987]) *The State: It's Historic Role*, translated by Vernon Richards, London, Freedom Press.

—— (n.d. [2005]), 'Revolutionary Government', in D. Guérin (ed.) *No Gods, No Masters: An Anthology of Anarchism*, Edinburgh, AK Press: 312–23.

Kuisma, M. (2007) 'Social Democratic Internationalism and the Welfare State After the "Golden Age"', *Cooperation and Conflict*, 42(1): 9–26.

Labour Party (1962) *Report of the annual conference of the Labour Party*, London, Labour Party.

—— (1976) *Report of the annual conference of the Labour Party*, London, Labour Party.

—— (1979) *Report of the annual conference of the Labour Party*, London, Labour Party.

—— (1980) *Report of the annual conference of the Labour Party*, London, Labour Party.

—— (1983) *The New Hope for Britain: Labour Party Election Manifesto*, London, Labour Party.

—— (1988a) *Social Justice and Economic Efficiency*, London, Labour Party.

—— (1988b) *Report of the annual conference of the Labour Party*, London, Labour Party.

—— (1989a) *Meet the challenge, Make the change: A new agenda for Britain: Final report of Labour's Policy Review for the 1990s*, London, Labour Party.

—— (1989b) *Report of the annual conference of the Labour Party*, London, Labour Party.
—— (1990) *Looking to the Future*, London, Labour Party.
—— (1992) *It's time to get Britain working again: Labour Party Election Manifesto 1992*, London, Labour Party.
—— (1995) *Labour Party Constitutional Rules*, London, Labour Party. Online. Available HTTP < http://labourcounts.com/constitution.htm#4> (accessed November 2008).
—— (1997) *New Labour: Because Britain Deserves Better*, London, Labour Party.
Ladrech, R. (1993) 'Social Democratic Parties and EC Integration: Transnational Party Responses to Europe 1992', *European Journal of Political Research*, 24(2): 195–210.
—— (1998) 'Party Networks, Issue Agendas and European Union governance', in D.S. Bell and C. Lord (eds) *Transnational Parties in the European Union*, Aldershot, Ashgate: 51–86.
—— (2000) *Social Democracy and the Challenge of European Union*, Colorado, Lynne Rienner.
—— (2001) 'Europeanization and French Social Democracy', *Journal of Southern Europe and the Balkans*, 3(1): 37–48.
—— (2003) 'The Left and the European Union', *Parliamentary Affairs*, 56(1): 112–24.
Ladrech, R. and Marlière, P. (eds) (1999) *Social Democratic Parties in the European Union: History, Organization, Politics*, Basingstoke, Macmillan.
Landman, T. (2008), *Issues and Methods in Comparative Politics: An Introduction*, 3rd edition, London, Routledge.
Leggett, W. (2007) 'British Social Democracy beyond New Labour: Entrenching a Progressive Consensus', *British Journal of Politics and International Relations*, 9(3): 346–64.
Leibfried, S. (2005) 'Social Policy: Left to the Judges and Markets?', in H. Wallace, W. Wallace, and M.A. Pollack (eds) *Policy-Making in the European Union*, 5th edition, Oxford, Oxford University Press: 243–78.
Leibfried, S. and Pierson, P. (2000) 'Social Policy: Left to Courts and Markets?', in H. Wallace and W. Wallace (eds) *Policy-Making in the European Union*, 4th edition, Oxford, Oxford University Press: 267–92.
Lenin, V.I. (1902 [1999]) *What is to be Done? Burning Questions of our Movement*, Lenin Internet Archive. Online. Available HTTP: <http://www.marxists.org/archive/lenin/works/1901/witbd/> (accessed 26 September 2008).
Levy, J.D. (2000) 'France: Directing Adjustment?', in F.W. Scharpf and V.A. Schmidt (eds) *Welfare and Work in the Open Economy: Volume II. Diverse Responses to Common Challenges*, Oxford, Oxford University Press: 308–50.
Li, Y. and Marsh, D. (2008) 'New Forms of Political Participation: Searching for Expert Citizens and Everyday Makers', *British Journal of Political Science*, 38(2): 247–72.
Lightfoot, S. (2005) *Europeanizing Social Democracy?: The Rise of the Party of European Socialists*, London, Routledge.
Lindbom, A. (2001) 'Dismantling the Social Democratic Welfare Model? Has the Swedish Welfare State Lost Its Defining Characteristics?', *Scandinavian Political Studies*, 24(3): 171–93.
López, J. (2003) 'Critical realism: the difference it makes, in theory', in Cruickshank (2003) 75–89.
Lordon, F. (2001) 'The Logic and Limits of Désinflation Competitive', in Glyn (2001) 110–37.
Luxembourg, R., (1900 [1999]), *Reform or Revolution*, Marxist Internet Archive. Online.

Available HTTP: <http://www.marxists.org/archive/luxemburg/1900/reform-revolution/index.htm> (accessed 25 September 2008).
McGowan, F. (2001) 'Social Democracy and the European Union: Who's Changing Whom?', in Martell *et al.* (2001) 74–106.
Mandelson, P. and Liddle, R. (1996 [2002]) *The Blair Revolution*, London, Politico's Publishing.
Marks, M. P. (1997) *The Formation of European Policy in Post-Franco Spain: The Role of Ideas, Interests and Knowledge*, Aldershot, Avebury.
Marlière, P. (1999) 'Introduction: European Social Democracy in situ', in Ladrech and Marlière (1999) 1–15.
—— (2001) 'Introduction', *Journal of Southern Europe and the Balkans*, Special Issue: Social Democracy in southern Europe and the challenge of European integration, 3(1): 5–10.
Martell, L., van den Anker, C., Browne, M., Hoopes, S., Larkin, P., Lees, C., McGowan, F. and Stammers, N. (eds) (2001) *Social Democracy: Global and National Perspectives*, Basingstoke, Palgrave.
Martin, D. (1988) *Bringing Commonsense to the Common Market: A Left Agenda for Europe*, London, Fabian Society.
Marx, K. (1867 [1976]) *Capital: A Critique of Political Economy: Volume One*, London, Penguin.
—— (1894 [1981]) *Capital: A Critique of Political Economy: Volume Three*, London, Penguin.
May, T. (1994) *The Political Philosophy of Poststructuralist Anarchism*, Pennsylvania, Pennsylvania State University Press.
Méndez Lago, M. (2006) 'Turning the Page: Crisis and Transformation of the Spanish Socialist Party', *South European Society and Politics*, 11(3–4): 419–37.
Merkel, W., Petring, A., Henkes, C. and Egle, C. (2008) *Social Democracy in Power: The Capacity to Reform*, London, Routledge.
Miller, V., Taylor, C. and Potton, E. (2003) 'The Swedish Referendum on the Euro', *House of Commons Library Research Paper 03/68*. Online. Available HTTP: <http://www.parliament.uk/commons/lib/research/rp2003/rp03-068.pdf> (accessed 25 September 2008).
Möller, T. (1999) 'The Swedish Election 1998: A Protest Vote and the Birth of a New Political Landscape?', *Scandinavian Political Studies*, 22(3): 261–76.
Molina, O. and Rhodes, M. (2007) 'Industrial Relations and the Welfare State in Italy: Assessing the Potential of Negotiated Change', *West European Politics*, 30(4): 803–29.
Morgan, K. (1984) *Labour in Power, 1945–1951*, Oxford, Clarendon Press.
Moschonas, G. (2002) *In the Name of Social Democracy: The Great Transformation, 1945 to the Present*, London, Verso.
Motta, S.C. and Bailey, D.J. (2007) 'Neither Pragmatic Adaptation nor Misguided Accommodation: Modernization as Domination in the Chilean and British Left', *Capital and Class*, 92: 107–36.
Nedergaard, P. (2007) 'Blocking Minorities: Networks and Meaning in the Opposition Against the Proposal for a Directive on Temporary Work in the Council of Ministers of the European Union', *Journal of Common Market Studies*, 45(3): 695–717.
Newell, J.L. (2006) 'The Italian Election of May 2006: Myths and Realities', *West European Politics*, 29(4): 802–13.
Newell, J.L. and Bull, M.J. (2002) 'Italian Politics after the 2001 General Election: *Plus ça change, plus c'est la même chose?*', *Parliamentary Affairs*, 55(4): 626–42.

Newman, S. (2001) *From Bakunin to Lacan: Anti-Authoritarianism and the Dislocation of Power*, Maryland, Lexington.
Nielsen, P. (2002) 'Reflections on critical realism in political economy', *Cambridge Journal of Economics*, 26(6): 727–38.
Norris, P. (2004) *Democratic Phoenix: Reinventing Political Activism*, Cambridge, Cambridge University Press.
OECD (1999) *OECD Economic Surveys 1998–1999: Italy*, Paris, OECD publications.
OECD.stat, various pages. Online. Available HTTP: <http://stats.oecd.org/wbos/Index.aspx?usercontext=sourceoecd> (accessed August 2008).
Olsen, G. (1992) *The Struggle for Economic Democracy in Sweden*, Aldershot, Avebury.
Olsson, S. (1987) 'Sweden', in P. Flora (ed.) *Growth to Limits: The Western European Welfare States Since World War II: Volume 4 – Appendix (Synopses, Bibliographies, Tables)*, Berlin, de Gruyter: 1–64.
Oppermann, K. (2008) 'The Blair Government and Europe: The Policy of Containing the Salience of European Integration', *British Politics*, 3(2): 156–82.
Outhwaite, W. (1987) *New Philosophies of Social Science: Realism, Hermeneutics and Critical Theory*, London, Macmillan.
Panitch, L. (1976) *Social Democracy and Industrial Militancy: The Labour Party, the Trade Unions and Incomes Policy, 1945–1974*, Cambridge, Cambridge University Press.
Panitch, L and Leys, C. (2001) *The End of Parliamentary Socialism: From New Left to New Labour*, 2nd edition, London, Verso.
Pasquino, G. (1980) 'From Togliatti to the Compromesso Storico: A Party with a Governmental Vocation', in S. Serfaty and L. Gray (eds) *The Italian Communist Party: Yesterday, Today, and Tomorrow*, London, Aldwych Press: 75–106.
Paterson, W. and Sloam, J. (2006) 'Is the Left Alright? The SPD and the Renewal of European Social Democracy', *German Politics*, 15(3): 233–48.
Patomäki, H. and Wight, C. (2000) 'After Postpositivism? The Promises of Critical Realism', *International Studies Quarterly*, 44(2): 213–37.
Pennetier, J.M. (1997) 'A "New Deal" in Europe? Reflections on the French Socialists' Victory', *Renewal*, 5 (3/4): 131–8.
Persson, G. (2002) *Statement of Government Policy presented by the Prime Minister, Mr Göran Persson, to the Swedish Riksdag on Tuesday, 1 October 2002*.
PES (1993) Declaration of the Leaders of the Party of European Socialists: 'The European Employment Initiative', leaders' meeting of the PES, Brussels, 9 December 1993, Brussels, PES.
—— (1994) *Manifesto for the Elections to the European Parliament of June 1994*, Brussels, PES.
—— (1995) 'Report of the PES Working Party on the 1996 Intergovernmental Conference'. Brussels, PES.
—— (1999a) *A European Employment Pact: For a New European Way*, PES, Fourth Congress Milan 1 and 2 March 1999, Brussels, PES.
—— (1999b) *Party of European Socialists: Manifesto for the 1999 European Elections*, Brussels, PES.
—— (2001a) *Security in Change*, Text adopted by the 5th PES Congress, 7–8 May 2001, Berlin, Brussels, PES.
—— (2001b) *The Future of Europe: PES Laeken Declaration*, Brussels, PES.
—— (2006) *New Social Europe: Ten Principles for Our Common Future*, Brussels, PES.
Pierson, C. (2001) *Hard Choices: Social Democracy in the Twenty-First Century*, Cambridge, Polity.

Pinder, J. (1969) 'Problems of European Integration', in G. Denton (ed.) *Economic Integration in Europe*, London, Weidenfeld and Nicolson.

Pollack, B. and Hunter, G. (1987) *The Paradox of Spanish Foreign Policy: Spain's International Relations from Franco to Democracy*, London, Pinter.

Pontusson, J. (1992) *The Limits of Social Democracy*, Ithaca, NY, Cornell University Press.

—— (1995) 'Explaining the Decline of European Social Democracy: The Role of Structural Economic Change', *World Politics*, 47(4): 495–533.

Powell, M. (2004), 'Social Democracy in Europe: renewal or retreat?' in G. Bonoli and M. Powell (eds) *Social Democratic Party Policies in Contemporary Europe*, London, Routledge: 1–20.

Przeworski, A. (1985) *Capitalism and Social Democracy*, Cambridge, Cambridge University Press.

—— (2001) 'How Many Ways Can Be Third?', in Glyn (2001) 312–333.

Przeworski, A. and Sprague, J. (1986) *Paper Stones: A History of Electoral Socialism*, Chicago, University of Chicago Press.

Przeworski, A. and Wallerstein, M. (1988) 'Structural Dependence of the State on Capital', *American Political Science Review*, 82 (1): 11–29.

PSOE (2004) *Merecemos una España mejor: Programa Electoral: Elecciones Generales 2004*, Madrid, PSOE.

Quaglia, L. and Radaelli, C.M. (2007) 'Italian Politics and the European Union: A Tale of Two Research Designs', *West European Politics*, 30(4): 924–43.

Quinn, T. (2006) 'Choosing the Least-Worst Government: The British General Election of 2005', *West European Politics*, 29(1): 169–78.

Raveaud, G. (2007) 'The European Employment Strategy: Towards More and Better Jobs?', *Journal of Common Market Studies*, 45(2): 411–34.

Recio, A. and Roca, J. (1998) 'The Spanish Socialists in Power: Thirteen Years of Economic Policy', *Oxford Review of Economic Policy*, 14 (1): 139–58.

—— (2001) 'The Spanish Socailists in Power: Thirteen Years of Economic Policy', in Glyn (2001) 173–99.

Reid, A.J. and Pelling, H. (2005) *A Short History of the Labour Party*, 12th edition, Basingstoke, Palgrave.

Rhodes, M. (2000), 'Restructuring the British Welfare State: Between Domestic Constraints and Global Imperatives' in F.W. Scharpf and V.A. Schmidt (eds.), *Welfare and Work in the Open Economy: Volume II. Diverse Responses to Common Challenges*, Oxford, Oxford University Press: 19–68.

Robinson, N. (2007) 'More than a Regulatory State: Bringing Expenditure (Back) into EU Research', *Comparative European Politics*, 5(2): 179–204.

Roder, K. (2003) *Social Democracy and Labour Market Policy: Developments in Britain and Germany*, London, Routledge.

Ross, G. (1995) *Jacques Delors and European Integration*, Cambridge, Polity.

—— (1998a) 'The Euro, The "French Model of Society," and French Politics', in *French Politics and Society*, 16(4): 1–16.

—— (1998b) 'French Social Democracy and EMU', ARENA Working Paper NO. 19.

Ross, G. and Jenson, J. (1994) 'France: Triumph and Tragedy', in P. Anderson and P. Camiller (eds) *Mapping the West European Left*, London, Verso: 158–88.

Rothstein, B. (1996) *The Social Democratic State: The Swedish Model and the Bureaucratic Problem of Social Reforms*, Pittsburgh, University of Pittsburgh Press.

Royo, S. (2000) *From Social Democracy to Neoliberalism: The Consequences of Party Hegemony in Spain 1982–1996*, New York, St. Martin's Press.

Rucht, D. (2006) 'Political Participation in Europe', in R. Sakwa and A. Stevens (eds) *Contemporary Europe*, 2nd *edition*, Palgrave, Macmillan: 110–37.

Rueda, D. (2007) *Social Democracy Inside Out: Partisanship and Labor Market Policy in Industrialized Democracies*, Oxford, Oxford University Press.

Ryner, J.M. (2002) *Capitalist Restructuring, Globalization and the Third Way: Lessons from the Swedish model*, Routledge, London.

—— (2004) 'Neo-liberalization of Social Democracy: The Swedish Case', *Comparative European Politics*, 2(1): 97–119.

SAP (2000) *Congress Guidelines extra Congress 2000: Swedish Social Democratic Party Guidelines For Development and Equality*, adopted by the Extra Party Congress, Stockholm, 10–12 March 2000.

—— (2002) *Working Together for Security and Development: The Election Manifesto of the Swedish Social Democrats, 2002–2006*, Stockholm, SAP.

Sapir, A. (2006) 'Globalization and the Reform of European Social Models', *Journal of Common Market Studies*, 44(2): 369–90.

Sassoon, D. (1981) *The Strategy of the Italian Communist Party: From the Resistance to the Historic Compromise*, London, Frances Pinter.

—— (1996) *One Hundred Years of Socialism: The West European Left in the Twentieth Century*, London, Fontana Press.

Sayer, A. (1992) *Method in Social Science: A Realist Approach*, 2nd edition, London, Routledge.

Scharpf, F.W. (1991) *Crisis and Choice in European Social Democracy*, London, Cornell University Press.

—— (1999) *Governing in Europe: Effective and Democratic?*, Oxford, Oxford University Press.

—— (2002) 'The European Social Model: Coping with the Challenges of Diversity', *Journal of Common Market Studies*, 40(4): 645–70.

—— (2006) 'The Joint-Decision Trap Revisited', *Journal of Common Market Studies*, 44(4): 845–64.

Schmidtke, O. (2002) 'Transforming the Social Democratic Left: The Challenges to Third Way Politics in the Age of Globalization', in O. Schmidtke (ed.), *The Third Way Transformation of Social Democracy: Normative claims and policy initiatives in the 21st century*, Aldershot, Ashgate: 3–27.

Scruggs, L. (2004) *Welfare State Entitlements Data Set: A Comparative Institutional Analysis of Eighteen Welfare States, Version 1.2*. Online. Available HTTP: <http://www.sp.uconn.edu/~scruggs/wp.htm> (accessed August 2008).

Seyd, P. (1987) *The Rise and Fall of the Labour Left*, Basingstoke, Macmillan.

Seyd, P. and P. Whiteley (1992) *Labour's Grass Roots: The Politics of Party Membership*, Oxford, Clarendon Press.

Share, D. (1989) *Dilemmas of Social Democracy: The Spanish Socialist Workers Party in the 1980s*, New York, Greenwood Press.

Shaw, E. (1988) *Discipline and Discord: Politics of Managerial Control in the Labour Party, 1951–86*, Manchester, Manchester University Press.

—— (1996) *The Labour Party since 1945: Old Labour–New Labour*, Oxford, Blackwell.

Smith, W.R. (1998) *The Left's Dirty Job: The Politics of Industrial Restructuring in France and Spain*, Pittsburgh, University of Pittsburgh Press.

Socialist Parties of the European Community (1973) *9th Congress of the Socialist Parties of the European Community*, Bonn 26 and 27 April 1973.

Stammers, N. (2001) 'Social Democracy and Global Governance', in Martell *et al.* (2001) 27–48.

Streeck, W. (2001) 'International competition, supranational integration, national solidarity: The emerging constitution of "Social Europe"', in M. Kohli, and M. Novak (eds) *Will Europe Work? Integration, Employment and the Social Order*, London, Routledge: 21–34.

Svensson, T. (2002) 'Globalization, Marketisation and Power: The Swedish Case of Institutional Change', *Scandinavian Political Studies*, 25 (3): 197–229.

Taylor, G.R. (1997) *Labour's Renewal? The Policy Review and Beyond*, London, Macmillan.

Teague, P. (1985) 'The Alternative Economic Strategy: A Time to go European', *Capital and Class*, 26: 43–71.

Thompson, N. (1996) 'Supply-Side Socialism: The Political Economy of New Labour', *New Left Review*, 216: 37–54.

Thomson, S. (2000) *The Social Democratic Dilemma: Ideology, Governance and Globalization*, Basingstoke, Macmillan.

Threlfall, M. (2002) 'Social Integration in the European Union: Towards a Single Social Area?', in M. Farrell, S. Fella and M. Newman (eds) *European Integration in the 21st century*, London, Sage: 135–57.

Tilton, T. (1991) *The Political Theory of Swedish Social Democracy: Through the Welfare State to Socialism*, Oxford, Clarendon Press.

Tormey, S. (2006) '"Not in my Name': Deleuze, Zapatismo and the Critique of Representation', *Parliamentary Affairs*, 59(1): 138–54.

TUC (1988) *Maximising the Benefits, Minimising the Costs: TUC Report on Europe 1992*, London, TUC.

Vandenbroucke, F. (1999) 'European Social Democracy: Convergence, Divisions, and Shared Questions', in A. Gamble and T. Wright (eds) *The New Social Democracy*, Blackwell, Oxford: 37–52.

Vartiainen, J. (2001) 'Understanding Swedish Social Democracy: Victims of Success?, in Glyn (2001) 21–52.

Verdier, D. and Breen, R. (2001) 'Europeanization and Globalization: Politics Against Markets in the European Union', *Comparative Political Studies*, 34(3): 227–62.

Visser, J. (2006) 'Union Membership Statistics in 24 Countries', *Monthly Labor Review*, January 2006.

Volkens, A. (2004) 'Policy changes of European Social Democrats, 1945–98', in G. Bonoli and M. Powell (eds) *Social Democratic Party Policies in Contemporary Europe*, London, Routledge: 21–42.

Wahl, A.V. (2005) 'Liberal, Conservative, Social Democratic, or … European? The European Union as Equal Employment Regime', *Social Politics*, 12(1): 67–95.

Watson, M. and Hay, C. (2003) 'The Discourse of Globalization and the Logic of No Alternative: Rendering the Contingent Necessary in the Political Economy of New Labour', *Policy and Politics*, 31(3): 289–305.

Weiler, J.H.H. (1999) *The Constitution of Europe: 'Do the New Clothes Have an Emperor?' and other essays on European integration*, Cambridge, Cambridge University Press.

Weinberg, L. (1995) *The Transformation of Italian Communism*, New Brunswick, Transaction Publishers.

Whickam-Jones, M. (2003) 'From Reformism to Resignation and Remedialism? Labour's Trajectory Through British Politics', in E.C. Hargrove (ed.) *The Future of the Democratic*

Left in Industrial Democracies, Pennsylvania, Pennsylvania State University Press: 26–45.

Wright, E.O. (1999) 'Alternative Perspectives in Marxist Theory of Accumulation and Crisis', *Critical Sociology*, 25(2/3): 115–42.

Zeitlin, J. (2008) 'JCMS Symposium: EU Governance After Lisbon: Is there a Convincing Rationale for the Lisbon Strategy?', *Journal of Common Market Studies*, 46(2): 436–50.

Index

Anarchist theories of the state 36–40; classical anarchism 37–8; poststructuralist anarchism 38–9

Bakunin, M. 38
Bebel, August 4
Benn, Tony 51
Bernstein, Eduard 4
Beumer, Ton 133
Bevan, Aneurin 45
Blair, Tony 53, 103, 105

Confederation of the Socialist Parties of the European Community 130–2
critical realism: causation 17, 21; change 24; compared with interpretivism 24–5; compared with positivism 21, 23; explanation 21–6; real definitions 25–6
Crosland, Anthony 27, 44–5

Deleuze, Gilles 38–9
Delors, Jacques 10, 69–70, 101
Democratic Party (PD) 169
Democrats of the Left (DS) 80–2, 118–21, 167–9; D'Alema Government 80, 120–1; Prodi Government (2006–8) 168

Erlander, Tage 57–8
European integration: Amsterdam Treaty 147; budget 149; Employment Chapter 147; EU social policy 144–55; EU economic policy 144–55; Lisbon Strategy 147–8, 152–4; Nice Treaty 147–8; Single European Act 146; Social Chapter 147

Fabius, Laurent 72–3, 165
Fassino, Piero 120, 168

Gaitskell, Hugh 44, 95
Goldberg, Daniel 114, 167
Gonzalez, Felipe 82, 121, 123, 169
Guerra, Alfonso 87
Guesde, Jules 4
Guterres Report 135

Hansson, Per Albin 56–7

International Workingmen's Association: First International 3; Second International 3, 4, 5; Socialist International 4; Third International 4
Italian Communist Party (PCI) 74–9, 117–9; Berlinguer, Enrico 77; Cossutta, Armando 78–9; 'democratic alternative' 78; Gramsci 75; 'historic compromise' 77; *il nuovo corso* 75–6; *nuovo corso* 78; Occhetto, Achille 78–9; ; *riformismo forte* 78; Togliatti, Palmiro 75–6

Jaurés, Jean 4
Jospin, Lionel 73–4, 115–7

Kautsky, Karl 4
Kinnock, Neil 52, 98–100, 103, 105
Kropotkin, P. 37–8

Labour Party 42–55, 162–3; Attlee Government 43–4, 95; Blair Government 162; Brown Government 162; Callaghan Government 49–50, 96; Campaign for Labour Party Democracy 51; European policy of 10, 95–106, 132, 147; New Labour 53–5, 103–6, 162–3; 1988–91 policy review 52–3, 102; Wilson Government (1964–70) 45–8, 96; Wilson Government (1974–6) 48–9,

96; Larsson, Allan 108–9, 132; Larsson Report 132–4
Lenin, V.I. 4
López Aguilar, Juan Fernando 124
Lisbon Strategy 12; Kok Report 12
Luxembourg, Rosa 4

Marxist theories of capitalist crisis 32–6
Mitterrand, François 67–8, 70–3, 112
Mollet, Guy 66, 111–2

'new' social democracy: adoption of 7–8; explanations for 14–17, 157–9; real definition of 94

Office of the Socialist Parties of the European Community 129–30

Parti Communist Français (PCF) 66–8, 71
Parti Socialiste 67–74, 165–7; Arche Congress 73; European Policy 111–7, 147, 166–7; Épinay Congress 67; Fabius Government 72–3; Issy-les-Moulineaux Congress 67; Nantes Congress 67; CERES 67, 71, 114; Jospin Government 74, 115–7, 147, 165; Mitterrand Presidency 68, 113–5; Mauroy Government 68–72, 113–4; Party of European Socialists 11, 108, 129, 132–44
Party of the Democrats of the Left (PDS) 79–82, 118–21, 167, 169; Prodi (*Ulivio*) Government (1994–98) 79–80, 119–20

Refoundation Communists (*Rifondazione Comunista*) 79–80, 119, 168
Rocard, Michel 67, 73

SFIO (*Section française de l'Internationale ouvrière*) 66–7
social democratic parties: definition of 9–10; 'reformist' social democracy 3, 4; 'revisionist' social democracy 4–5; 'revolutionary' social democracy 3
Social Democratic Party of Germany (SPD) 3; and Bad Godesberg 27
Solchaga, Carlos 85
Spanish Socialist Workers Party (PSOE) 82–90, 169–71; European policy 121–5, 169–71; Gonzalez Government 83–90, 169; *Manifesto of the Programme 2000* 87–9, 123; and Marxism 82–3; *plan de convergencia* 88
Stability and Growth Pact (SGP) 116
Swedish model: EFO model 61; Rehn-Meidner model 57–8, 62; Saltsjöbaden Accords 56
Swedish Social Democratic Party (SAP) 5, 55–66, 163–4; Carlsson Government (1986–91) 63–4; Carlsson Government (1994–96) 64; European policy of 11, 106–11, 147, 164; Erlander Government 57–9; Palme Government (1969–76) 61; Palme Government (1982–86) 62–3; Persson Government 64–5, 147, 164; 1944 Programme 57

Thorez, Maurice 67
'traditional' social democracy: adoption of 5; policy content 5; definitions of 6, 27–31; real definitions of 31, 36, 39–40

Wigforss, Ernst 56
Wilson, Harold 45

Zapatero, José Luis Rodríguez 170

eBooks – at www.eBookstore.tandf.co.uk

A library at your fingertips!

eBooks are electronic versions of printed books. You can store them on your PC/laptop or browse them online.

They have advantages for anyone needing rapid access to a wide variety of published, copyright information.

eBooks can help your research by enabling you to bookmark chapters, annotate text and use instant searches to find specific words or phrases. Several eBook files would fit on even a small laptop or PDA.

NEW: Save money by eSubscribing: cheap, online access to any eBook for as long as you need it.

Annual subscription packages

We now offer special low-cost bulk subscriptions to packages of eBooks in certain subject areas. These are available to libraries or to individuals.

For more information please contact webmaster.ebooks@tandf.co.uk

We're continually developing the eBook concept, so keep up to date by visiting the website.

www.eBookstore.tandf.co.uk

9780415604253